Christoph Rathfelder

AF239064

Modelling Event-Based Interactions in Component-Based Architectures for Quantitative System Evaluation

The Karlsruhe Series on Software Design and Quality

Volume 10

Chair Software Design and Quality
Faculty of Computer Science
Karlsruhe Institute of Technology

and

Software Engineering Division
Research Center for Information Technology (FZI), Karlsruhe

Editor: Prof. Dr. Ralf Reussner

Modelling Event-Based Interactions in Component-Based Architectures for Quantitative System Evaluations

by
Christoph Rathfelder

Dissertation, Karlsruher Institut für Technologie (KIT)
Fakultät für Informatik
Tag der mündlichen Prüfung: 19.12.2012
Erster Gutachter: Dr.-Ing. Samuel Kounev
Zweiter Gutachter: Prof. Dr. Ralf Reussner

Impressum

Karlsruher Institut für Technologie (KIT)
KIT Scientific Publishing
Straße am Forum 2
D-76131 Karlsruhe
www.ksp.kit.edu

KIT – Universität des Landes Baden-Württemberg und
nationales Forschungszentrum in der Helmholtz-Gemeinschaft

KIT Scientific Publishing 2013
Print on Demand

ISSN 1867-0067
ISBN 978-3-86644-969-5

Karlsruher Institut für Technologie

Modelling Event-Based Interactions in Component-Based Architectures for Quantitative System Evaluation

Zur Erlangung des akademischen Grades eines

Doktors der Ingenieurwissenschaften

von der Fakultät für Informatik
des Karlsruher Instituts für Technologie (KIT)

genehmigte
Dissertation

von

Christoph Rathfelder

aus Villingen-Schwenningen

Tag der mündlichen Prüfung: 19. Dezember 2012
Erster Gutachter: Dr.-Ing. Samuel Kounev
Zweiter Gutachter: Prof. Dr. Ralf Reussner

Abstract

The event-based communication paradigm is used increasingly often to build loosely-coupled distributed systems in many different industry domains. The application areas of *Event-based Systems* (EBS) range from distributed sensor-based systems, over emergency and rescue systems, up to large-scale business information systems. Compared to synchronous communication using, for example, *Remote Procedure Calls* (RPCs), event-based interactions among components promise several benefits such as high scalability and improved system adaptability and extendability due to the loose coupling of components.

With the growing proliferation of event-based interactions in mission-critical systems, *Quality-of-Service* (QoS) attributes like performance, availability and scalability of such systems are becoming a major concern. Although the event-based communication model promises many advantages in terms of higher flexibility and scalability, this comes at the cost of higher system complexity compared to RPC-based communication since the application logic is distributed among multiple independent event handlers with decoupled and parallel execution paths. This increases the difficulty of modelling EBS for evaluating their QoS attributes at system design and deployment time. Most general-purpose performance meta-models for component-based systems provide limited support for modelling event-based interactions at the architecture-level and do not explicitly consider the influence of the underlying communication middleware on the QoS attributes of the system. Furthermore, existing performance prediction techniques specialised for EBS are focused on modelling the routing of events in the system as opposed to modelling the interactions and event flows between the communicating components.

In this thesis, we present a novel modelling and prediction approach that combines architecture-level modelling of event-based interactions with detailed platform-aware QoS prediction techniques for quantitative system evaluation. The contributions presented in this thesis, can be summarised as follows:

- **Modelling Abstractions for Event-based Interactions at the Architecture-level.** The abstractions developed in this thesis enable architects to model event-based interactions at the system architecture-level independent of the employed underlying communication middleware. While abstracting platform-specific details about the communication middleware and its implementation, the developed modelling abstractions contain sufficient information to support the evaluation of system QoS attributes.

- **Two-step Refinement Transformation for Platform-aware QoS Evaluation and Prediction.** The developed two-step refinement approach enables platform-aware QoS evaluation. The refinement transformation first substitutes event-based interactions modelled at the architecture-level with a detailed chain of generic event processing components. These components provide extension points to integrate platform-specific components defined in a separate middleware repository as part of the second transformation step. The resulting model can serve as input for multiple existing analytical and simulative prediction techniques.

- **Implementation, Evaluation, and Validation.** An implementation of the developed modelling and prediction techniques in the context of the *Palladio Component Model* (PCM) as a mature and representative *Architecture Description Language* (ADL) for component-based systems serves as basis for the successful validation of the proposed approach. The detailed evaluation of the contributions presented in this thesis in the context of several real-world case studies based on a traffic monitoring system developed at the University of Cambridge and the SPECjms2007 benchmark demonstrates the applicability and accuracy of the proposed modelling and prediction approach. In all case studies, the prediction error, compared to measurements on the running system, was less than 20% in most cases. Furthermore, applying the developed modelling and prediction techniques in different system evolution stages demonstrated the efficiency of our approach, which reduces the modelling effort by more than 80% compared to the use of manual workarounds.

In addition to the detailed case studies presented in this thesis, the developed modelling and prediction techniques have already been applied in two external projects for evaluating the design of a distributed control system for power plants and for analysing the architecture and behaviour of a control unit for solar orbiters, respectively. Applying the developed modelling and prediction approach to PCM, we extended it to enable the modelling and evaluation of event-based interactions in addition to the already supported RPC-based communication. These extensions, which have been included in the official PCM Release[1] since version 3.3, open up a new domain of systems that can be modelled and evaluated using the Palladio approach. Furthermore, we are currently working on the integration of the developed modelling abstractions into the *Descartes Meta-Model* (DMM)[2], a meta-model enabling the self-aware run-time management of distributed systems.

---

[1] http://www.palladio-simulator.com
[2] http://www.descartes-research.net

Kurzfassung

Ereignisbasierte Kommunikation wird in vielen verschiedenen Anwendungsdomänen verwendet. Die Einsatzbereiche reichen dabei von verteilten Sensornetzen zur Verkehrsüberwachung oder für das Notfallmanagement bis zu komplexen betrieblichen Informationssystemen. Im Vergleich zu synchroner Kommunikation mit z.B. *Remote Procedure Calls* (RPCs) verspricht ereignisbasierte Kommunikation mehrere Vorteile wie z.b. eine verbesserte Skalierbarkeit sowie eine höhere Flexibilität und Anpassbarkeit durch die lose Kopplung zwischen Komponenten.

Durch den zunehmenden Einsatz ereignisbasierter Interaktionen innerhalb sicherheits- und geschäftskritischer Anwendungen nimmt die Dienstgüte der Systeme und der erbrachten Funktionalität (wie z.B. Verfügbarkeit oder Antwortzeitverhalten) einen immer wichtigeren Stellenwert ein. Neben all den Vorteilen, die aus der losen Kopplung zwischen Komponenten resultieren, ergeben sich durch den Einsatz ereignisbasierter Kommunikation jedoch auch neue Herausforderungen für den Entwurf der Systeme. Im Vergleich zu RPC-basierter Kommunikation steigt die Komplexität der Systeme, da Ereignisse oft in mehreren parallelen und asynchronen Verarbeitungspfaden in unterschiedlichen Systemteilen verarbeitet werden. Diese Komplexität erschwert neben der Modellierung vor allem die Qualitätsvorhersage eines ereignisbasierten Systems (EBS) zur Entwurfszeit. Existierende Modellierungs- und Vorhersagetechniken für Software-Architekturen bieten meist keine Unterstützung für ereignisbasierte Interaktionen auf der Architekturebene und vernachlässigen den Einfluss der eingesetzten Middleware auf die Dienstgüte des Gesamtsystems. Im Gegensatz dazu bieten Vorhersagetechniken für EBS meist keine entwurfsnahe Modellierung der

Software-Architektur und sind sehr stark auf die Modellierung und Vorhersage der Verarbeitung innerhalb der Middleware fokussiert und vernachlässigen die Modellierung und Vorhersage kompletter Interaktionen zwischen den einzelnen Komponenten des Systems. Im Rahmen dieser Arbeit habe ich einen neuen Ansatz entwickelt, der die beiden Aspekte *Modellierung ereignisbasierter Kommunikation auf Architekturebene* und *Qualitätsvorhersagen unter Berücksichtigung plattformspezifischer Einflussfaktoren* kombiniert. Die Beiträge meiner Arbeit können wie folgt zusammengefasst werden:

- **Abstraktionen zur Modellierung ereignisbasierter Interaktionen auf der Architekturebene.** Die im Rahmen der Arbeit definierten Elemente ermöglichen es, die Architektur eines EBS unabhängig von eingesetzten Kommunikationstechnologien und Middleware-Realisierungen zu modellieren. Plattformspezifische Details über die Zustellung der Ereignisse innerhalb der Middleware und deren eigene Architektur werden dabei abstrahiert, ohne die Möglichkeiten von Qualitätsvorhersagen einzuschränken.

- **Eine 2-stufigen Verfeinerungstransformation zur Integration plattformspezifischer Einflussfaktoren.** Die entwickelte 2-stufige Verfeinerungstransformation ermöglicht detaillierte Dienstgüte Vorhersagen für EBS unter Berücksichtigung der Einflüsse der eingesetzten Middleware-Lösung. Die Transformation verfeinert im ersten Schritt die Modellierungselemente auf Architekturebene durch die Einwebung einer generalisierten Ereignisübertragungskette für jede Kommunikationsverbindung. Diese Übertragungskette bildet die Basis für die im zweiten Schritt durchgeführte Integration plattformspezifischer Komponenten aus einem dedizierten und wiederverwendbaren Middleware-Repository. Das Ergebnis der Verfeinerungstransformation kann als Eingabe für verschiedene existierende Vorhersagetechniken verwendet werden.

- **Umsetzung, Evaluation und Validierung.** Eine Umsetzung des entwickelten Modellierungs- und Vorhersageansatzes als Erweiterung des Palladio-Komponentenmodells (PCM), einer ausgereiften und repräsentativen Architektur-Beschreibungssprache (ADL) für die Modellierung und QoS-Vorhersage komponentenbasierter Systeme, dient als Basis für die erfolgreiche Validierung des präsentierten Ansatzes. Die detaillierte Evaluation im Kontext realistischer Fallstudien basierend auf einem Verkehrsüberwachungssystem, welches an der Universität Cambridge entwickelt wurde, und dem SPECjms2007 Benchmark demonstrieren die Anwendbarkeit des vorgestellten Modellierungsansatzes und die Genauigkeit der entwickelten Vorhersagetechniken. In fast allen Fällen konnte ein maximaler Vorhersagefehler von unter 20% nachgewiesen werden. Des Weiteren konnte gezeigt werden, dass der Modellierungsaufwand im Vergleich zu einer Fallstudie basierend auf dem ursprünglichen PCM mit manuellen Hilfskonstrukten ohne die entwickelten Erweiterungen für ereignisbasierte Interaktionen um ca. 80% reduziert werden konnte.

Neben den in dieser Arbeit präsentierten detaillierten Fallstudien, wurden die entwickelten Modellierungs- und Vorhersagetechniken bereits in zwei weiteren externen Projekten eingesetzt. Es handelte sich hierbei um die Bewertung des Entwurfs eines Kontrollsystems für Kraftwerke sowie die Analyse der Architektur und des Verhaltens der Steuereinheit eines neuen Satelliten für die Sonnenbeobachtung. Durch die Umsetzung der entwickelten Modellierungs- und Vorhersagetechnik als Erweiterung des PCM, untersützt dieses nun neben RPC-basierter Kommunikation auch die Modellierung and Analyse ereignisbasierter Interaktionen. Mit diesen Erweiterungen, welche seit Version 3.3 offizieller Bestandteil des PCM Release[3] sind, konnte ein neue Domäne von

---

[3]http://www.palladio-simulator.com

Systemen für den Palladio Ansatz erschlossen werden. Darüber hinaus werden die entwickelten Modellierungsabstraktionen aktuell als Erweiteung des Descartes Metamodells (DMM)[4], einem Modell für das dynamische Laufzeitmanagement verteilter Systeme, umgesetzt.

---

[4]http://www.descartes-research.net

Acknowledgements

Completing a dissertation is truly a marathon event, and I would not have been able to complete this journey without the aid and support of countless people over the past years. First of all, I would like to thank my two supervisors Samuel Kounev and Ralf Reussner. Ralf laid the foundation for my research and gave my the opportunity to work as a member of his research group in a very enjoyable and fruitful working atmosphere and supported me with very constructive feedback in individual discussions and in many doctoral rounds. For me, it is an honor to be Samuel's first "doctor child", and I would like to thank him for his guidance, his inspiring ideas and motivation when writing my thesis and multiple papers but also when working together in projects and writing project proposals at the FZI.

My special thanks goes to Benjamin Klatt, whose diploma thesis forms the basis for the implementation of my approach. The constructive discussions when supervising his thesis but also when being colleagues at the FZI helped me to shape and refine my approach.

The two case studies presented in my thesis would not have been possible without the support of two persons. I would like to thank David Evans for his support when realizing the traffic monitoring system and instrumenting the PIRATES middleware. Kai Sachs supported me with his vast knowledge of the SPECjms2007 benchmark. I thank him for providing me access to detailed measurements forming the basis of my validation but also for the enjoyable and long evenings when meeting at different conferences.

Furthermore, I would like to thank my former and current department heads, Steffen Becker, Mircea Trifu, and Klaus Krogmann for providing me with solid funding combined with the space and time for preparing and finishing my thesis. Furthermore, I would like to my former and current colleagues at the FZI for their support when working together in multiple projects, their feedback and the fruitful discussions, but also the various foosball matches and the positive and enjoyable working atmosphere. In alphabetical order: Steffen Becker, Martin Blersch, Franz Brosch, Oliver Denninger, Zoya Durdik, Giovanni Falcone, Thomas Goldschmidt, Henning Groenda, Jens Happe, Michael Hauck, Benjamin Klatt, Anne Koziolek, Klaus Krogmann, Martin Küster, Volker Kutruff, Christof Momm, Thomas Schuster, Simon Spinner, Johannes Stammel, Gabor Szeder, Peter Szulman, Adrian Trifu, Mircea Trifu, and Jan Wiesenberger. Additionally, I would like to thank my colleagues of the Descartes research group and the chair of Software Design and Quality (SDQ) for their feedback and the various constructive discussions in multiple research meetings and doctoral rounds as well as the enjoyable and productive retreats together with the FZI colleagues in Dagstuhl, Freudenstadt and other locations. Again in alphabetical order: Fabian Brosig, Erik Burger, Lucia Happe, Jörg Henß, Matthias Huber, Nikolaus Huber, Rouven Krebs, Michael Kuperberg, Michael Langhammer, Philipp Merkle, Aleksandar Milenkoski, Qais Noorshams, Fouad ben Nasr Omri, Michael Papez, Andreas Rentschler, Piotr Rygienski, and Dennis Westermann. (hoping very much that I did not forget other names to mention).

Furthermore, I would like to thank all the students that supported me in multiple projects as part of their diploma thesis (Stefan Becker, Nikolaus Huber, and Varvara Kolovou) or as research students (Christian Busch, Carolin Gärtner, and Joakim Gunnarsson von Kistowski).

Finally, I would like to thank my parents for their support and encouragement throughout the years, which made it all possible.

Contents

1. Introduction

1.1. Motivation

The event-based communication paradigm is used increasingly often to build loosely-coupled distributed systems in many industry domains. The application areas of *Event-based Systems* (EBS) range from embedded systems like traffic monitoring systems or automotive control systems, over emergency and rescue systems, up to large-scale business information and supply-chain management systems [Hinze 10b]. Furthermore, event-based communication serves as enabling technology for several emerging application domains as for example ubiquitous sensor actor networks or ambient assisted living [Hinze 09]. Event-based communication is often used to build loosely coupled and highly distributed systems. Compared to synchronous communication using, for example, *Remote Procedure Calls* (RPCs), event-based interactions among components promise several benefits [Hohpe 08]. Being asynchronous in nature, they allow a *send-and-forget* approach, i.e., a component that publishes information in form of an event can continue its execution without waiting for the receivers to acknowledge the event or react on it. Furthermore, the loose coupling of components achieved by the mediating communication middleware that encapsulates the event routing and delivery leads to an increased extensibility of the system as components can easily be added, removed, or substituted.

With the growing proliferation of event-based interactions in business- and mission-critical systems, the provisioning of *Quality-of-Service* (QoS) guarantees with respect to availability, performance, or efficiency plays an increasingly important role. The application of event-based interactions in the context of distributed rescue and emergency applications as described in [Skjeksvik 10] places high demands on the QoS attributes of such systems and the communication middleware in particular, given that the high availability and responsiveness of such applications can often be of life-saving importance. Even in cases where physical safety is not influenced by the system, poor QoS can often be a business- and mission-critical aspect. The first release of SAP's solution for medium-sized businesses called A1S, which also includes event-based communication, showed that bad performance can be a significant threat for the success of a product [Briegleb 07]. Just recently, the initial public offer of Facebook was overshadowed by the unavailability of NASDAQ's software system, which was caused by "poor design" [Bloomberg 12], resulting in the loss of several million US dollars. In the past and at present, such problems have typically being handled in an adhoc manner using a trial and error approach but this often does not address the issues and may become too expensive considering the business constraints and scale of modern enterprise applications [Williams 03]. Furthermore, in today's data centres, software systems are often deployed on server machines with significantly over-provisioned capacity in order to guarantee highly available and responsive operation [Kaplan 08], which automatically leads to low system efficiency. Moreover, this "kill it with iron" approach can only solve performance problems caused by insufficient hardware resources and cannot address problems that have their root in the design of the system [Smith 02].

Although the event-based programming model promises many advantages in terms of increased flexibility, scalability, and elasticity to handle peak loads, the system complexity compared to using RPC-based communication is higher since the application logic is distributed among multiple independent event handlers with decoupled and parallel execution paths. This increases the difficulty of modelling event-based interactions for QoS prediction at system design and deployment time. However, due to the often mission-critical importance of system QoS attributes, the latter should be considered already in the system design phase as argued for example by Clements and Northrop: *"Whether or not a system will be able to exhibit its desired (or required) quality attributes is largely determined by the time the architecture is chosen."* [Clements 96]. Early stage architecture evaluation helps to avoid costly redesigns and implementation delays. The evaluation of EBS requires specialised techniques that consider the different characteristics and features of event-based interactions. This thesis introduces an integrated approach supporting the modelling of EBS combined with prediction techniques enabling system architects evaluate system QoS attributes at system design and deployment time.

1.2. Problem Statement

Event-based communication is an important part of modern software architecture styles like *Service-Oriented Architecture* (SOA) [Krafzig 06], *Event-Driven Architecture* (EDA) [Etzion 11], or *Complex Event Processing* (CEP) [Chandy 10] and it is natively supported by common implementation frameworks as for example the *Java Platform, Enterprise Edition* (Java EE), Microsoft .NET, or the *Common Object Request Broker Architecture* (CORBA). Especially in the case of large scale and distributed systems where event-based interactions are typically used, the complexity of system architectures is high. Using an *Architecture Description Language* (ADL) enables architects to define and describe the system architecture at a higher level of abstraction. In addition to their descriptive role, such architecture models can serve as a basis for a model-based quality prediction process as described in [Becker 08a] in the context of component-based systems. Performance modelling techniques for component-based systems, surveyed in [Koziolek 10], support system architects in evaluating the prototype architectures and comparing different design alternatives with respect to their QoS attributes. However, they often provide only limited support for modelling event-based interactions. On the other hand, existing performance modelling and analysis techniques specialised for EBS (e.g., [Sachs 11, Mühl 09, Kounev 08, Carzaniga 01]) are focused on modelling and evaluating the processing of events within the communication middleware only, as opposed to modelling the entire system including the behaviour and interactions of all its components. QoS evaluation for complex and large scale systems using event-based communication requires a specialised ADL that allows the description of the system architecture including the specific characteristics of event-based interactions at a high abstraction level. The ADL needs to be accompanied by analysis techniques to support the QoS evaluation of the modelled system. In summary, the two high level research questions addressed by this thesis are:

- How to describe and model event-based interactions in component-based systems at the architecture-level?

- How to predict the expected QoS of an EBS at design and deployment time, based on its architecture-level model?

1.3. Goals and Success Criteria

The goal of this thesis is to support the QoS evaluation of component-based systems with event-based interactions. The increasing application of event-based communication in business- and mission-critical systems requires detailed QoS evaluation techniques supporting system architects in designing and optimising the system architecture and determining the required hardware resources. The responsiveness of EBS is one of the most important and critical QoS attributes and can heavily influence the business success as demonstrated in [Briegleb 07] and

[Bloomberg 12]. Furthermore, recent research reports list performance modelling and evaluation in the context of EBS as one of the most urgent and critical research areas to be addressed [Hinze 10a].

For these reasons, the focus of this thesis is placed on enabling the analysis and prediction of performance metrics like response time, resource utilisation, and throughput, which additionally are the common metrics based on which system efficiency is evaluated. Although, this thesis is focused on performance prediction, the developed approach is intended to be generic and extensible to support other QoS attributes such as reliability. Our ultimate goal is the development of an integrated methodology and framework that enables the modelling and evaluation of EBS based on architecture-level models. This goal can be broken down into the following sub-goals:

- **Derivation and specification of modelling abstractions to capture event-based interactions at the architecture-level.** Describing event-based interactions at the architecture-level aims at hiding as much details related to the underlying communication protocols and mechanisms as possible while still giving the architect the possibility to specify all information needed for analysing the system's behaviour and QoS attributes. For this reason, finding an adequate abstraction level is an important aspect. Enabling the modelling of complete systems requires the formalisation of the identified modelling abstractions and their integration into an ADL for component-based systems.

- **Platform-aware QoS prediction techniques for EBS.** In EBS, the processing of events between interacting components is done by a communication middleware. Implementations of such middleware systems range from simple client libraries up to complex and distributed routing systems. Since the architecture and behaviour of the communication middleware significantly influence the QoS

5

attributes of the system running on top of it [Sachs 09], our performance prediction techniques for EBS should explicitly consider such influence factors. According to the model-based prediction process presented in [Becker 08a], architecture-level models are used as input to analytical or simulation-based prediction techniques, which provide different trade-off between prediction accuracy and overhead. Our proposed modelling approach should support the use of existing prediction techniques as far as possible and thus retain the flexibility in being able to trade-off between prediction accuracy and overhead when evaluating system architectures.

- **Integration of the modelling and prediction capabilities into a state-of-the-art modelling and prediction tool.** In order to be applicable both in industrial and research settings, the modelling and prediction techniques developed as part of this thesis should be combined to build an integrated state-of-the-art modelling and prediction framework. Only a smooth integration of the modelling approach and the corresponding QoS prediction techniques would enable external users to apply the results developed as part of this thesis in real-world projects. The integration should close the gap between the abstract descriptions at the architecture-level and the prediction models, which include platform-specific details about the event processing within the communication middleware.

With the aim of being applicable and usable in real-world scenarios, our approach should fulfil the following success criteria that are considered essential for every modelling and prediction approach:

- **Expressiveness:** The approach should be applicable to the various types of event-based communication used in practice. Furthermore, the prediction techniques should take into account the influences of the communication middleware.

- **Accuracy:** The developed modelling and prediction techniques should provide results with good accuracy compared to the actual system's performance. Normally, deviations within 35% from measurements taken on the real system are considered acceptable for design-time performance analysis and capacity planning [Menascé 04].

- **Efficiency:** The approach should reduce the manual modelling and prediction effort as well as lower the required expert knowledge compared to the existing approaches for modelling and evaluating EBS based on workarounds using conventional modelling constructs or specialised performance models such as *Queueing Petri Nets* (QPNs) or *Layered Queueing Networks* (LQNs).

- **Scalability:** The approach should support the modelling and evaluation of systems of realistic size and complexity.

- **Automation:** The approach should allow a high degree of automation, meaning that most activities except for the modelling task, which we assume to be a manual activity, should be supported and automated by tools as much as possible.

1.4. Approach and Contributions

In this thesis, we developed a novel modelling and performance prediction approach for component-based systems with event-based interactions. Our approach for the first time combines modelling of event-based interactions at the architecture-level with detailed platform-aware performance prediction techniques. The modelling abstractions proposed in this thesis allow the specification of event-based interactions between components. So far existing architecture-level modelling and prediction approaches provide only limited support for event-based interactions. With the novel and unique support for explicitly modelling different interaction types, i.e., direct *Point-to-Point* (P2P) connections and decoupled *Publish/Subscribe* (Pub/Sub) interactions, at the architecture-level, our approach opens up the area of EBS for QoS prediction techniques based on architecture-level models. Given that multiple mature ADLs for component-based systems supporting model-based performance prediction exist in the literature (e.g., as surveyed in [Koziolek 10]), our approach aims at extending existing ADLs in such a way that existing prediction techniques can be leveraged.

Our novel platform-aware prediction process extends the model-based performance prediction process defined in [Becker 08a]. As illustrated in Figure 1.1, an EBS is described by an architecture-level software model that conforms to a specific *base ADL* extended with the modelling abstractions developed in this thesis. According to the original process, the software model is annotated with additional attributes such as resource demands, input parameter characterisations, or workload specifications. Depending on the existence of a system implementation, these attributes can be derived either based on measurements or using estimation techniques.

At the architecture-level, platform-specific details about the underlying communication middleware are abstracted away. However, given that the employed middleware significantly influences the QoS attributes of the system built on top of it [Happe 09, Sachs 11], platform-specific details need to be taken into account by the prediction techniques. To realise a platform-aware QoS prediction technique, our approach extends the model-based prediction process by introducing the novel two-step refinement transformation. In the refinement step, the transformation first refines event-based interactions between components with a detailed chain of components each representing one of

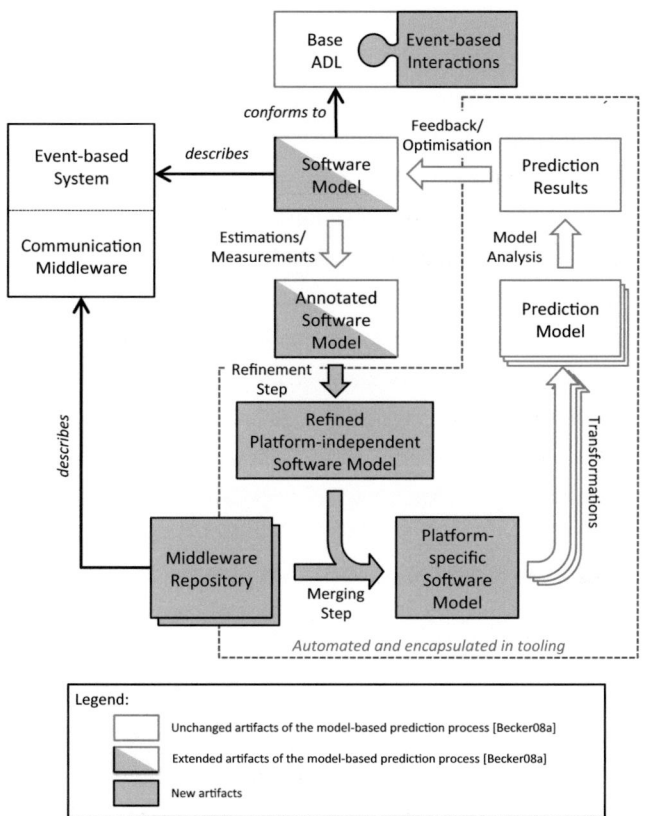

Figure 1.1: Extended Model-based Performance Prediction Process

the different processing stages that are common for the event processing within a communication middleware. The integrated components serve as extension points to integrate additional platform-specific components. These components, which are specified in a separate middleware repository, describe the platform-specific behaviour and resource demands of the employed communication middleware. The second transformation step, merges the middleware repository with the refined software model and integrates the platform-specific components into the platform-independent event processing chain. The described two-step transformation extends the general idea of performance completions introduced by Woodside [Woodside 02] with a strict separation of platform-specific and platform-independent aspects.

Given that the refinement step substitutes the introduced architecture-level abstractions for event-based interactions with the mentioned generic event-processing chain, the refined platform-specific model conforms to the *base ADL* und can thus be used as input to existing prediction techniques available for the respective *base ADL*. The developed two-step refinement transformation is encapsulated in the tooling and integrated into the automated prediction process. This automated and transparent execution of the two-step refinement transformation allows system architects for concentrating on modelling the considered EBS at a high level of abstraction, while platform-specific details are automatically integrated based on the selected middleware repository.

1.4.1. Contributions

The contributions of the work presented in this thesis can be classified into conceptual and technical contributions. Figure 1.1 highlights the various areas of contributions which are summarised in the following. These contributions are supplemented by additional work and publications in the context of performance modelling and prediction that influenced the work and results presented in this thesis.

10

Conceptual Contributions

- **Specification of abstractions enabling the modelling of event-based interactions at the architecture-level.** The modelling of event-based interactions at the architecture-level requires the identification of a set of adequate modelling abstractions. As part of this thesis, we analyse the different characteristics of event-based interactions and derive a set of generic architecture-level abstractions that enable the modelling of event-based interactions at the architecture-level while abstracting implementation and platform-specific details. With the support of direct P2P connections as well as decoupled Pub/Sub communication, the proposed modelling abstractions cover the major types of EBS used in practice. The results in this area were published in [Rathfelder 09b], [Rathfelder 09c], and [Rathfelder 13].

- **Definition of a generic event processing chain abstracting from implementation-specific details.** Transmitting events from producers to consumers requires several processing steps within the communication middleware as well as at the producer and consumer sides. Based on an analysis of the event processing process, we identify a set of generic processing stages existing in any EBS. Aligned with these processing stages, we define the generic event processing chain that serves as foundation for refining event-based interactions following the idea of completions [Woodside 02]. In contrast to existing completion-based approaches (e.g., [Happe 08], [Kapova 10a]), our proposed event processing chain is platform-independent and explicitly considers the different event processing stages. Although it is defined to be platform-independent, it contains enough details and structure to integrate individual platform-specific components implementing the different event processing stages. The event process-

11

ing chain was initially published in [Rathfelder 10b] and refined in [Rathfelder 13].

- **Development of a generic and flexible evaluation methodology based on a two-step refinement transformation.** Enabling QoS evaluation of EBS modelled at the architecture-level requires the integration of platform-specific details about the underlying transmission system into the prediction models. With the developed two-step refinement transformation, our approach strictly separates the platform-independent architecture-level model from platform-specific details of the underlying communication middleware. While the first step of the proposed two-step transformation refines event-based interactions by introducing a chain of platform-independent components representing the different event processing stages, the second step integrates platform-specific components specified in separate middleware repositories that describe the behaviour and resource demands of a specific middleware implementation. With this separation, we achieve a substantial improvement in flexibility concerning the evaluation of different middleware implementations and their impact on the system performance compared to existing approaches (e.g., [Woodside 02], [Kapova 11]) where platform-specific details are often hard coded in middleware-specific completions. The proposed two-step refinement transformation substitutes all modelling elements describing event-based interactions at the architecture-level with a chain of platform-independent and platform-specific components. The resulting model conforms to the original *base ADL* and thus is compatible with all existing prediction techniques. The initial idea of using a refinement transformation was published in [Rathfelder 10b] and further refined in [Kounev 12b] and [Rathfelder 13].

Technical Contributions

- **Application of the proposed modelling abstractions to a representative ADL for component-based systems.** The *Palladio Component Model* (PCM) [Becker 09, Happe 11] is a mature design-oriented ADL for component-based software architectures. PCM is accompanied by a graphical modelling and prediction tool and provides support for a number of different performance prediction techniques including techniques based on LQNs [Koziolek 08b], QPNs [Meier 11] and simulation models [Becker 09, Becker 08a]. Due to its maturity and the multiple available different prediction techniques, we selected PCM as a representative example. Applying our modelling approach to PCM, we extended it to enable the modelling of event-based interactions in addition to the already supported RPC-based communication. This extension opens up a completely new domain of systems that can be modelled and evaluated using the Palladio approach. We demonstrated the modelling and prediction capabilities of the extended PCM in [Rathfelder 11a].

- **Implementation of a performance prediction technique based on the two-step refinement transformation in the context of PCM.** Based on the extended version of PCM, we implemented a model-to-model transformation according to the developed two-step refinement approach. The transformation is realised as in-place transformation based on the *QVT Operational Mapping Language* (QVT-O). The integration of the transformation into the prediction workflow enables an automated and transparent execution of the transformation. The extensions of PCM, which form the basis for our validation, were published in [Klatt 11b].

- **Development of a realistic traffic monitoring system as event-based reference system.** In order to validate and evaluate our work, we developed a novel reference system based on the traffic monitoring system developed as part of the *Transport Information Monitoring Environment* (TIME) project [Bacon 08] at the University of Cambridge. We implemented configurable workload drivers that are able to reproduce real-world event streams collected in the city of Cambridge. The system is highly adaptable and can be setup on a single machine or distributed over multiple servers. To support the automated setup and execution of experiments, we implemented a central control application responsible for deploying the system and the event generators on the different servers, executing the experiments, and finally collecting all measurement data. Due to this high automation and the adaptability of the system, it can be used as a general reference application for validating research results in the context of EBS and architecture evaluation and optimisation approaches in general. The traffic-monitoring system combined with a validation of our approach was initially published in [Rathfelder 10a] and then later on as extended version with additional components in [Rathfelder 11c].

- **Evaluation of our methodology and framework in the context of two real-world systems.** The validation of our approach is based on an evaluation plan that addresses both the accuracy of the prediction results and the applicability of the developed modelling abstractions. We selected two real-world systems, the traffic monitoring system described above and the SPECjms2007 standard benchmark. The two selected systems represent different types of EBS, i.e., a distributed peer-to-peer system and a centralised system with a mixture of P2P and Pub/Sub interactions and thus can be considered as representative for a large set of existing EBS. Following the evaluation plan, we conduct several experiments and apply the developed methodology and framework in multiple architecture evaluation scenarios. Based on the collected metrics, we evaluate our approach with focus on the defined success criteria expressiveness, accuracy, efficiency, scalability, and automation.

The results of the evaluation show that the prediction error of our prediction technique is less than 20% in most cases and thereby significantly better than the generally accepted prediction error of 35% [Menascé 04]. The introduced modelling abstractions substantially reduce the modelling effort compared to using manual workarounds as described in [Rathfelder 10a]. System variations and evolutions typical for loosely coupled EBS can be reflected in architecture-level models in less than 30 minutes. The evaluation demonstrates the effectiveness of our proposed methodology and respective prediction techniques for evaluating realistic systems with complex event-based interactions.

1.4.2. Related Activities and Publications

The above described contributions in the area of event-based interactions in component-based systems form the focus of this thesis. At the same time, as a byproduct of this work some additional contributions were made in several related areas as summarised in the following.

- **Architecture evaluation and certification.** We presented an approach to evaluate the architecture documentation of a software system with the aim to derive indicators on its maintainability in [Rathfelder 08b]. In [Rathfelder 09a], we extended this idea and developed the *Architecture Documentation Maturity Model (ADM2)*, a multi-dimensional maturity model to evaluate the architecture documentation with indicators on the architecture's maintainability. Furthermore, in [Rathfelder 08c] we described the application of component quality certificates in the context of software industrialisation and distributed development processes.

- **QoS prediction in service-oriented systems.** We studied different service-oriented systems and demonstrated that the consideration of QoS characteristic is an important success factor when migrating to a *Service-Oriented Architecture* (SOA) as presented in [Rathfelder 07, Schuster 10]. This research led to the development of the *independent SOA Maturity Model* (iSOAMM) [Rathfelder 08a]. In [Rathfelder 11b, Klatt 11a], we showed how prediction techniques can be employed to evaluate services and service compositions in *Service Level Agreement* (SLA) management frameworks.

- **Evaluating the applicability and effectiveness of performance modelling techniques in the context of real-life industrial systems.** We conducted two industrial case studies using PCM for modelling and performance prediction. We demonstrated PCM's applicability in two realistic industrial scenarios,namely IBM's storage virtualisation layer and 1&1's email system. In [Huber 10], we evaluated and compared two different design alternatives of a storage virtualisation system that is part of IBM's mainframe systems. In [Rathfelder 12], we demonstrated the use of PCM to enable continuous performance monitoring in the context of the email system operated by the 1&1 Internet AG, which is with more than 2000 servers providing services for more than 40 million users is currently one of Europe's largest email systems.

1.5. Application Scenarios

The developed modelling and QoS prediction approach can be applied in different stages of the lifecycle of a software system ranging from the design and development over operation up to maintenance and evolution. Due to its integrated nature, our approach supports multiple of these scenarios and enables the reuse of the described architecture models in different application scenarios throughout the system lifecycle.

1.5.1. Evaluation of Design Alternatives

Designing a system based on a set of requirements often results in several different design alternatives, which provide the same functionality however differing in QoS attributes such as service availability and responsiveness. The loose coupling between components introduced by using Pub/Sub-based communication opens up a wide range of design alternatives as removing, changing or adding new components, does not have any impact on the other components, their interfaces, and existing connections. Although the individual components are not influenced, the end-to-end performance of the system can be significantly impacted by such changes. Evaluating and comparing different design alternatives is often done based on prototypical implementations. Using a model-based QoS prediction approach as presented in this thesis enables the evaluation at the model-level and does not require expensive and time consuming prototypical implementations. The use of a design-oriented ADL instead of specialised prediction models allows architects to easily model the architecture and its variations without requiring special knowledge in low-level prediction models. Combined with the automation of the QoS prediction process, the required effort for evaluating different design alternatives is significantly reduced compared to using prototypical implementations as shown in [Huber 10]. The typical questions that can be answered by applying a model-based prediction approach like the one presented in this thesis are:

- What is the response time or event processing time of a given design alternative?

- How does the integration of an additional component impact the system performance?

- How is the performance influenced by the substitution of component A with component B?

1.5.2. System Sizing and Capacity Planning

EBS promise high system scalability and the flexibility to handle varying workloads. Combined with the simplified adaptation of the system's structure and deployment by adding new components, replicating components or moving components to other servers, the evaluation of the system performance in different workload situations often requires expensive and time-consuming load testing. The developed modelling and prediction approach enables architects to evaluate the system performance in different hardware environments, to analyse the influences of the used communication middleware as well as to compare different deployment alternatives in terms of their performance and efficiency. The developed techniques help to answer the following questions that arise frequently both at system deployment time and during operation:

- What would be the average utilisation of system components and the average event processing time for a given workload and deployment scenario?

- How much would the system performance improve if a given server is upgraded?

- What would be the performance impact of changing the used communication middleware?

- How many servers are needed to ensure adequate performance under the expected workload?

1.5.3. Scalability / Impact Analysis of Workload Changes

High scalability combined with elasticity with respect to workload peaks are two of the benefits of using event-based interactions. However, high scalability does not mean that the system can handle every workload without problems. In EBS, events can be queued up, which enables handling higher peak loads but also increases the complexity of detecting an overload situation. The approach developed in this thesis allows architects to easily specify and vary the workload used in the evaluation of the system behaviour and performance. In contrast to performance tests, the model-based approach allows evaluating the system without setting up a realistic testbed and implementing the required workload drivers. The automated prediction process providing detailed evaluation results enables both determining the maximal system throughput as well as detecting potential bottlenecks as demonstrated in one the case studies presented as part of this thesis and in [Rathfelder 11c]. The questions that arise in this scenario and that can be answered by applying the modelling and prediction techniques developed in this thesis are:

- What maximum load level can the system sustain for a given resource allocation?

- How does the system behave if the workload is increased?

- Which component or resource is a potential bottleneck?

1.5.4. Run-time Performance Testing and Monitoring

Existing software monitoring and management solutions support the definition of rules and conditions evaluated at run-time to detect potential performance problems and to identify malfunctions of the system. Most of these solutions use fixed thresholds as upper or lower bounds to differentiate between normal system operation and a potentially problematical system state [Cherkasova 09]. However, the performance of a system in terms of response times or resource utilisation depends on the workload, which especially in the context of EBS can significantly vary over time. Workload-aware performance monitoring approaches like the one presented in [Rathfelder 12] enable a more fine-grained monitoring. The methodology and techniques developed in this thesis enable the realisation of such workload-aware monitoring processes for EBS. Questions that can be answered by combining the workload-aware monitoring process with the methodologies and techniques developed in this thesis are:

- Does the system behave as expected under the current workload?

- What is the root cause of observed unexpected performance changes (varying workload or mal-operation)?

- What is the expected CPU utilisation of a server or the response time of a service for a given workload?

1.5.5. Automated Architecture Evaluation and Optimisation

The loose coupling between components introduced by using event-based interactions opens up a large space of different design and deployment alternatives for implementing a component-based system. Automated architecture evaluation and optimisation methods, such as the scalability analysis presented in [Rathfelder 11c], or automated architecture optimisation frameworks like PerOpertyx [Koziolek 11b] reduce the manual effort for evaluating and comparing different alternatives and support the selection of the best alternatives. Due to the lack of formal ADLs that provide support for modelling event-based interactions, these automated evaluation and optimisation techniques have so far been limited to component-based systems with synchronous method invocations only. The modelling abstractions for event-based interactions combined with the prediction technique introduced in this thesis make it possible to apply such automated evaluation and optimisation techniques to EBS, which were not supported before. The combination of the techniques developed in this thesis with existing automated architecture evaluation and optimisation techniques promise to answer the following questions:

- What is the most efficient deployment of a system for a given resource environment?

- What is the optimal system structure and deployment for a given set of constraints in terms of available resources?

- What is the most cost efficient design and deployment of a system for a given QoS level that should be guaranteed?

1.6. Thesis Organisation

The thesis is organised as follows. In Chapter 2, we present the foundations, upon which the developed methodology and techniques are based. First, we give an overview of the domain of EBS. This overview starts with the introduction of basic terminology followed by the presentation of a classification schema for EBS. Applying this classification schema to existing systems, we demonstrate the large variety of different types of EBS used in practice. Second, we introduce the area of model-driven engineering. After a general overview, we present the two transformation languages used in this thesis. Following a brief introduction into the domain of software performance engineering, we finally present the *Palladio Component Model* (PCM), which we use as basis for the presented implementation and validation of our approach.

Chapter 3 reviews related work in the two research areas architecture-level modelling and performance prediction techniques with a focus on the provided support for modelling and evaluating event-based interactions in component-based systems.

Chapters 4 through 6 constitute the core of this thesis and present the main contributions. In Chapter 4, we present the developed modelling methodology and introduce a set of architecture-level abstractions for specifying event-based interactions between components. In the second part of this chapter, we apply the developed modelling abstractions to an existing and representative ADL for component-based systems.

In Chapter 5, we introduce the two-step refinement transformation we developed to enable platform-aware performance predictions for EBS. After presenting the generic event processing chain, which provides the basis for the following two-step refinement transformation, we present more details on the transformation including the integration of platform-specific components. Next, we present a detailed and formalised specification of the transformation. The chapter ends with a short overview of the transformation's implementation and its integration into the PCM tool chain.

In Chapter 6, we evaluate the contributions of this thesis in the context of two real-world case studies, a traffic monitoring system and the official SPECjms2007 benchmark. The chapter begins with the definition of evaluation goals, which form the basis for the evaluation presented in the following sections. Section 6.2 introduces the traffic monitoring system and demonstrates the application of our approach in different evolution stages of the system. The results show that the prediction accuracy with mostly less than 20% error is significant better compared to the generally accepted 35%–40% error range considered as acceptable for model-based performance prediction techniques [Menascé 04]. The application of our modelling approach to different design alternatives demonstrates its efficiency since the required modelling adaptation could be realised in less than 30 minutes. Section 6.3 presents the SPECjms2007 benchmark which includes different interaction types with a complex mixture of events designed to be representative for industrial supply chain management systems. The case study demonstrates the applicability of our approach to such complex systems and the good prediction accuracy, which was mostly within 25%. In Section 6.4, we give an overview of two external projects in which the contributions presented in this thesis are currently applied, followed by a summary of the evaluation results in Section 6.5.

Finally, Chapter 7 summarises the contributions presented in this thesis and concludes with an outlook on future work.

2. Foundations

This chapter introduces the general terminology, describes the context of *Event-based Systems* (EBS), and presents an overview of the foundations our approach is based on. More specifically, Section 2.1 describes the domain of EBS. It first introduces a generic set of term and definitions followed by a detailed characterisation schema for EBS. The section closes with an overview of existing middleware implementations for EBS based on the introduced classification schema. Section 2.2 presents the area of model-driven engineering in general and the two transformation languages used in this thesis in particular. Section 2.3 gives an overview of software performance engineering followed by a detailed introduction to the *Palladio Component Model* (PCM) providing the basis of our implementation.

2.1. Event-based Systems

Event-based systems are used in a variety of different domains and their size ranges from small embedded systems up to large-scale and world-wide distributed systems [Hinze 09]. Nevertheless, most systems that use event-based interactions have the four core elements *Source*, *Sink*, *Transmission System*, and *Event*, illustrated in Figure 2.1, in common [Carzaniga 98b]. Chandy [Chandy 06] defined an *Event* as *"a significant change in state"*, where by significant only those changes are meant that influence the system or application. This definition is one of the most widely used in the IT world [Chandy 10, Hinze 10b]. Detecting such changes leads to the instantiation of events, which are emit-

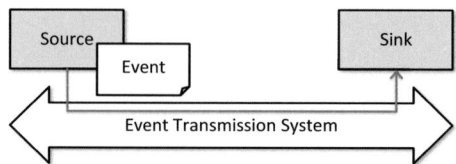

Figure 2.1: Core Elements of Event-based Systems

ted by a *Source*. In the literature, the *Source* is also known as *Producer* [Hinze 09, Mühl 06], *Publisher* [Eugster 03], *Sender* [Pietzuch 04], *Generator* [Carzaniga 98b], or *Monitoring Component* [Sachs 11]. The *Transmission System* is responsible to deliver events from sources to connected sinks that have registered for receiving the events. The transmission system encapsulates the communication between the sources and sinks. The communication can be push-based, pull-based or completely decoupled following the *Publish/Subscribe* (Pub/-Sub) paradigm [Mühl 06]. In push-based systems, the source is the active part responsible to invoke the event processing behaviour within the sink. In pull-based systems, the sink actively asks for new events that should be processed [Sachs 11]. In the literature, the transmission system is also known as *Notification Service* [Hinze 09, Mühl 06], *Event Service* [Eugster 03], *Event-based Middleware* [Pietzuch 04], *Channel* [Hohpe 08] or *Event Bus* [Carzaniga 98b]. The *Sinks*, also known as *Reactive Components* [Hinze 09, Sachs 11], *Consumers* [Mühl 06], *Subscribers* [Eugster 03], or *Receivers* [Carzaniga 98b, Pietzuch 04], contain the business logic for processing incoming events. Although most EBS share this common structuring in sink, source and transmission system, they differ in many different aspects. In the following, we present and discuss a characterisation schema, which highlights these differentiating factors.

2.1.1. Characterisation Schema for Event-based Systems

The characterisation schema developed as part of this thesis systematically structures the different characteristics of an EBS. We use feature models [Czarnecki 00] to group and visualise these characteristics. In Figure 2.2, we present an overview of the different categorisation dimensions. In the following, these dimensions are explained in more detail, each with its own sub-model.

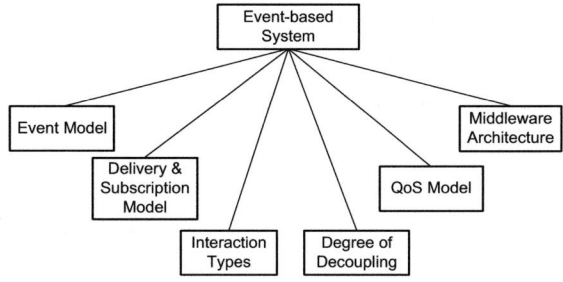

Figure 2.2: Characterisation Overview

Event Model The *Event Model*, depicted in Figure 2.3, focuses on the characteristics of the events used within the system. We differentiate between *Notifications/Triggers, Messages,* and *Typed Events.* The distinguishing feature is the type of content events encapsulate referred to as

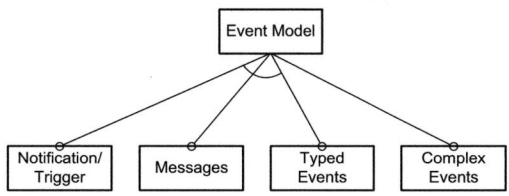

Figure 2.3: Characterisation: Event Model

payload. Notifications and triggers do not contain any data, they comprise only a notification that something happened, without providing further data. In contrast, messages as well as typed events contain a payload, which can be used to transmit data from sources to sinks. The contained data can range from a simple value of a certain sensor up to complex business data objects. Messages are envelopes that need to be unwrapped in order to analyse the content and the included metadata to differentiate messages. The possible message content ranges from unstructured text as used in *Java Message Service* (JMS) text messages [Hapner 02], over key value pairs [Carzaniga 01] and structured XML data, up to serialised objects [Eugster 03]. In contrast to messages, *Typed Events* are data objects [Oki 93] as used in object-oriented programming languages. In [Eugster 01], typed-events are called *Obvents* to highlight the fusing of data objects and events. The access to typed events is usually integrated into the programming languages used on the source and sink side, thus an explicit serialisation or de-serialisation is not required. Additionally, the transmission system is able to determine the type of a certain event and thus adjust the handling and routing of events depending on their type.

Some EBS allow to define *Complex Events* also known as composite events, which are an aggregation of basic or other complex events [Mühl 06]. The detection of event patterns described using an event correlation language leads to the instantiation and sending of a complex event [Hinze 09].

Delivery & Subscription Model Figure 2.4 illustrates the different characteristics of the *Delivery & Subscription Model.*

It differentiates between *Point-to-Point* (P2P) and *Publish/Subscribe* (Pub/Sub) communication, which are illustrated in Figure 2.5. P2P communication, is built around the concept of queues which form a virtual communication channel. Each event is sent to a specific queue and

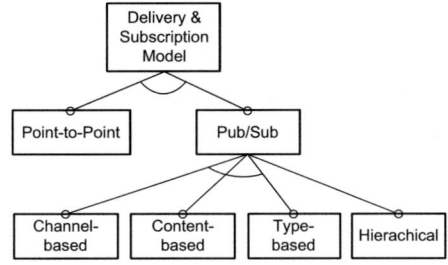

Figure 2.4: Characterisation: Delivery & Subscription Model

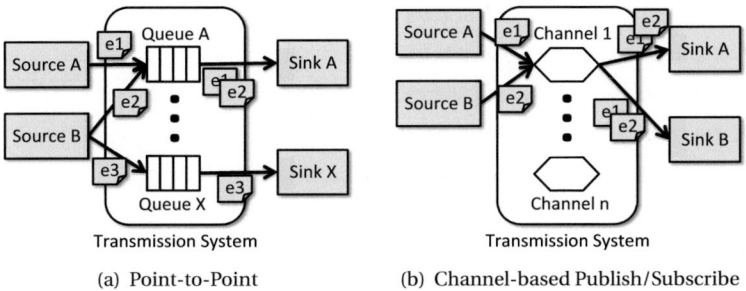

Figure 2.5: Event-based Interactions

later retrieved from there and processed by a sink [Sachs 11]. Usually a queue is associated with a single sink. However, in the most general case multiple sinks can be connected to a queue and events are then de-queued from the queue on a *first-come-first-serve* (FCFS) basis resulting in the fact, that each event is received and processed by exactly one sink. In *Pub/Sub* interactions, the sink connects to the transmission system and subscribes for the events of interest by defining a set of conditions that the respective events should fulfill [Eugster 03]. Event subscriptions can address different aspects of an event. Our classification schema differentiates between three different subscription models *Channel-based,*

Content-based, and *Type-based.* In order to allow a fine-grained selection of events, EBS often support a mixture of different subscription models. All subscription models have in common that an event is delivered to all sinks whose selection conditions are satisfied by the event.

With *Channel-based* subscriptions, the transmission system offers different event channels that sinks can connect to as illustrated in 2.5(b). When emitting an event, the source is responsible to select the channel that is used to publish the event. The transmission system forwards the event to all sinks subscribed to this channel. Channels are independent of the employed event model and the event content and thus they allow a logical grouping of events. This logical grouping can be used to reflect for example the geographical distribution of the system like the grouping of events within a traffic monitoring system based on the districts in which emitting sensors are located.

In *Type-based* subscriptions [Eugster 01], the events of interest are identified by their data type, which means that the transmission system delivers to the subscribed sinks all events that conform to a specified type or a subtype. Obviously, this requires the support of typed events within the transmission system.

Often a sink's interest in an event depends on the content of the event. For these reasons, *Content-based* subscriptions allow the definition of filtering rules that refer to the content and payload of events. Content-based subscription can only be used with messages or typed-events as event model. Content-based subscriptions enable a fine-grained selection of events, however, they induce more processing overhead within the transmission system compared to the other subscription models. Each event needs to be examined in order to route the event to all subscribed sinks that have issued matching subscriptions. With the aim to combine fine-grained event selection with simplified event routing, channel- or type-based subscriptions are often used in combination with a content-based subscription model.

Channel-based as well as type-based subscriptions can be *hierarchical*. In a hierarchical channel-based subscription, a sink not only receives the events published on the specified channel, but it also receives all events published on one of the sub-channels. Hierarchical channel-based subscriptions are also known as *subject-based* subscriptions [Mühl 06, Sachs 11]. In a hierarchical type-based subscriptions, the sink receives all events which conform with the defined type or are a subtype of this type.

Interaction Types   The number of sources and sinks that can participate in an event-based interaction is an additional characteristic of the interaction. Our characterisation schema differentiates between four interaction types, depicted in Figure 2.6. *One-to-one* interactions are interactions between exactly one source and one sink. In *one-to-many* interactions only one source but several sinks are allowed also known as centralised broadcasting of events. In contrast *many-to-one* interactions allow several event sources participating in an event-based interaction, however the emitted events are consumed by exactly one sink. The last and most powerful interaction type is the *many-to-many* interaction, which does not restrict the number of participating sources and sinks. Thus, it subsumes all other interaction types.

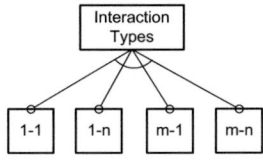

Figure 2.6: Characterisation: Interaction Types

Degree of Decoupling   The decoupling of components is one of the benefits promised by event-based communication. In analogy to the

31

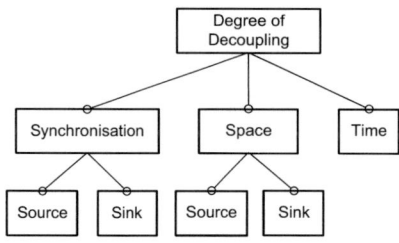

Figure 2.7: Characterisation: Degree of Decoupling

characterisation used in [Eugster 03], we differentiate three aspects of decoupling namely *Synchronisation, Space,* and *Time.* As illustrated in Figure 2.7, the first two are further subdivided into decoupling on the source and sink side.

Synchronisation decoupling means that the control flow of sources and sinks is decoupled. In the case of source decoupling, the event source is blocked only until the event is handed over to the transmission system and does not have to wait until the event is delivered to and processed by the receiving sinks. In the case of sink decoupling, the event delivery is often realised by using callback functions invoked by the transmission system. However, there also exist event-based systems that use blocking event pulling mechanisms, e.g., the PIRATES middleware (described in Section 2.1.2), which provide synchronisation decoupling on the source side but not on the sink side. In contrast, the event listener concept often used to build graphical user interfaces provides decoupling of sinks while the event source is often blocked until all event listeners are executed.

In systems decoupled in *Space,* the sources do not know which and how many sinks are receiving the events. Similarly, sinks do not know which and how many sources are producing events. Pub/Sub-based systems are always decoupled in space both on the source and on the sink side [Eugster 03]. However, other event-based systems, especially P2P-based systems might be decoupled only on the source side or the sink side or provide no space decoupling at all.

The last aspect of decoupling is *Time* decoupling. Following the definition in [Eugster 03], sources and sinks do not need to be active at the same time to interact via sending events. Thus, a sink can consume events that have been emitted by a source which was deactivated before the receiving sink became active. In the case of time decoupling there is no differentiation between the source side and sink side, as in contrast to the other aspects of decoupling, the source sides and sink sides cannot be considered in isolation in this case.

QoS Model A lot of different quality models for software can be found in the literature with the ISO/IEC 9126 [ISO/IEC 03] as one of the most prominent representatives. In contrast to those general software quality models, our characterisation focuses on the run-time behaviour of EBS and thus it does not consider quality characteristics like usability

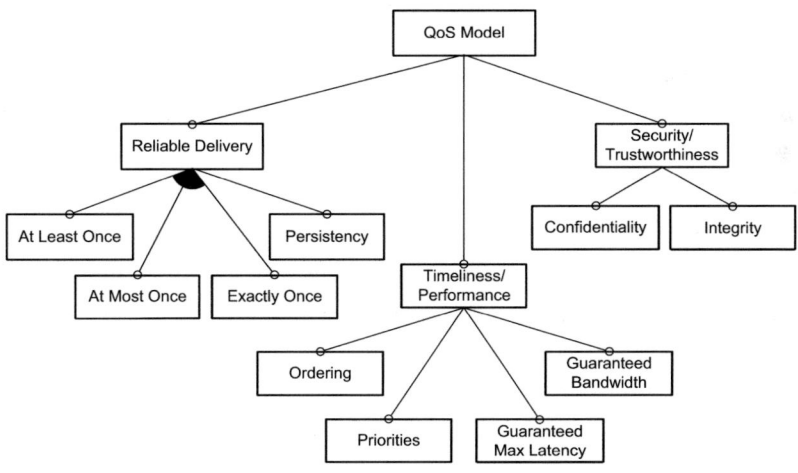

Figure 2.8: Characterisation: QoS Model

or maintainability. Corsaro et al. [Corsaro 06] classified the *Quality-of-Service* (QoS) attributes of EBS into the domains reliable delivery, timeliness, security, and trust. As illustrated in Figure 2.8, our classification schema refines these domains resulting in the characteristics *Reliable Delivery*, *Timeliness/Performance*, and *Security/Trustworthiness*. We rearranged and refined the QoS metrics specialised for EBS defined in the literature (e.g., [Behnel 06], [Appel 10], [Corsaro 06]) according to our schema.

According to [Behnel 06], we differentiate between three guaranteed types of *Reliable Delivery*. *At Least Once* guarantees that an event is delivered to the subscribed components, however, the same event might be transferred several times to a receiving component. In contrast, the *At Most Once* guarantee forbids such multiple delivery of events, but it also allows that events might be dropped and not delivered to the sinks. *Exactly Once* is a combination of the two previous guarantees, thus it guarantees that all events are delivered to the sinks and each event is delivered only once. The guaranteed delivery of events requires a *Persistency* mechanism that prevents the loss of events. Given that an EBS can offer a persistent storage of events without supporting any delivery guarantees, it is an additional and separat aspect of the *Reliable Delivery* characteristic.

Timeliness/Performance focuses on the temporal aspects of the event delivery as well as on performance aspects of the delivery mechanisms. In the case of *Ordering*, the transmission system guarantees, that the ordering of the events delivered to sinks corresponds to the order in which the events have been published. This means that if event A was published before event B, A will always be delivered first. Often transmission systems do not guarantee an ordered delivery in order to increase the optimisation opportunities within the routing algorithms and to avoid expensive synchronisation mechanisms. In some EBS, sources can assign *Priorities* to events, which are considered within the transmission system and influence the processing and routing of events. Events with high priorities are processed faster and might overtake events with lower priorities. The event delivery latency and the bandwidth or event throughput respectively are two important QoS metrics of EBS [Behnel 06]. Especially when using event-based communication in real time systems (e.g., [Iwai 00], [Kaiser 05]), the transmission system should be able to guarantee a certain QoS level. In our classification schema, we differentiate between the two optional characteristics *Guaranteed Max Latency*, the ability to guarantee an upper bound of the delivery latency, and *Guaranteed Bandwidth*, which is the ability of the transmission system to guarantee a given event throughput. Our schema only considers the ability to guarantee such behaviours and not the values of the respective metrics themselves. Thus, we do not differentiate between fast and slow EBS, as the performance of a system is always context dependent.

With the use of event-based communication in business- and mission-critical systems, the security and trustworthiness of the communication mechanisms became an increasingly important aspect. In analogy to [Behnel 06], we differentiate between the two aspects *Confidentiality* and *Integrity*. In the case of confidentiality, the transmission system has to ensure that events and the data they carry can only be read by the sources and sinks that participate in the respective interactions and not by other components that intercept the communication. As described in [Fiege 04], confidentiality can be realised by using a trusted transmission system combined with encrypted data connections between sources, sinks, and the transmission system. In order to ensure the integrity of events, the transmission needs to provide authentication functionalities to identify each component. In combination with techniques like digital signatures, the source of an event can be identified and it can be ensured that the event has not been modified.

Middleware Architecture The architecture of the underlying communication middleware and respectively the transmission system is an additional differentiating factor. As illustrated in Figure 2.9, the characterisation schema differentiates between three architecture types. In *Peer-to-Peer* architectures, there is no dedicated server or set of servers hosting the transmission system. The functionality provided by the transmission system is integrated into the communicating components of the sources and sinks in the form of local libraries. The *centralised* middleware is characterised by a transmission system running as one central process all sources and sinks are connected to. Most industrial event-based systems are based on a centralised middleware like for example JMS-based servers. In *distributed* architectures, the transmission system is distributed over several independent event brokers [Mühl 06]. The brokers use specialised routing algorithms to deliver the published events to all subscribed sinks that can be connected to different brokers.

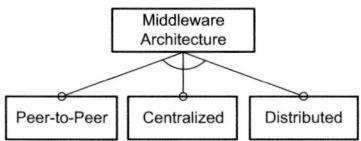

Figure 2.9: Characterisation: Middleware Architecture

2.1.2. Overview of Existing Event-based Systems

In this section, we apply the derived categorisation schema to existing EBS. As seen in the previous section, the variations between different systems especially with respect to the underlying communication middleware is high. In the following, we survey existing EBS considering both industrial systems and research prototypes and classify them according to our categorisation schema. The selected systems we consider serve as representative examples and demonstrate the large variation ranging from centralised large scale systems up to highly distributed embedded systems. Several similar surveys exist in the literature, however, they focus on other aspects and do not evaluate all dimensions in our categorisation schema. [Liu 03], [Baldoni 06], and [Pietzuch 07] present surveys on existing Pub/Sub systems, which in the case of [Baldoni 06] is focused on distributed Pub/Sub systems. Schmidt et al. [Schmidt 08] present an overview of the area of *Complex Event Processing* (CEP). [Mühl 06] and [Hinze 10b] give a more generic overview of existing EBS, however, lacking a common categorisation schema to compare different systems.

CORBA Notification Service

The *Common Object Request Broker Architecture* (CORBA) [OMG 11] defines a platform- and language-independent object-oriented middleware architecture. CORBA is a mature middleware technology that is widely used in the financial and telecommunication domains. In 1994, the *Object Management Group* (OMG) introduced the CORBA Event Service [OMG 94] as a new CORBA service, with its latest version 1.2 released in 2004 [OMG 04a]. Events are defined as CORBA objects using the *Interface Definition Language* (IDL), which is part of the CORBA standard. The Event Service decouples sources and sinks by introducing an event channel, which can be accessed by components in a pull- as well as push-based manner. This channel allows components to participate in many-to-many interactions. The asynchronous communication is implemented on top of the already existing synchronous method invocations provided by the CORBA framework. The event service does not provide any filtering mechanisms, which in combination with some other shortcomings has led to the development of the Notification Service [OMG 04b]. As successor of the Event Service, it introduces new functionality like event filtering, QoS, and a new event type called structured events. Structured events are divided into header and body, which both can contain a filterable list of key-value pairs. The Notification Service specification defines several parameters to configure reliable and persistent delivery. Furthermore, the parameters allow to assign priorities and configure the ordering of events.

Java Message Service (JMS)

The *Java Message Service* (JMS) [Hapner 02] is a standardised *Application Programming Interface* (API) for Java applications to access the facilities of *Message-Oriented Middleware* (MOM) servers. It is part of the *Java Platform, Enterprise Edition* (Java EE) standard [(Sun) 09], which defines a set of standards for building large enterprise applications. In the terminology of JMS, the communication middleware that provides the JMS API is referred to as JMS server while applications using the API to exchange messages are referred to as JMS clients. Nearly all industrial enterprise application servers (e.g., IBM's WebShpere, SAP's Netweaver platform, or Oracle's Weblogic server) support event-based communication using the JMS API, resulting in JMS being the de facto standard in Java-based enterprise messaging applications.

JMS is based on messages as event model and supports different message types, e.g., text, byte object, or map messages, depending on the payload that should be transferred. In addition, JMS allows to define message attributes using key value pairs. When subscribing to a channel, each sink can specify individual filtering rules called *selectors* applied to the event attributes on the server side. JMS supports P2P communication through JMS-Queues as well as channel-based Pub/Sub communication using JMS-Topics in a many-to-many interaction style. JMS decouples sources and sinks with respect to synchronisation and space. With durable subscriptions, JMS additionally allows decoupling sources and sinks with respect to time. JMS differentiates between non-persistent and persistent delivery modes. In non-persistent mode, pending messages are kept in main memory buffers while they are waiting to be delivered resulting in low messaging overhead at the cost of losing un-delivered messages in case of a server crash. In persistent mode, the JMS server ensures that no messages are lost by logging messages to persistent storage such as a database or a file system. In non-persistent mode, each message is guaranteed to be delivered at most once, whereas in persistent mode it is guaranteed to be delivered exactly once. JMS ensures the ordering of messages which belong to one session. Furthermore, it allows the specification of message priorities, however it does not guarantee any quality attributes, neither performance guarantees with respect to latency or bandwidth nor security aspects.

WS Eventing and WS Notification

Web Services have been designed to allow platform-independent access to web-based services based on synchronous request/reply inter-actions. With their growing popularity and their integration into business applications, the need for an asynchronous push-based service interface was recognised. Sending messages to a service requires that the service can be addressed and contacted using a communication endpoint. *Web Service Addressing* (WS-Addressing) [W3C 04], a standard defined by the *World Wide Web Consortium* (W3C), introduces service endpoint references for Web services. Such endpoints can be passed as message parameters to a source service to register for an event stream. *Web Service Eventing* (WS-Eventing) [W3C 06], which is based on WS-Addressing, standardises the direct communication between Web Service sources and Web Service sinks. Events are realised as *Extensible Markup Language* (XML) messages, which can contain a simple value as well as complex data types. Sources and sinks are not decoupled with respect to synchronisation nor with respect to space and time. The event sink can define an event filter, which is a boolean XPath expression. As an alternative to WS-Eventing, the *Organisation for the Advancement of Structured Information Standards* (OASIS) introduced the *Web Service Notification* (WSN) [OASIS 04] standard. Similarly to WS-Eventing, WSN builds on top of WS-Addressing. In contrast to WS-Eventing, which is a pure peer-to-peer based solution, WSN allows direct peer-to-peer based connection between sources and sinks using *Web Service Base Notification* (WS-BaseNotification) [OASIS 06a] as well as space decoupled communication using *Web Service Brokered Notification* (WS-BrokeredNotification) [OASIS 06b] or *Web Service Topics* (WS-Topics) [OASIS 06c]. WS-BrokeredNotification introduces broker intermediaries to decouple sources and sinks. WS-Topics addresses the features related to a channel-based Pub/Sub delivery. Similarly to WS-Eventing, WSN supports the specification of content-based filtering rules. However, neither WS-Eventing nor WSN provide any support for QoS-related characteristics.

PIRATES

The *Peer-to-peer Implementation of Reconfigurable Architecture for Typed Event Streams* (PIRATES) [Ingram 09b] middleware was designed to support distributed component-based applications. The traffic monitoring system that we later use in one of our case studies in Section 6.2 is built on top of the PIRATES middleware. Its peer-to-peer based architecture is illustrated in Figure 2.10. The basic entity is the *component*. Each component is divided into a *wrapper*, provided by the PIRATES framework, and the business logic that encapsulates the component's functionality. The wrapper manages all communication between components including handling of the network I/O, registration of endpoints and management of their schemas, and reporting on the component's status. Each *endpoint* can be a *client*, a *server*, a *source*, or a *sink*. Clients and servers implement *Remote Procedure Call* (RPC) functionality providing synchronous request/reply operations and are attached in many-to-one relationships. The communication between sources and sinks is entirely asynchronous based on many-to-many interactions. Each end-

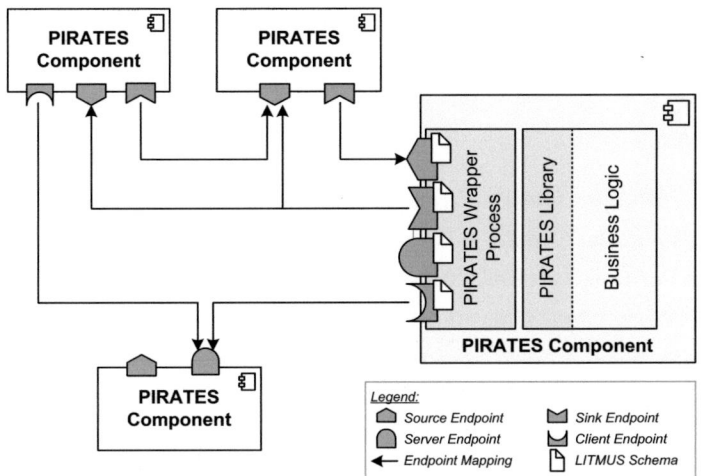

Figure 2.10: Schematic Overview on PIRATES Components

point specifies the data schema of the messages that it will emit and accept. The event type specification is based on the *Language of Interface Types for Messages in Underlying Streams* (LITMUS) [Ingram 09a], which is integrated into the PIRATES framework. PIRATES enforces matching of sender and receiver schemas ensuring that only compatible endpoints are connected. The act of connecting two endpoints is called *mapping*. The separation of the wrapper is intentional as it insulates business logic from dealing with network communication issues such as providing resilience in the face of failure of connected components. The business logic specifies its endpoints' mappings and the wrapper takes care of sending an event to all connected sinks as well as forwarding received events to the business logic. The interaction with the wrapper process is encapsulated within the *PIRATES Library,* which decouples the control flow of the source while the event handler of the sink is blocked until the next event is received. Furthermore, the PIRATES wrappers decouple

41

sources and sinks in the space domain. PIRATES does not provide any QoS guarantees, neither reliability nor performance or security-related.

SIENA

The Scalable Internet Event Notification Architecture (SIENA) [Carzaniga 98a, Carzaniga 01] was one of the first distributed content-based Pub/Sub systems. SIENA is based on a distributed multi-broker architecture targeted at an Internet-scale deployment. In SIENA, brokers are called servers. Sources connect to one of the SIENA servers to publish an event. Sinks register by placing content-based subscriptions at one of the servers. The latter is not required to be the same as the one the source is connected to. SIENA servers build a logical overlay network and route events through this network to the target servers that host matching subscriptions. The topology of the overlay network of event brokers is static and must be specified at deployment time. In SIENA, events are a set of typed attributes while the event itself is not typed. SIENA supports only content-based subscriptions applying filtering rules to the attributes contained in an event. When a subscription reaches a server (either from a client or from another server), the server forwards the subscription only if the set of addressed events is not subsumed by one of the sets addressed by existing subscriptions. The routing paths of events are defined based on these subscriptions at subscription time. The communication in SIENA is many-to-many. Since SIENA does not contain any persistence mechanisms, it decouples sources and sinks only with respect to synchronisation and space. There exists no precise specification of the semantics of event delivery [Mühl 06]. The content-based routing algorithms hamper any further security mechanisms like encryption [Wang 02].

SCRIBE

Scribe [Castro 02] is a scalable channel-based Pub/Sub system developed at Microsoft Research. Its architecture is a decentralised peer-to-peer architecture based on Pastry [Rowstron 01], a generic peer-to-peer object location and routing overlay network. Each node within the Scribe network can act as an event source or sink but it can also define a channel or act only as a forwarding relay node. In Scribe, channels are called groups, each identified through a unique ID. All messages can contain data and are thus classified as messages following our schema. Groups are not limited to only one source and thus allow many-to-many communication. Event delivery in Scribe is a best-effort approach and does not guarantee any QoS characteristics. Any reliable and/or ordered delivery of events has to be implemented on top of Scribe, which provides a dedicated extension interface. Similarly to SIENA, Scribe does not provide any persistence mechanisms and thus only decouples sources and sinks with respect to synchronisation and space but not with respect to time.

REBECA

The *Rebeca notification service* [Mühl 02, Parzyjegla 10] realises a content-based Pub/Sub system. Its distributed architecture is comparable to the broker-based architecture of SIENA. Events in Rebeca are a set of key-value pairs. Since Rebeca was designed to be extendible, which is a distinguishing feature compared to other approaches, it allows the integration of additional data types and filtering models [Mühl 06]. Rebeca distinguishes three types of brokers: local, border, and inner brokers. Local brokers are usually part of a local communication library, which encapsulates the communication with the Rebeca middleware. Each local broker is connected to one of the border brokers that form the boundary of the distributed overlay network. The network itself consists of border brokers handling the connections with sources and sinks and inner brokers forwarding events to other inner or border brokers. Local brokers forward messages created by sources into the Rebeca network. The routing among the border and inner brokers is based on filter-based routing tables and extendable routing strategies. Finally, the messages are sent through the local brokers to the subscribed sinks. This message flow decouples components with respect to synchronisation and space but not with respect to time. In its original version, QoS-related guarantees have been considered as future work [Mühl 02]. Given that the design of Rebeca allows the integration of new routing algorithms, the Rebeca middleware can be extended to support for example reliable delivery or encrypted communication as described in [Parzyjegla 10].

HERMES

Hermes [Pietzuch 04] is similarly to the previously described approaches based on a distributed broker network. However, in contrast to other systems, Hermes supports type-based subscriptions that can be combined with content-based rules. Hermes aims at an easy integration into existing *object-oriented* (OO) programming languages and supports type-checking of event data and event type inheritances. Similarly to Scribe, Hermes builds on top of a variation of the Pastry routing algorithm. Hermes has a layered architecture inspired by the ISO/OSI network stack. Each layer builds on top of the functionality provided by the layer underneath and provides an explicitly defined interface to the layer above. Thanks to this layered architecture, the implementations of the different layers can be replaced individually or adapted without affecting the other layers. The top layer provides extension points to plugin additional high level middleware services, which can be used for example to enforce QoS properties such as performance, reliability or security [Mahambre 08]. As Hermes does not provide persistence mechanisms, it decouples sources and sinks only with respect to synchronisation and space but not with respect to time.

2.1.3. Summary

The previous sections gave an overview of area of EBS. After introducing the general terminology, we presented a detailed characterisation schema for EBS. We introduced the six categorisation dimensions *Event Model, Delivery & Subscription Model, Interaction Types, Degree of Decoupling, QoS Model,* and *Middleware Architecture* each including multiple sub-characteristics. We applied the developed characterisation schema to different existing middleware implementations for EBS with the aim to present a survey on the large variety between existing EBS. Table 2.1 summarises the survey and lists the identified characteristics for each dimension. We selected the surveyed systems to represent different classes of EBS and thus to allow us demonstrating the large variety between existing systems. Several further middleware implementations for EBS not covered in our survey have been developed by research and industry, e.g., Ahkera [Fromm 09], *Cambridge Event Architecture* (CEA) [Bacon 00], Corona [Ramasubramanian 06], Echo [Eisenhauer 06], *Java Event-based Distributed Infrastructure* (JEDI) [Cugola 01], Gryphon [IBM 01], NaradaBrokering [Pallickara 03], READY [Gruber 00], and XMessages [Slominski 02].

While the presented overview of EBS introduced the context our approach is applied in, the following sections on model-based engineering and software performance engineering describe the foundations that our approach builds on.

2.2. Model-Driven Engineering

The aim of *Model-driven Engineering* (MDE) and more specific *Model-driven Software Development* (MDSD) is to leverage the role of models

	Event-Model	Delivery Model	Interaction Types	Decoupling	QoS Model	Middleware
CORBA	• Messages with typed payload	• Pub/Sub: *channel- and content-based*	• Many-to-many	• Synchronisation • Space	• Configurable Rel. Delivery • Ordering • Priorities	• Centralised
JMS	• Messages	• P2P • Pub/Sub: *channel- and content-based*	• Many-to-one (Queues) • Many-to-many (Topics)	• Synchronisation • Space	• Configurable Rel. Delivery • Ordering • Priorities	• Centralised
WS-Eventing	• Messages	• P2P	• One-to-many	• Synchronisation sink side	-	• Peer-to-Peer
WSN	• Messages	• P2P • Pub/Sub: *channel-based*	• Many-to-many	• Synchronisation • Space	-	• Peer-to-Peer • Centralised
PIRATES	• Messages • Types Events	• P2P	• Many-to-many	• Synchronisation *(only source)* • Space	-	• Peer-to-Peer
SIENA	• Messages with attributes	• Pub/Sub: *content-based*	• Many-to-many	• Synchronisation • Space	-	• Distributed
Scribe	• Messages	• Pub/Sub: *channel-based*	• Many-to-many	• Synchronisation • Space	-	• Peer-to-Peer
Rebeca	• Messages with attributes but extendable	• Pub/Sub: *content-based*	• Many-to-many	• Synchronisation • Space	• extendable	• Distributed
HERMES	• Typed-Events • Hierarchical	• Pub/Sub: *type-based*	• Many-to-many	• Synchronisation • Space	• Confidentiality • Integrity	• Distributed

Table 2.1: Categorisation of Existing Event-based Systems

in the software development process. Models describe the software at a higher level of abstraction. Compared to source code, implementation specific details and complexity are abstracted. Model transformations support the translation of high-level models into models at a lower abstraction level, which might include source code. In doing so, MDSD aims to handle the increasing complexity and flexibility in today's software systems by allowing low level implementation tasks like coding to be substituted by modelling activities like the specification of domain or problem specific high-level models [Schmidt 06]. In the following, we first introduce the foundational concepts of MDE including definitions of central terms like model and meta-model. Second, we present a general introduction to model transformations and then introduce the two transformation languages used in the context of this thesis namely *MOdel transformation LAnguage* (MOLA) and *Query/View/Transformation* (QVT).

2.2.1. Basic Concepts

Models are the central artifact in MDE. A common definition of the term *Model* is given in [Uhl 07] and [Becker 08a]:

Definition 2.1 (Model [Becker 08a]). *"A formal representation of entities and relationships in the real world (abstraction) with a certain correspondence (isomorphism) for a certain purpose (pragmatics)."*

This definition is based on the three characteristics of a model identified by Stachowiak [Stachowiak 73] namely abstraction, isomorphism, and pragmatism. *Abstraction* refers to the property of a model to hide details of the real-world objects (entities and relationships) it represents. The selection of included and abstracted aspects is guided by the goal for which the model is created. The relation between the model and the respective real-world objects can be seen as a projection. This projection must be an *isomorphism* to allow drawing conclusions from the model that can be translated in the context of the real-world objects. Again, the definition of this projection should be guided by the goal for which the model is built. This *pragmatism* in the definition of a model is the last important characteristic of models. Models are not defined for their own sake but are always designed for a given specific purpose.

MDE aims at the automated processing of models, which requires a formal definition of rules and constraints that should be satisfied by models in a given target domain. In MDE, such rules and constraints are specified by means of meta-models.

Definition 2.2 (Meta-Model [Ernst 99]). *"A meta-model is a precise definition of the constructs and rules needed for creating semantic models."*

A meta-model contains rules that are either syntactic or semantic [Völter 06]. Rules defining the semantic can again be split into rules defining the concrete syntax or the abstract syntax of model instances. Following the description of Becker [Becker 08a], the abstract syntax defines the concepts of a meta-model independently of concrete encoding specifics, while the concrete syntax defines encoding rules to store and visualise the abstract concepts. The semantics of a model comprises static and dynamic rules. Static semantics define further constraints on the model that can be checked without "executing" the model or knowing its intention. In contrast, the dynamic semantics define the intention of the meta-model concepts and describe how to interpret a model instance in a given context. However, the borderline between the different types of rules is not always strict.

With the aim to increase the adoption of MDSD in industrial software projects, the OMG developed the *Model-Driven Architecture* (MDA) approach [OMG 06b]. In the context of the MDA approach, the OMG defined a set of standards with the aim to ensure the interoperability between different MDSD tools. The central standard is the *Meta Object Facility* (MOF) [OMG 06c], which is a self-describing meta-meta-model providing a common language to specify meta-models. MOF has been developed in the context of the *Unified Modeling Language* (UML) [OMG 10] and was used to formally define the UML meta-model, which is the most well-known meta-model for software systems. With the *Object Constraint Language* (OCL) [OMG 06d], the OMG defined a language to specify the rules restricting the set of valid models as well as meta-models. Meta-model designers often use OCL expressions to define the static semantic.

Meta-models and models can be defined on different abstraction levels. The MDA guide [OMG 03] groups them into *platform-independent models* (PIMs) and *platform-specific models* (PSMs) defined as follows:

Definition 2.3 (*Platform-independent model* (PIM) [OMG 03]). *"A model of a subsystem that contains no information specific to the platform, or the technology that is used to realise it."*

Definition 2.4 (*Platform-specific model* (PSM) [OMG 03]). *"A model of a subsystem that includes information about the specific technology that is used in the realisation of it on a specific platform, and hence possibly contains elements that are specific to the platform."*

The term platform originally comes from technology platforms like Java EE, .NET, or CORBA, which offer middleware services and simplify the building of complex software systems. It is defined as:

Definition 2.5 (Platform [OMG 03]). *"A set of subsystems/technologies that provide a coherent set of functionality through interfaces and specified usage patterns that any subsystem that depends on the platform can use without concern for the details of how the functionality provided by the platform is implemented."*

According to the MDA guide, transformations bridge the semantic gap between a PIM and a PSM as illustrated in Figure 2.11. A transformation

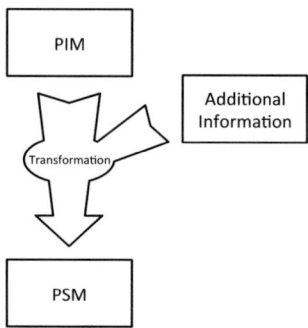

Figure 2.11: Transformation Pattern According to the MDA Guide [OMG 03]

takes the PIM together with optionally additional information and generates the PSM. The amount of additional information can vary from not taking any additional information to providing sets of additional models parameterising the transformation process. Although this generic pattern shows a direct mapping from PIM to PSM, a transformation can consists of several transformation steps generating a chain of PIMs followed by a chain of PSMs. Each model is a refinement of the previous model instance, which in case of a PIM is still platform independent. In the following section, we give an overview of techniques that can be used to implement such model transformations.

2.2.2. Model Transformations

In the domain of MDSD, model transformations are generally classified into two types, namely *Model-2-Text* (M2T) and *Model-2-Model* (M2M) transformations [Czarnecki 03], which we briefly describe in the following paragraphs. For a more detailed survey and characterisation of model transformations, we refer the reader to [Mens 06], [Czarnecki 06], and [Rose 12].

M2T transformations   M2T transformations receive a model that conforms to a certain meta-model as input. The result of the transformation is one or more arbitrary text files, which in the area of MDSD mostly contain source code in a given programming language. However, M2T transformations are not limited to source code and can also be applied to generate for example documentation or configuration files. According to the surveys presented in [Czarnecki 06] and [Rentschler 06], the most common approaches to realise M2T transformations are visitor-based and template-based approaches. Applying the visitor design pattern [Gamma 95], visitor-based approaches use a visitor object that traverses a graph of elements and writes text specific for the currently visited element to an output stream. Template-based approaches use templates that contain a combination of text artefacts and small code snippets. When executing the transformation, the included code is executed to query information from the source model and the result is inserted into the surrounding text artefact.

M2M transformations   As illustrated in Figure 2.12, M2M transformations transform a *Source Model* that conforms to a *Source Meta-Model* into a *Target Model* that conforms to a *Target Meta-Model*. In case of identical source and target meta-models, M2M transformations enable

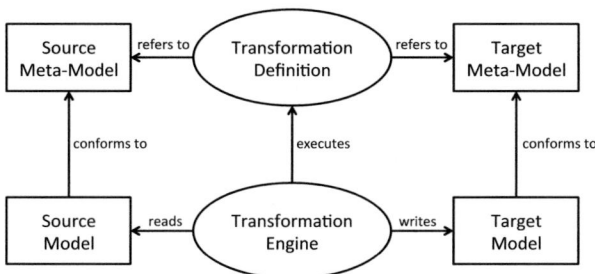

Figure 2.12: Concept of Model-2-Model Transformations [Czarnecki 06]

a direct manipulation of the input model, which is referred to as *in-place transformation*. Kleppe et al. [Kleppe 07] provide the following definitions:

Definition 2.6 (Transformation [Kleppe 07]). *"A transformation is the automatic generation of a target model from a source model, according to a transformation definition."*

Definition 2.7 (Transformation Description [Kleppe 07]). *"A transformation definition is a set of transformation rules that together describe how a model in the source language can be transformed into a model in the target language."*

Definition 2.8 (Transformation Rule [Kleppe 07]). *"A transformation rule is a description of how one or more constructs in the source language can be transformed into one or more constructs in the target language."*

As illustrated in Figure 2.12, transformation definitions are specified at the meta-level and refer to the elements defined within the meta-models. They describe the mapping between source and target element types. For example, a M2M transformation transforming UML class diagrams to *Entity Relationship* (ER) models would contain one rule to map UML classes to entities in the ER model and a second rule to map UML associations to ER relations. When executing such a transformation in the transformation engine, the rules are evaluated for each element and if they match, the corresponding elements in the target model are created. In the case of the example UML to ER transformation, an entity is created for each class defined within the source UML model as well as a relation for each association between classes.

According to the classification of Czarnecki et al. [Czarnecki 06], M2M transformations can be grouped into different types depending on the realisation of rules and their evaluation. The most important types are direct-manipulations, operational, relational, graph-based, and hybrid approaches.

Direct-manipulations require equal source and target meta-models. They are mostly implement as in-place transformations where the results of the transformation are directly stored in the source model. Such approaches provide an internal representation of the model extended with an API to manipulate the model elements. Often they are realised as an OO framework in multi-purpose programming languages like Java.

Operational approaches have similarities with direct-manipulations as they are also build out of operational methods used to manipulate the source model. However, operational approaches are normally based on a dedicated transformation language specialised for model transformations. Often they combine query languages like OCL with imperative programming constructs. The most well known transformation language representing operational approaches is the *QVT Operational Mapping Language* (QVT-O), which is part of OMG's QVT standard [OMG 07]. Section 2.2.4 presents more details on QVT in general and QVT-O in particular.

Relational approaches use a declarative language to define relations between source and target elements. The transformation engine takes the set of relations and either tests if the relationships are fulfilled or adapts the target model such that none of the relationships is violated. *QVT Relations Language* (QVT-R), which is the second transformation language defined within the QVT standard, is one of the most prominent representatives of this type of transformations.

Graph transformations operate on typed, attributed, labeled graphs [Andries 96]. Rules usually consist of a *left-hand-side* (LHS) and a *right-hand-side* (RHS) graph pattern. Whenever a LHS pattern can be matched, it is replaced by the structure given via the RHS pattern. The process is repeated until no more matching LHS patterns can be found. Several transformation approaches like *VIsual Automated model TRAnsformations framework* (VIATRA2) [Varro 07], Henshin [Arendt 10], Story Diagrams/Fujaba [von Detten 12], and MOLA (described in Section 2.2.3) extend the basic approach of graph mappings with additional elements to define an explicit scheduling of the different mapping rules.

Hybrid approaches combine different techniques of the previous approaches. Mostly, they allow a mixture of declarative and imperative rules. The *Atlas Transformation Language* (ATL) [ATLAS Group 07] represents this type of transformations as it support fully declarative, hybrid as well as fully imperative transformation rules.

The previous paragraphs, provided a brief overview of the different techniques that can be applied to implement transformations. In the following sections, we introduce the two transformation languages used in this thesis.

2.2.3. MOLA

The *MOdel transformation LAnguage* (MOLA) [Kalnins 04] represents the group of graph transformation based approaches. It has been developed at the University of Latvia. The main goal of MOLA was *"to provide an easy readable graphical transformation"* [Kalnins 04]. MOLA combines traditional structured programming using some kind of flowcharts with transformation rules based on relatively simple graph patterns. The results of the transformation tool contest published in [Rose 12] highlight that the developers reached their goal of providing a easy readable graphical transformation language that is still executable and applicable to implement realistic transformations. Before describing the MOLA syntax in more detail, we provide a short overview of the tool support for MOLA transformations.

The MOLA tool [Kalnins 06] that is publicly available from the project website [Latvia 12] is based on the METAclipse framework, which itself is based on the Eclipse platform. The tool consists of two main parts, the *Transformation Definition Environment* (TDE) and the *Transformation Execution Environment* (TEE). Both use a common repository to store transformations, meta-models and model instances. TDE provides

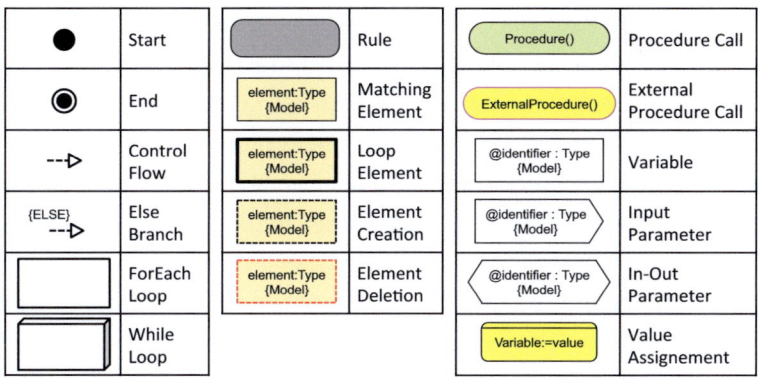

Figure 2.13: Syntax of MOLA

graphical editors supporting the modelling of MOLA-based transformations as well as a dedicated meta-model editor. However, the tool also supports importing externally defined meta-models. TEE provides different possibilities to execute MOLA transformations. The most often used variant is the execution within the MOLA tool, based on an interpreter directly working with the repository [Kalnins 06]. Additionally, TEE provides a compiler transforming MOLA transformation into executable libraries for Java and C++. The Java libraries are based on the JGraLab framework [JGraLab 12] while the C++ implementation uses the framework presented in [Barzdins 06]. For a more detailed description of the different transformation solutions, we refer the reader to [Sostaks 10].

Each MOLA transformation consists of a set of procedures with one marked as main procedure being the starting point of the transformation. Each procedure is specified using the elements provided by the graphical syntax of MOLA, shown in Figure 2.13. Similarly to UML activity diagrams, each procedure contains one *Start* node and depending on the control flow one or more *End* nodes. *Control Flow* arrows connect the different statements (namely loops, rules, procedure calls, and value assignments) with each other as well as the start and end nodes.

Rules are the most important statements within a MOLA procedure, as they contain the definition of graph patterns describing the transformation. Each rule contains a set of *Matching Elements* representing a certain type defined within the source meta-model. In addition to the direct referencing of meta-model elements, matching elements can also reference other matching elements defined in one of the previous rules. The addressing of an element in MOLA is specified with the @ symbol followed by the element's name. To define a matching pattern, matching elements are connected by drawing associations between these elements. The semantics of these associations, which have a corresponding association within the meta-model, is that the pattern matches if an instance of the respective meta-model association between the two elements exists within the source model. Matching elements can additionally be extended with constraints on the attributes of the elements. For example, they allow specifying that only elements with a certain attribute value are matched. When executing the transformation, the pattern matching algorithm tries to find the defined pattern within the source model. If the pattern can be matched the execution continues with the next statement following the control flow arrow. If it is not matched, the execution continues with the statement specified by the *Else Branch*. In addition to pure matching patterns, MOLA allows the specification of element instances as well as their deletion. The *Element Creation* is similar to the matching of elements, however, they have a thicker dashed border in red. *Element Deletions* are marked with a black dashed border. Element creation as well as element deletion can be mixed with matching elements to define the required context of the element instances in which the creation or deletion should be executed. Additionally, MOLA allows the creation and deletion of associations represented by red dashed and black dashed lines, respectively.

Providing explicit loop constructs is a unique selling point of the MOLA approach. MOLA provides two types of loops, a *ForEach Loop* and a

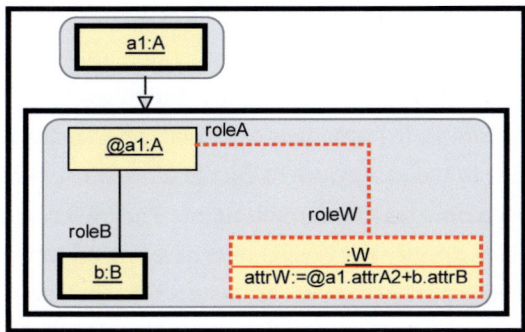

Figure 2.14: Exemplary MOLA Procedure based on [Kalnins 06]

While Loop. Each loop starts with a rule containing the declaration of the loop element. In order to distinguish the loop element from other classes in the mapping instances defining its context, the loop element has a thicker border. The semantics of both types of loops differ in the following way. A ForEach loop is executed only once for each valid instance matching the pattern. A While loop continues execution until there is no more matching variable instance, which means that the same loop variable instance may be processed several times.

Figure 2.14 provides an example containing two nested ForEach loops. The outer loop iterates over all elements of type A and executes the inner loop for each instance of A exactly once. The inner loop iterates over all elements of type B that are connected with the current instance of loop element `a1` of the outer loop. In addition to the pure definition of the loop element, the rule contains an element creation. For each matching tuple a new instance of type W together with an association to element `a1` is created. Additionally, the attribute `attrW` is set to the sum of `attrA2` of element `a1` and `attrB` of element `b`.

As already mentioned, MOLA transformations can be split over several procedures allowing to structure the transformation and thus improve its readability. *Procedure Call* statements are used to integrate these procedures into the control flow. Further to calls of MOLA procedures, MOLA additionally allows the integration of procedures that are implemented in Java. Within the MOLA syntax, they are integrated by means of *External Procedure Calls*. Both procedure calls allow referencing elements that are handed over to the procedure using the already explained combination of the @-symbol and the element name. The MOLA syntax provides two constructs to specify the parameters of a procedure. *Input parameters* are read-only parameters which means that the element instances received via such parameters as well as their attributes cannot be manipulated within the transformation. In contrast, *In-Out Parameters* follow the call by reference paradigm and manipulations on the received parameter within the procedure are visible for the calling procedure. With in-out parameters, it is possible to implement utility procedures for example creating and returning elements that are further processed outside the procedure. In addition to parameters, MOLA procedures can also include internal *Variables*. Similar to parameters, variables reference an element type defined within one of the meta-models. *Value Assignments* integrated in the control flow allow to store elements in variables.

Due to the easy readability of MOLA combined with its formalised and executable semantics, we selected MOLA as a formal language to specify the transformation developed in this thesis in a readable and at the same time formal manner. Although MOLA provides several transformation engine implementations, their integration into the Palladio tool chain confronted us with several technical issues discussed in Section 5.5 and therefore we decided to use another transformation language for our implementation, which is presented in the following section.

2.2.4. Query/View/Transformation Standard

In the context of the MDA approach, the OMG has developed the *Query/View/Transformation* (QVT) standard [OMG 07] including the two

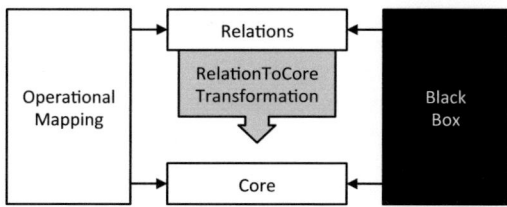

Figure 2.15: QVT Overview [OMG 07]

already mentioned transformation languages *QVT Relations Language* (QVT-R) and *QVT Operational Mapping Language* (QVT-O). The central concepts in QVT are *Queries* describing requests on the source model to identify the parts of the model that serve as input for the transformation, *Views* specifying the results in the source model, and *Transformations* describing the mapping between queries in the source model to views in the target model [Nolte 10].

As shown in Figure 2.15, QVT defines a common language core. This core provides a small set of operations supporting pattern matching over a flat set of variables by evaluating conditions over those variables. The core has the same expressiveness as the declarative transformation language QVT-R built on top of it. As QVT-R provides more complex language constructs mapped to a set of operations provided by the core, it allows a less verbose specification of transformations. This direct mapping between QVT-R and core operations can be compared with the transformation of Java source code into bytecode executed by the Java virtual machine. Operational mappings defined with QVT-O are partially mapped to either core operations or to relations later transformed to core operations. This combination of core and relational operations reduces the complexity of the transformations and allows to reuse the mappings defined between the relations and the core. Additionally, QVT allows the integration of custom black box language extensions that use either QVT or other multi-purpose programming languages like Java or C++. To allow an easy navigation within the models, QVT integrates the OCL standard [OMG 06d] supporting both the access to model elements and their attributes as well as the selection of elements based on conditional statements.

With QVT-R and QVT-O, the QVT standard provides two expressive and powerful transformation languages that highly differ in their language structure as being based on different transformation approaches. Both languages are still young and the number of reference projects and experience reports is still limited. However, the selection of the transformation language has a big impact on the implementation and requires weighing up advantages and disadvantages.

We selected QVT-O as language to implement the transformations developed in this thesis. Before presenting some insights into the QVT-O language, we first discuss the rationale behind our decision, which is based on our own experiences as well as on [Guduric 09] and [Nolte 10].

Transformation Structure Complex transformations grow to a reasonable amount of code. Similarly to programming languages, splitting the transformation into multiple files can reduce the complexity and simultaneously increase the maintainability and reusability. Only QVT-O allows structuring a transformation into multiple files. QVT-R requires having all relations to be defined within a single file resulting in files with more the 1.000 lines of code [Kapova 10b].

In-place Transformations The refinement transformation developed as part of this thesis is implemented as an in-place transformation (Chapter 5). Furthermore, the existing PCM prediction workflow following the pipeline pattern requires the manipulation of existing models instead of creating new instances. Implementing in-place transformations with QVT-R requires to create a complete clone using a generated copy transformation [Goldschmidt 08] which is later manually adapted to include the transformation rules that adapt the target model [Kapova 09]. QVT-O provides direct support of in-place transformations as well as copy operations for model elements and complete sub-models.

Branching   QVT-R supports only simple branches which means that an if-then-else-endif statement allows only one "if" and one "else" expression. This limitation results in multiple nested if-then-else constructs if more than a binary branch decision is required. In contrast, QVT-O provides an explicit else-if construct (elif) supporting unlimited branches.

Transformation Control Flow   QVT-R does not define an execution order in the case of multiple matching rules. To prevent an indeterministic execution of transformations, relations should be defined in a way that in every case only one rule matches, which requires additional marker relations and further increases the design complexity. Due to its operational structure, QVT-O provides several constructs to manage the control and data flow within the transformation. For example, QVT-O allows the iteration over a list of elements and the execution of different actions within each iteration.

Required Programming Skills   Nowadays most programmers are familiar with OO programming languages following an imperative programming style. Only a few programmers have experience with declarative programming styles like functional programming or logical programming supported by languages like Haskell or Prolog. For this reason, the learning curve for developers learning QVT-O based on the imperative programming style, raises much faster compared to QVT-R, which is based on a declarative programming style.

Eclipse Integration   The prediction tools that we extend as part of this thesis are all based on the Eclipse framework. For this reason, a smooth integration of the transformation engine into the Eclipse platform is an important aspect. The Eclipse Modeling Project [Eclipse Foundation 12] focuses on the evolution and promotion of model-based development technologies. The M2M sub-project, promises eventual support for QVT-O as well as QVT-R. However, the recent Eclipse releases only provided a stable version of the QVT-O engine since the QVT-R implementation is still under development. For this reason, executing QVT-R transformations within Eclipse requires additional third party transformation engines like mediniQVT [ikv++ 12] increasing the installation and maintenance complexity due to further dependencies.

Insights into QVT-O

In the following, we provide a brief introduction to QVT-O which, as mentioned above, was chosen for the implementation of the transformations developed in this thesis. For a detailed introduction to QVT-O, we refer the reader to [Nolte 10], which forms the basis for this introduction, as well as to the official QVT-O specification provided by the OMG [OMG 07].

Listing 2.1: QVT-O Transformation Definition

```
1   import myUtilityLibrary;
2
3   modeltype UML uses SimpleUml
4              ( "http://omg.qvt-examples.SimpleUml" );
5   modeltype RDBM uses SimpleRdbms
6              ( "http://omg.qvt-examples.SimpleRdbms" );
7
8   transformation exampleTransformation(
9                           in inputModel : UML,
10                          out outputModel : RDBM)
11                          access library myUtilityLibrary;
12  main() {
13      ...
14  }
```

QVT-O transformations contain as a minimum the three mandatory sections: model declarations, transformation declaration and the main operation. As shown in Listing 2.1, model declarations start with the keyword `modeltype` followed by an identifier that is assigned to this model. The keyword `uses` separates the assigned name from the meta-model specification. QVT-O allows importing externally defined meta-models using a *Uniform Resource Locator* (URL) as well as the inline definition as part of the QVT-O source code. Referencing an external meta-model as illustrated in Listing 2.1 is the preferable option as it allows to access and reuse the meta-model also from outside the transformation.

The transformation declaration, which begins with the keyword `transformation`, defines the name of the transformation followed by a comma separated list of models encapsulated in parentheses. An identifier put in front of each model's name defines the accessibility of the model. Possible identifiers are `in` for "source model only", `out` for "target model only" and `inout` for "source and target model at the same time" (in-place transformation). The models can be placed in this list without any need to order them in relation to the access modifiers. Each model is defined with a unique identifier to access them within the transformation followed by the meta-model type as defined in the model declaration section. The mandatory `main` operation is the starting point when executing the transformation.

In addition to these mandatory elements, Listing 2.1 includes the import of an external library. Libraries allow to partition the transformation into several files as well as to define common operations that can be reused in other transformations. To access such external files they first have to be imported using the `import` keyword followed by a reference to the file omitting the file extension. Second, the transformation declaration needs to be extended with an `access library` statement to gain access to the library defined in the external file.

Besides the `main()` operation which is the starting point of each transformation, QVT-O differentiates the following three types of operations that can be declared within the transformation itself or within an external library.

- **Mappings** are the standard operations to create new elements in the transformation.

- **Helpers** specify general functionality not focused on the creation of new elements. They have the same expressiveness as mapping operations.

- **Queries** are read-only operations. They are used to locate and access objects within a model.

Helper and mapping operations have a slightly different syntax but comparable expressiveness as both are able to receive one or more input parameters and able to return one or more output parameters. Additionally, both handle input parameters as references and are thus able to modify the referenced elements. The significant difference between these two operation types is the fact that mapping operations cache the returned results for each set of parameter values. This means that a mapping called a second time with the same parameters directly returns the results of the first execution without executing its internal operations.

The QVT-O specification provides the following definitions to further clarify the difference between mappings and helpers:

Definition 2.9 (Mapping [OMG 07]). *"A mapping operation is an operation implementing a mapping between one or more source model elements and one or more target model elements."*

Definition 2.10 (Helper [OMG 07]). *"A helper is an operation that performs a computation on one or more source objects and provides a result."*

Listing 2.2: QVT-O Operation Declaration

```
1   mapping myOperation(myClass: Class) : Entity @ targetmodel
        {
2     name = "name";
3   }
4
5   helper myOperation(myClass: Class) : Entity {
6     var myEntity : Entity @ targetmodel =
7                 Entity { name = "name" };
8     return myEntity;
9   }
10
11  query myOperation(myClass: Class) : Entity {
12    var myEntity : Entity = Entity { name = "name" };
13    return myEntity;
14  }
```

Additionally, the QVT-O specification states that helpers should not be used to create new objects except when they refer to sets, tuples, or intermediate properties. Helpers can also be used to combine a sequence of mappings when none or only one reference to a created element is returned.

Listing 2.2 shows an example for each of these operation types. The parentheses following the operation name contain a list of input elements in the form of tuples of identifiers and element types similar to well-known programming languages. A colon separates the set of input elements from the definition of the return type. Declaring multiple return types requires to separate them with a comma. If the operation does not return any elements the body which is encapsulated in curly braces begins directly after the specification of input parameters without any colon. If the parent transformation specifies more than one output model, the @ character followed by the name of the output model is used to identify the target model that the element should be created in. The @ syntax can also be used to identify the target model for inline object creation as shown in Listing 2.2.

Listing 2.3: QVT-O OCL example

```
1  container.containedElement->select(element | element.
       oclIsTypeOf(MyType))
```

With OCL [OMG 06d], QVT-O integrates a very expressive and powerful language supporting the selection and querying of elements within operations. Listing 2.3 demonstrates the querying of all instances of `MyType` contained in `container` element.

In QVT-O, operations can be executed on a single element or on each element of a provided set corresponding to an implicit foreach loop. A simple dot "`.`" specifies the single execution while the arrow operator "`->`" specifies the implicit for-each loop. In the example shown in Listing 2.4, the `mappingA()` operation is executed for each element contained in the list `elementList`, but the `oclIsTypeOf()` operation is applied only once for the whole `elementList`.

Listing 2.4: QVT-O Arrow Operator

```
1  elementList->map mappingA();
2  elementList.oclIsTypeOf(Collection);
```

In addition to this simplified notation using the arrow operator, QVT-O provides and explicit `forEach` construct, which allows specifying a set of instructions that should be executed for each element. Listing 2.5 provides an example of a `forEach` expression. The example first selects all instances of `MyElement` defined in `myModel`. Second, the foreach loop

Listing 2.5: QVT-O forEach Construct

```
1  myModel.objectsOfType(MyElement)->forEach(element){
2    myModel.removeElement(element);
3    log("element removed");
4  };
```

iterates over all selected elements. Within the loop body, the element is first removed from `myModel` and then a log entry of the successful deletion is created. Similarly to OO programming languages, the parentheses of the `forEach` construct contains the identifier to access the actual processed element within the block.

After briefly introducing MDE and MDSD in general and the two transformation languages applied in the context of this thesis, in the following section we present an overview of the application of model-driven techniques in the context of performance modelling and prediction.

2.3. Software Performance Engineering

Modelling and predicting extra-functional properties of software systems such as their performance and reliability is in the focus of research for a long time. Quality and especially performance issues are one of the root causes for serious problems that hamper the success of a software project as reported in [Glass 98],[Briegleb 07], and [Bloomberg 12]. In the past and at present, these problems are often targeted with a trial and error approach but this can be insufficient and become too expensive in matters of business constraints and scale of modern business applications [Williams 03].

Over the last years numerous approaches have been proposed for integrating performance prediction techniques into the software engineering process. Efforts were initiated with Smith's seminal work on *Software Performance Engineering* (SPE) [Smith 90]. In recent years, with the increasing adoption of *Component-based Software Engineering* (CBSE), the SPE community has focused on adapting and extending conventional SPE techniques to support component-based systems.

A number of architecture-level performance meta-models for component-based systems have been developed as surveyed in [Koziolek 10]. The most prominent examples are the UML SPT profile [OMG 05] and its successor the UML MARTE profile [OMG 06e], all of which are extensions of UML as the de facto standard modelling language for software architectures. Such meta-models provide means to describe the performance-relevant aspects of software components (e.g., internal control flow and resource demands) while explicitly capturing the influences of their execution context. The idea is that once component models are built they can be reused in multiple application and execution contexts.

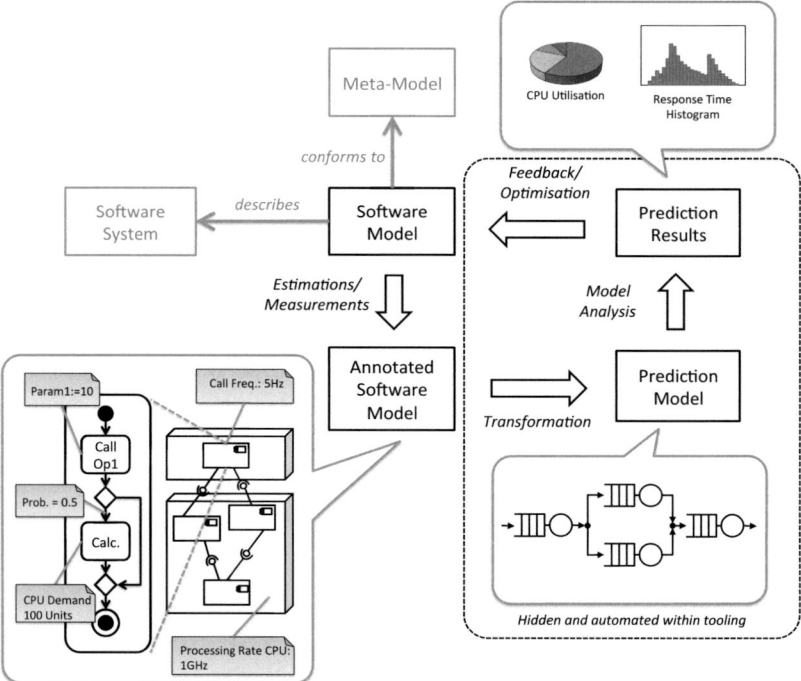

Figure 2.16: Model-based Prediction Process based on [Becker 08a]

2.3.1. Model-based Performance Prediction Process

To close the gap between architecture-level descriptions on the one hand and specific performance prediction techniques on the other hand, most approaches base upon a model-based prediction process [Becker 08a] as illustrated in Figure 2.16. This process starts with a *Software Model* that describes the *Software System* under study at the architecture-level. The modelled system can be an already existing system, but it needs not necessarily. Architecture-level meta-models like the already mentioned UML but also meta-models specially designed for model-based performance prediction techniques like CSM [Petriu 07], KLAPPER [Grassi 05], or PCM, which is described in more detail in Section 2.4, form the basis for modelling the system. Often, such architecture-level models already exist as part of the software engineering process. For a more detailed presentation and discussion of individual architecture-level meta-models for performance prediction and their support for modelling event-based interactions, we refer to Section 3.1.2.

In the second step, the model is annotated with additional information required for the performance prediction resulting in the *Annotated Software Model*. As sketched in Figure 2.16 these annotations cover different aspects and range from workload specifications over brach probabilities and parameter characterisations up to resource demands for internal calculations and the processing rate of hardware resources. Generic design languages like UML require additional profiles like the already mentioned SPT or MARTE profile extending the language with the required annotation elements. Designated architecture-level meta-models for performance prediction like PCM or KLAPPER already foresee such annotation elements and supersede the extension with additional profiles. Depending on the existence of a system implementation, the annotated values can be based on measurement on a running instance of the system or estimated by the architect or software developer.

The following steps are encapsulated and executed within an automated tool chain. First the *Annotated Software Model* is transformed into a *Prediction Model*, which serves as input for a specific performance prediction technique. Figure 2.16 sketches a Queueing Network as exemplary representative of a *Prediction Model*. However, a multitude of different prediction techniques exists. Applying the solver or simulators belonging to a prediction technique returns different performance metrics like resource utilisation, throughput or processing times. These *Prediction Results* serve as feedback to the architect to evaluate the system and its architecture. Furthermore, the results enable optimising the system architecture regarding one or more extra-functional properties, which can be conducted manually by the architect or automated in architecture optimisation frameworks like PerOpteryx [Koziolek 11a].

In the following section, we present an overview of different prediction techniques that can be integrated in the model-based prediction process.

2.3.2. Performance Prediction Techniques

Performance prediction techniques can be categorised into simulation-based and analytical approaches. However, this classification is no clear cut [Kounev 09a]. Both approaches have in common, that they require a dedicated prediction model as input.

In *Simulation-based approaches* the prediction models are software programs that mimic the behaviour of a system as requests arrive and get processed at the various system resources. For this reason, they require very detailed information about the system behaviour and the available resources. The structure of a simulation program is based on the states of the simulated system and simulated resources (e.g. CPU) used by the system. The simulation programs records the duration of time spent in different states. Based on these data, performance metrics of interest (e.g., the average time a request takes to complete or the average system throughput) can be estimated at the end of the simulation run. The main advantage of simulation models is that they are very general and can be made as accurate as desired. However, this accuracy comes at the cost of the time taken to develop and run the simulation.

Different approaches for realising a simulation-based performance prediction exist [Kounev 12a]. The most time consuming approach is the manual implementation based on general purpose programming languages like C++ or Java, which might be extended with specialised simulation libraries (e.g., DESMO-J [DESMO-J 12], SSJ [Simard 11] or OMNET++ [OMNeT 12]). Applying model-driven techniques to generate the simulation code as for example demonstrated in [Becker 08a] significantly reduces the implementation effort. Other simulation approaches use specialised languages to specify the simulation. These language range from simple textual representations (e.g., SPSS [Gordon 78] or MODSIM III [Goble 97]) up to graphical languages with specialised modelling tools like ExtendSim [extendsim 12], Arena [Kelton 10] or QPME [Kounev 10b]. A comprehensive treatment of simulation techniques can be found in [Banks 04] and [Law 99].

Analytical approaches use mathematical laws and algorithms to solve the prediction model and calculate the performance metrics. They are usually less expensive and more efficient to analyse compared to simulation-based approaches. However, because the analytical models are defined at a higher level of abstraction, they are normally less detailed and information about the system behaviour and structure are lost. Queueing networks and generalised stochastic Petri nets are perhaps the two most popular types of models used in practice. Queueing networks provide a very powerful mechanism for modelling hardware contention (contention for CPU time, disk access, and other hardware resources) and scheduling strategies.

A number of efficient analysis methods have been developed for product-form queueing networks, a special subclass of queueing networks. The downside of queueing networks is that they are not expressive enough to model software contention and synchronisation aspects accurately. Extended queueing networks [MacNair 94] and *Layered Queueing Networks* (LQNs) (also called stochastic rendezvous networks) [Woodside 95] provide some support for modelling software contention and synchronisation aspects, however they are often restrictive and inaccurate. In contrast to queueing networks, generalised stochastic Petri nets can easily express software contention, simultaneous resource possession, asynchronous processing, and synchronisation aspects. However, they do not provide any support for scheduling strategies. With *Queueing Petri Nets* (QPNs) [Bause 93], which combine the modelling power and expressiveness of queueing networks and stochastic Petri nets, this disadvantage can be eliminated. A major hurdle to the practical use of QPNs, however, is that their analysis suffers from the state space explosion problem limiting the size of the models that can be solved. Currently, the only way to circumvent this problem is by using simulations for model analysis [Kounev 06].

All of the above performance prediction techniques have in common, that detailed knowledge about the used prediction models is required, so performance prediction could only be carried out by performance experts. The integration of these techniques into the model-based performance prediction process in combination with the use of design-oriented software models, enable software architects and developers, which lack the required expert knowledge, evaluating the performance of the system as part of the development cycle.

2.4. Palladio Component Model

This section introduces the *Palladio Component Model* (PCM) [Becker 09, Happe 11], which provides the technical foundation for implementing and validating the concepts presented in this thesis. The discussion of

PCM's meta-model is not exhaustive but reduced to the core concepts that are required for understanding the following thesis chapters. For more details, we refer to the technical report [Reussner 11], which provides a full discussion of the PCM meta-model.

The development of PCM started in 2003 at the University of Oldenburg, and since 2006 it has been further developed at the *Karlsruhe Institute of Technology* (KIT) and the *Forschungszentrum Informatik* (FZI). PCM is accompanied by an integrated modelling and prediction tool, the *PCM-Bench* [PCM 12]. It is build on top of the Eclipse technology stack extensively using the *Eclipse Modeling Framework Project* (EMF) and *Graphical Modeling Framework* (GMF). PCM-Bench provides graphical editors aligned with the UML syntax, a simulation engine as well as several transformations into analytical prediction models and different visualisations of the prediction results. PCM is one of the most advanced and mature solutions in the field of model-based performance prediction techniques for component-based system architectures (surveyed in [Koziolek 10]). The applicability and prediction accuracy of Palladio approach has been validated in several industrial case studies (e.g., [Huber 10], [Koziolek 11c], [Rathfelder 12], and [Gouvêa 12]) as well as empirical experiments [Martens 08b, Martens 08a, Martens 11].

The PCM meta-model is structured into several loosely coupled sub models. This separation respectively parameterisation of a PCM model, allows an individual variation of the different influence factors on the performance of component-based systems [Becker 06a], which are:

1. **Implementation** Obviously, the implementation of algorithms and data structures within a component has an impact on the processing and memory demands and thereby on the performance of the whole system.

2. **Required Services** Components or complete systems that require services provided by other components respectively systems de-

pend not only functionally on these services. As the requiring component has to wait until the service call is executed, the performance is influenced by the performance of the required services.

3. **Resource Environment and Deployment** The resource environment, which consists of different hardware resources, like servers with CPUs, memory and hard disks, but also the network infrastructure and the different middleware systems, has an impact on the system performance. Often, but not always, more or faster CPUs, memory, or network connections promise an improved performance of a system, which results in the *"Kill it with iron"* approach [Weikum 02]. This approach tries to solve performance problems with increasing the number and speed of available hardware resources.

4. **Usage Profile** The dependency between the execution time of an algorithm and the input parameters is known for a long time. Especially in the area of algorithm theory, the Big-O notation ($O(n)$) [Landau 09] is often used to describe such dependency between execution time and a characterisation n of the input parameters. In addition to the characterisation of input parameters, the usage profile also covers the number of system calls as well as their frequency. It is obvious, that a concurrent use of the system by several users induces more load on the resources than one single user with only one request.

In order to enable an individual variation of these influence factors within one model, PCM defines the overall five different sub-models, which are depicted in Figure 2.17. The *Repository Model* specifies a library of system components and their provided and required interfaces. To specify the internal behaviour of components providing a services, PCM provides the *Resource Demanding Service Effect Specification* (RD-SEFF) language, which additionally includes specifications of

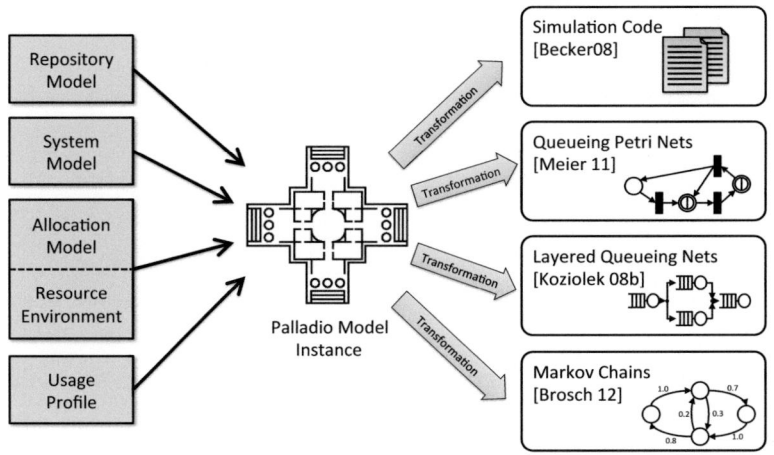

Figure 2.17: Overview on the Palladio Approach

resource demands and parameter dependencies. The *System Model* describes the structure of the system by connecting components via their provided and required interfaces. In the *Allocation Model*, the components that are part of the system are allocated to physical resources described in the *ResourceEnvironment*, which specifies the hardware environment the system is executed on, e.g., servers, processor speed, network links. The *Usage Model* describes the workload induced by the system end-users. For example, it specifies how many users access the system, the inter-arrival time of requests, or characterisations of input parameters. Usage profiles within the model represent individual user behaviours. As illustrated in Figure 2.17, the combination of al these models forms an instance of a Palladio model. To predict the performance of the modelled system, several transformation into prediction models have been developed. Becker developed a transformation into a Java-based simulation [Becker 08a], called SimuCom. The generated Java code, which builds on the DESMO-J simulation framework, is compiled on-the-fly and executed. SimuCom is tailored to directly support all PCM elements and thus is the most expressive prediction technique for PCM models. Meier et al. presented a transformation into a QPN model [Meier 11] that enables using simulative as well as analytical prediction techniques developed for QPNs [Kounev 06]. Koziolek et al. developed a transformation into LQNs [Koziolek 08b] that can be solved with low overhead however with less accuracy compared to QPN-based predictions [Meier 11]. Brosch developed a transformation into Markov Chains [Brosch 12] that enables a combined evaluation of performance and reliability as demonstrated in [Martens 09]. The following sub-sections provide a detailed presentation of the different sub models.

2.4.1. Repository Model

The PCM *Repository Model* contains all information required to specify the individual components, namely component types, interfaces, required and provided relations between components and interfaces, and component behaviours. Figure 2.18 gives a high-level overview of the meta-model classes involved in component definitions. For the sake of clearance, we abstract some multi-level inheritances. The `Repository`, which is the root element of the *Repository Model*, contains a list of `RepositoryComponents`, `Interfaces`, and `DataTypes`.

Each `Interface` contains a list of `Signatures`, defining input `Parameters` and a `DataType` as `returnType` of an operation. PCM supports the specification of `PrimitiveDataTypes`, `CollectionDataTypes`, and `CompositeDataTypes`. `PrimitiveDataTypes` conform to one out of a list of given types including "int", "string", "bool", and others. `CollectionDataTypes` represent a set of data items of a specific `innerType`. `CompositeDataTypes` contain a list of `InnerDeclarations`, each pointing to one contained `DataType`.

`RepositoryComponents` are a specialised `InterfaceProvidingRequiringEntity`, which means that they can provide or require interfaces through the specification of contained `ProvidedRoles` and

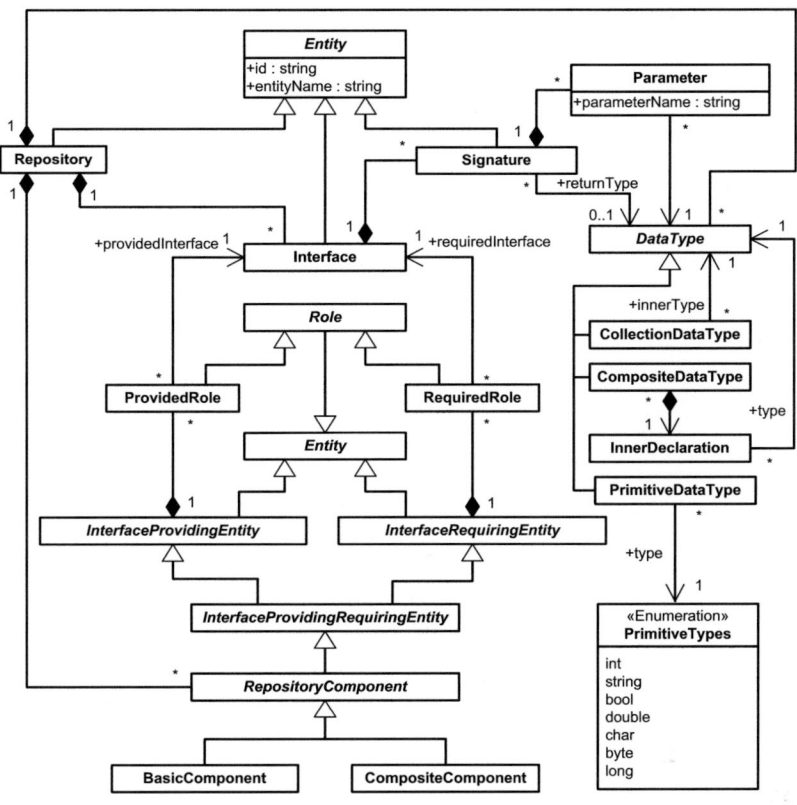

Figure 2.18: Meta Model of PCM Repository Model

RequiredRoles. This concept of Roles allows reusing interface definitions within multiple component specifications. A RepositoryComponent is either a BasicComponent or a CompositeComponent. While the first one cannot be further decomposed, the latter one is a composition of existing components. Section 2.4.2 provides more details on the composition of components. Moreover, the Repository itself and most of the described elements are Entities, equipped with a unique id and a name.

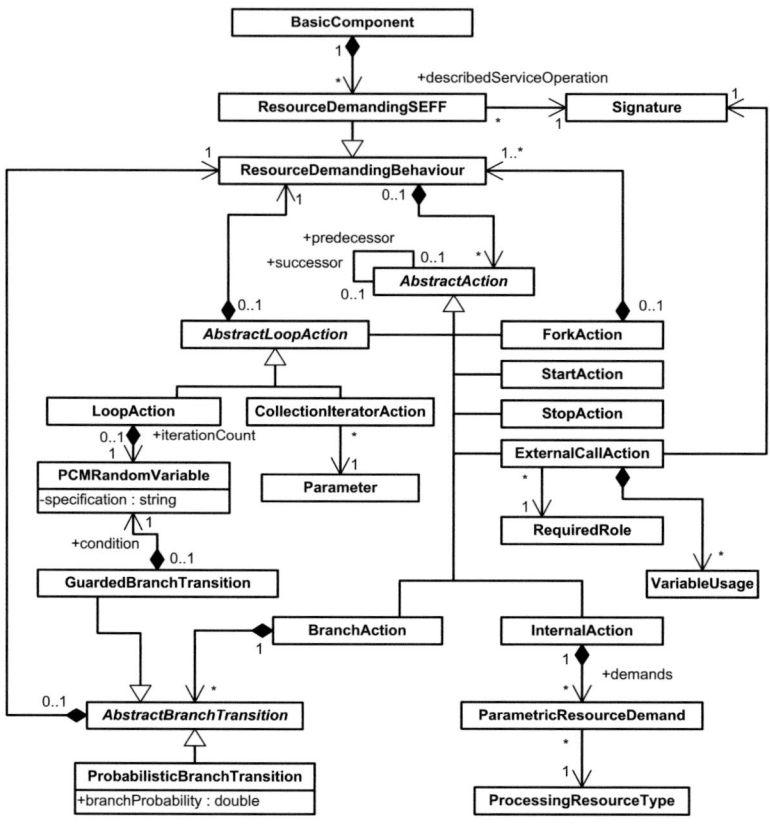

Figure 2.19: Meta Model of Resource Demanding Service Effect Specifications

Each service operation offered by a `BasicComponent` through its `ProvidedRoles` must be accompanied by a corresponding behavioural specification that describes the reaction of the component when the service operation is invoked. In PCM, the component behaviour is represented by a contained `ResourceDemandingSEFF` (where "SEFF" stands for service effect specification), which is, as illustrated in Figure 2.19, a subtype a `ResourceDemandingBehaviour`. Each behaviour contains a set of `AbstractActions`, with each Ab-

`stractActions` pointing to its `predecessor` and `successor`. Different action types represent different kinds of execution steps. `StartActions` and `StopActions` act as delimiters of action sequences. The `AbstractLoopAction` represents a repeated execution of a referenced internal `ResourceDemandingBehaviour`. Normal `LoopActions` contain a loop iteration counter specified through a `PCMRandomVariable` while `CollectionIteratorActions` reference a `Parameter` with a `CollectionDataType` and iterate over the size of this parameter. `BranchActions` represent decisions within the control flow. They contain a set of `AbstractBranch-Transitions` each including exactly one `ResourceDemandingBehaviour`. `ProbabilisticBranchTransitions` contain a fixed value expressing the probability for executing this branch. `GuardedBranchTransitions` contain a `PCMRandomVariable` representing a boolean expression. `ForkActions` include a set of `ResourceDemandingBehaviours`, which are concurrently executed. An `InternalAction` represents a computational step during service execution. It abstracts the algorithmic details and lists the associated resource consumption in form of `ParametricResourceDemands`. A resource demand refers to a certain `ProcessingResourceType` (e.g. a CPU or hard disk). `ExternalCallActions` describe the invocation of an operation provided by another component. They reference the `RequiredRole` of the current component and the `Signature` of the invoked operation to avoid a direct wiring between components. To hand over parameters, `ExternalCallActions` contain a set of `VariableUsages`.

As illustrated in Figure 2.20 `VariableUsages` include an `AbstractNamedReference` to identify the parameter and a characterisation of a parameter property through a `VariableCharacterisation`. The identification is a `VariableReference`, which contains the name of the parameter on its own or encapsulated in `Namespac-`

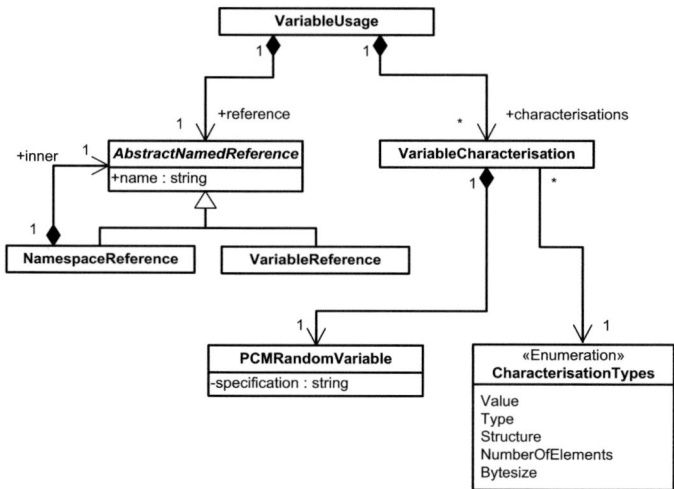

Figure 2.20: Meta Model of Variable Usages

eReferences, which in case of a complex data type address the outer data type. Each VariableCharacterisation specifies one out of a given set of properties (such as "Value", "Type", "Bytesize", "Structure", or "NumberOfElements") and provides the value of this property through a PCMRandomVariable. The PCMRandomVariable contains a string based on the *Stochastic Expression* (StoEx) language [Koziolek 08a]. This language, which is part of PCM, allows expressions, which range from single numbers, probability distributions up to mathematical and logical expressions that contain references to parameters available in the current execution context.

2.4.2. System Model

The PCM *System Model* captures the instantiation of components including their interconnections to describe the system architecture. Figure 2.21 shows the involved meta-model classes with the System as root element. It is both an InterfaceProvidingRequiringEn-

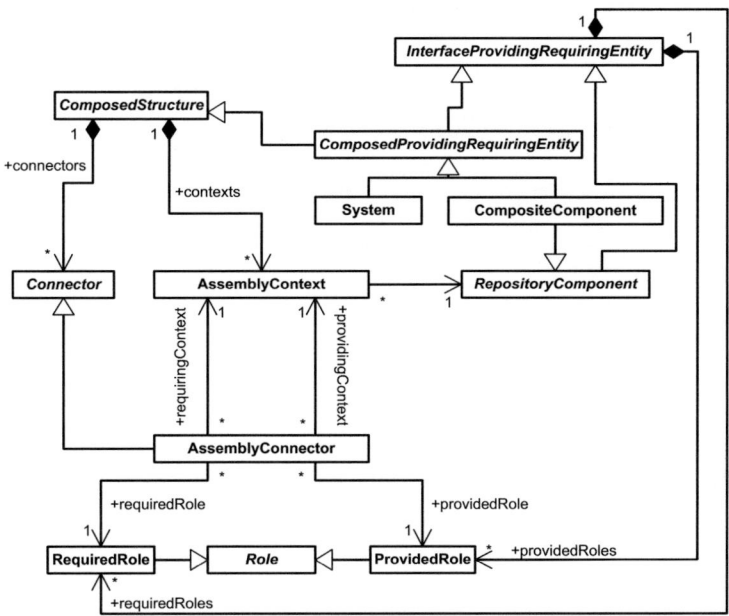

Figure 2.21: Meta Model of PCM System Model

tity and a ComposedStructure. As ComposedStructure, it provides the ability to instantiate RepositoryComponents through AssemblyContexts. These contexts can be connected through AssemblyConnectors. Connectors contain references to the providing and requiring contexts as well as to the belonging provided and required roles. While systems represent the highest level of composition, the corresponding meta-model concepts can also be used to express composition on lower levels through CompositeComponents, which are contained in a PCM *Repository Model*.

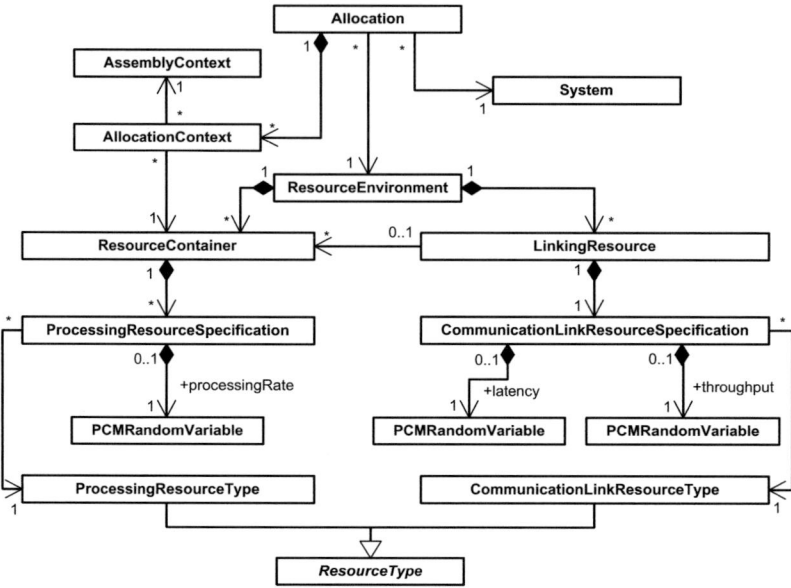

Figure 2.22: Meta Model of PCM Allocation Model and Resource Environment

2.4.3. Resource Environment and Allocation Model

PCM includes modelling constructs for a physical resource environment and the allocation of software components to computing nodes in form of the *Resource Environment* and the *Allocation Model*. As they are tightly coupled, Figure 2.22, presents a merged overview of the two metamodels. The *Allocation Model* maps components of a system to computing nodes and resources. For each `AssemblyContext` defined within the *System Model*, the *Allocation Model* contains an `AllocationContext` associated with the `AssemblyContext` and additionally with a `ResourceContainer` that represents the computing node.

The *Resource Environment* defines a set of `ResourceContainers` that can be connected through `LinkingResources`. Each `ResourceContainer` hosts physical resources declared as `Process-`

ingResourceSpecifications. ProcessingResourceSpecifications refer to one specific ProcessingResourceTypes (e.g., CPU or HDD) and contain a PCMRandomVariable specifying the processing rate of the resource. A LinkingResource contains a single CommunicationLinkResourceSpecification that references a CommunicationLinkResourceType such as LAN and includes a specification of latency and throughput by means of two PCMRandomVariables.

2.4.4. Usage Model

With the *Usage Model*, PCM offers explicit modelling constructs depicted in Figure 2.23 to express the usage profile of a system. A UsageModel contains a list of UsageScenarios, each scenario describing a certain use case of the system. The behaviour itself is captured through ScenarioBehaviours, similar to ResourceDemandingBehaviours used to describe the component behaviour. To specify the execution frequency, each UsageScenario contains an abstract Workload, which can either be an OpenWorkload or a ClosedWorkload. OpenWorkloads specify the execution frequency by means of an interArrivalTime specified as PCMRandomVariable. ClosedWorkloads contain an Integer attribute to specify the size of the population pool and an additional PCMRandomVariable to specify the thinkTime between each service invocation. Each ScenarioBehaviour includes a set of AbstractUserActions, referencing each other as successors and predecessors. Similarly to ResourceDemandingBehaviours, the *Usage Model* foresees elements for begin and end of behaviour (Start, Stop), loops (Loop), decisions (Branch), and invocations of operations provided by the system (EntryLevelSystemCall). Furthermore, the *Usage Model* allows the specification of waiting or sleep times in form of the DelayAction, which includes a PCMRandomVariable as timeSpecification.

Loops specify iteration counts through PCMRandomVariables and branches contain BranchTransitions with individual branch probabilities. Both loops and branch transitions include nested internal behaviours. An EntryLevelSystemCall references one of the ProvidedRoles belonging to the system and a Signature identifying a certain operation.

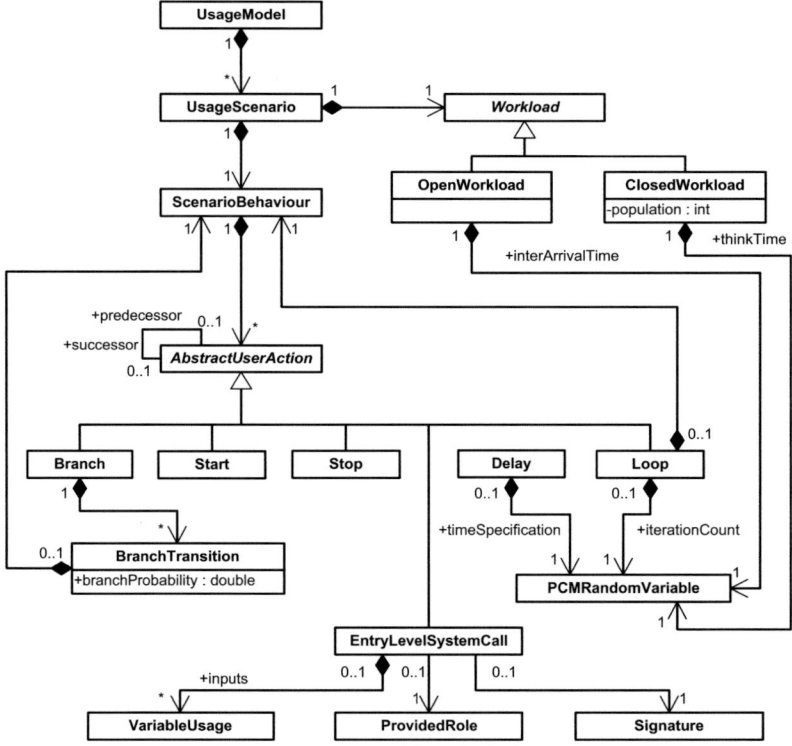

Figure 2.23: Meta Model of PCM Usage Model

2.5. Concluding Remarks

In this chapter we provided the background needed for the understanding of this thesis. We started with the concept of events and EBS. As part of this discussion, we introduced a categorisation schema for EBW and applied it to multiple existing middleware implementations to demonstrate the variations between different existing systems. This overview of the context of our work was followed by an introduction into the domain of MDE and MDSD including a detailed description of the two transformations languages (MOLA and QVT-O) applied in this thesis. Furthermore, we introduced the area of SPE. At the end of this chapter, we gave an overview of PCM, which forms the basis for our implementation described in Section 4.4.

3. Related Work

The approach presented in this thesis combines architecture-level modelling of event-based interactions (Chapter 4) with a detailed platform-specific performance prediction technique (Chapter 5) which are both independent research areas on their own. The following overview of related work starts with a presentation of different approaches that target modelling at the architecture-level in Section 3.1. Following this in Section 3.2, we present related work in the area of performance prediction techniques specialised for EBS, while finally Section 3.3 concludes with a summary.

3.1. Architecture-level Modelling

Architecture-level models for component-based systems (e.g., surveyed in [Lau 06], [Lau 07], [Feljan 09], and [Crnkovic 11]) can be classified into two areas depending on the goal for which the models are used. The first area covers component and architecture models that are designed with the goal to support the implementation. They are often complemented with M2T transformations to generate source code, configuration files, or deployment descriptors. The second area contains models that have beed designed to enable QoS prediction. Compared to the implementation-oriented approaches, these models often include additional information required by the prediction techniques. The classification schema for component models introduced in [Crnkovic 11] explicitly addresses the support of modelling Pub/Sub interactions. However, none of the more than 20 models surveyed in [Feljan 09] and

[Crnkovic 11] using this classification schema provides any support for modelling Pub/Sub interactions.

3.1.1. Implementation-oriented Approaches

With the goal to simplify the implementation and structuring of systems, several component models have beed developed in research and industry. These implementation-oriented models can be categorised into platform-specific and platform-independent models. Platform-specific models are defined to enable the specification of components executed in a specific execution container or technical framework, while platform-independent models describe components on a higher level of abstraction without assuming a specific execution environment. In the following overview, we focus on models that provide an explicit support of event-based communication. For a more comprehensive survey of component models in general, we refer to [Lau 06] and [Feljan 09].

Platform-specific Models

Platform-specific component models have mostly been defined by industry. They often build on existing programming languages and extend them with the definition of explicit component boundaries including provided and required interfaces. The most prominent examples of industrial component models are Microsoft's *Component Object Model* (COM) [Microsoft 07], *Enterprise JavaBeans* (EJB) [DeMichiel 06], which are based on Java EE, and the language independent *CORBA Component Model* (CCM) [OMG 06a] standardised by the OMG.

CORBA   The *Common Object Request Broker Architecture* (CORBA) [OMG 11] is a framework specified by the OMG for building distributed component-based applications. It enables software components written in different languages and running on multiple computers to work together. The *CORBA Component Model* (CCM) [OMG 06a], which is one part of the CORBA standard, defines the general structure of components and their possible interfaces. CCM explicitly distinguishes between method calls and events. It supports four kinds of component ports that enable components communicating with each other.

- **Facets** are operational interfaces respectively methods provided by a component.

- **Receptacles** define the interfaces required by a component. The receptacles are later connected with facets.

- **Event Sources** define the ports of a component that emit events of a specific type.

- **Event Shrinks** specify sink ports through which a component receives events of a given type from one or more sources.

For Facets and Receptacles, it is necessary to define the interfaces that specifies the input and output parameters. Event Sources and Shrinks require only the definition of the event's data type. Composition of components is done by connecting Facets with matching Receptacles or Event Sources with Event Shrinks. Although CORBA supports channel-based interactions between event sources and sinks based on the Notification Service [OMG 04b] standard as described in Section 2.1.2, CORBA and CCM in particular do not provide any support for specifying such interactions at the architecture-level.

AUTOSAR The *Automotive Open System Architecture* (AUTOSAR) [aut 07] is an open and standardised automotive software architecture, jointly developed by automobile manufacturers, suppliers and tool developers. In contrast to CORBA, which is often used for large business information systems, AUTOSAR focuses on embedded systems for automotive industries. The aim of AUTOSAR is to provide a common framework that enables and supports the integration and interaction of software components from different vendors in a car. Although CORBA and AUTOSAR are developed for completely different domains, the included component models bear large resemblance. AUTOSAR also distinguishes between method invocations and event-based communication. In AUTOSAR they are called client-server and sender-receiver. In addition to these two communication types, the AUTOSAR component model defines a third port type, the calibration ports. Calibration ports are not involved in component interactions, they rather allow components access to static calibration parameters. In addition to the three port types *client-server*, *sender-receiver*, and *calibration*, ports are additionally differentiated by providing or requiring data. Similarly to CORBA, it is only allowed to connect required and provided ports of the same type. Furthermore, a required *client-server* port can be connected with only one provided port. In contrast, both required and provided *sender-receiver* ports may be connected to several provided respectively required ports. Similar to CORBA, AUTOSAR does not provide any support for modelling Pub/Sub interactions.

SCA The *Service Component Architecture* (SCA) [OASIS 07b] is a set of specifications that allow the modelling and specification of applications and systems using a *Service-Oriented Architecture* (SOA). SCA combines component-based development with the paradigm of service-orientation. In contrast to the component models presented before, SCA components do not distinguish between event-based communication and synchronous method invocation. SCA differentiates between required and provided interfaces only. As shown in Fig. 3.1, SCA components have additionally the possibility to configure a component from the outside. Similar to AUTOSAR, SCA components provide a special properties port. Although, SCA considers only provided and required interfaces, it is also possible to use message-based communication us-

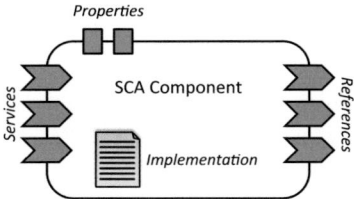

Figure 3.1: Schematical Overview of an SCA Component [OASIS 07b]

ing JMS [Hapner 02]. The JMS Binding Specification [OASIS 07a] defines how to map the provided and required interfaces to a JMS-based communication. As this mapping is done after specifying a component, it is not possible to explicitly specify that certain interfaces of a component have to use message-based communication or emit respectively handle events. Furthermore, an explicit modelling of one-to-many or many-to-many interactions is not supported.

The presented platform-specific component models have in common that they enable the specification of component boundaries but mostly neglect the composition of components. The definition of an intermediate event channel and Pub/Sub interactions is supported by none of these component models.

Platform-independent Models

With the aim to allow platform-independent specifications, several *Architecture Description Language*s (ADLs) have been developed. The most prominent representative is the *Unified Modeling Language* (UML). Such platform-independent ADLs are on the one hand often used to document the architecture of a software system in an abstract but formal way. On the other hand, they are often accompanied by (semi-)automated transformations, that directly generate code or refine the model to a platform-specific model as described in Section 2.2.2. The following overview focuses on a selection of representative platform-independent models, which have not yet been covered in one of the referenced surveys, and their capabilities to model event-based interactions.

UML The *Unified Modeling Language* (UML) more specifically UML 2.0 [OMG 10], defines several views on a software system. Component diagrams aim at illustrating the structure of a system. A UML component represents a modular unit of a system with explicitly defined provided and required interfaces. In UML, *"An interface declares a set of public features and obligations that constitute a coherent service offered by a classifier"* [OMG 10], which does not limit interfaces to a pure request/reply behaviour. Nevertheless, UML does not allow an explicit differentiation between RPC-style and event-based communication. When describing the behaviour of a system using activity diagrams, UML provides dedicated action elements to emit and receive events, which can be connected with Ports that belong to a Classifier element and, following the inheritance hierarchy, to interfaces as well. Similarly to the other component models, UML does not support the modelling of Pub/Sub communication using one or multiple intermediating event channels. As already described in Section 2.2, UML forms the basis of the MDA approach. Furthermore, extended with profiles, UML is used as platform-independent modelling language for several performance prediction approaches.

QImPrESS SAMM The *Quality Impact Prediction for Evolving Service-oriented Software* (QImPrESS) project, a European research project, developed methodologies and tools to provide service-orientation to critical application domains with guaranteed end-to-end quality. The *Service Architecture Meta-Model* (SAMM) [Becker 08b] is one of the results of the project. This meta-model is similar to PCM but extended with a couple of modifications specific to the requirements of the QImPrESS project. The design goal of SAMM was to provide a general ADL to describe service-oriented systems, which is not limited to predictions of a certain quality attribute. SAMM contains elements for event-based communication including support for many-to-many relationships between connected components. Although SAMM allows many-to-many connections, it does not provide any elements for specifying Pub/Sub interactions. The QImPrESS tools support performance prediction based on the PCM tool-chain. Nevertheless, the event-based part of the meta-model is not supported by the included performance prediction techniques.

PICML The *Platform-independent Component Modeling Language* (PICML) [Balasubramanian 07] is part of the *Component Synthesis with Model Integrated Computing* (CoSMIC) framework [Gokhale 02] developed at Vanderbilt University. PICML provides a language to describe components in a platform-independent way. Automated transformations generate platform-specific code skeletons, deployment descriptors, and configuration files. As the main goal of CoSMIC and PICML is the generation of implementation artefacts, it lacks information required for performance prediction, like an explicit usage model of the system or a description of the component's internal behaviour. Furthermore, PICML only supports direct connections between components and does not provide meta-model elements to modelling individual event channels or a central event bus.

MontiArch MontiArch [Haber 12] is a framework for modelling and simulation of distributed interactive systems developed at RWTH Aachen. It contains a textual language to describe components and their composition. Components in MontiArch communicate only by interchanging events, which is one of the characteristics distinguishing MonitArch from other models. Each component contains a set of ports associated with an event type. In addition to the explicit definition of connectors between source and sink ports, MontiArch allows an implicit definition, which automatically connects a sink with all sources that offer a compatible event type. According to our classification schema for EBS, implicit definition of connectors are type-based subscriptions. Synchronous RPC-style interactions are not supported in MontiArch. The specification of a component's behaviour is based on declarative invariants using Java or OCL. More complex behaviours need to be directly implemented using Java.

Although some of the presented implementation-oriented approaches are accompanied by prediction and simulation techniques, they have been designed with the main goal to support the implementation of a system. The architecture-level performance prediction approaches described in the following, use models that have been explicitly been designed to enable performance prediction.

3.1.2. Analysis-oriented Approaches

Following the SPE [Smith 90] approach, a number of architecture-level performance meta-models have been developed. Several approaches use model transformations to derive performance prediction models (e.g., [Marzolla 04, Petriu 00, Di Marco 04, Becker 09]). A survey on performance meta-models [Cortellessa 05] led to a conceptual MDA framework of model transformations for the prediction of different extra-functional properties [Cortellessa 07b, Cortellessa 07a].

CB-SPE [Bertolino 04] applies the original SPE method of Smith et al. to component-based systems with the limitation that impacts of the internal processing and input parameters are not considered. Resource demands are modelled probabilistically and dependencies on input parameters are neglected. The ROBOCOP [Gelissen 03] framework and the associated performance prediction techniques [Bondarev 04] are focused on the area of embedded systems. They allow the description of component internals in relation to the parameters of external services and resources. Due to the focus on embedded systems, resource parameters can only be specified as constant values and software layers are not supported at all. Communication in ROBOCOP can be either synchronous or asynchronous, however always limited to the request/reply paradigm. SAPS [Balsamo 03] uses annotated UML models as input for the performance prediction technique. The annotations are based on a proprietary annotation model and require manual model adaptations. Since the approach is based on UML, it provides no support for modelling and analysing event-based interactions. A recent survey of methods for component-based performance engineering was published in [Koziolek 10]. Although some of the approaches support asynchronous communication between components, none of them supports the modelling and performance prediction of Pub/Sub-based interactions.

Since the communication middleware can have significant influence on the performance of the system, several approaches, which build on existing architecture-level prediction techniques, explicitly address the refinement of connectors and the integration of middleware-specific performance influence factors into prediction models.

Woodside et al. [Woodside 02] introduced the idea of performance completions. Completions are used to refine an abstract software model by integrating annotations, sub-models or patterns that describe performance relevant factors on a lower level of abstraction. One of the presented examples is a CORBA-based RPC that is refined by integrating multiple interactions with the object request broker. Based on this idea, several approaches that use model transformations to integrate platform-specific details into architecture-level models have been developed.

Wu et al. [Wu 04] envision a repository of common platform-specific components, such as database or middleware servers. Based on a set of rules, the required components are selected and integrated into the model. Although, they identified the importance of automating this process, it seems that they have discontinued their work on this approach.

Verdickt et al. [Verdickt 05] developed a framework to automatically consider the impact of CORBA middleware on the performance of distributed systems. Transformations integrate CORBA-specific details into high-level middleware-independent UML models. The work focuses on the influence of RPCs as implemented in CORBA, Java *Remote Method Invocation* (RMI), and *Simple Object Access Protocol* (SOAP) and neglects event-based communication. Dependencies on service parameters were not considered.

The approach developed by Grassi et al. [Grassi 06] transforms architecture-level UML models into the intermediate *Kernel LAnguage for PErformance and Reliability analysis* (KLAPER) [Grassi 08]. When transforming the UML models into KLAPER, QVT-R-based transformations refine the typed UML connectors with additional processing steps for marshalling or calling a name service within the KLAPER model. Similarly to Verdickt's approach, the selection of using UML as specification language limits the approach to direct RPC-style communication.

Coupled Transformations [Becker 08a] combine automated performance completions with model-driven code generation. A dedicated configuration model attached to connectors in a PCM model specifies the realisation (e.g., SOAP or RMI) of the respective connector. Using this annotated PCM model as input, Coupled Transformations generate both the implementation code and the refined performance model in parallel. Since component interactions in PCM have been limited to RPC-style communication before introducing the extensions presented in this thesis, event-based interactions have never been in the focus of Coupled Transformations.

A method for modelling JMS-Queues using performance completions is presented in [Happe 10]. Modelling patterns are used to refine component connectors with asynchronous communication. Again the use of the original PCM as a basis limits this approach to direct P2P connections. A case study based on the SPECjms2007 benchmark is presented as a validation of the approach. However, no interactions involving multiple message exchanges or interaction mixes are included and their case study considers only a small subset of the benchmark functionality tailored to a specific workload scenario. In [Happe 10], the combination with Coupled Transformations enabling a configurable automated model refinement is demonstrated. This refinement transformation has never been completely implemented and integrated into the Palladio tool, but the underlying idea was one of the starting points for the approach presented in this thesis.

In [Kapova 10a], a refinement transformation for concurrent systems is presented based on PCM. The authors introduce one-to-many connectors between operational interfaces to model Pub/Sub interactions, which limits the approach to one-to-many interactions. Since in realistic systems using Pub/Sub communication, the interactions are often many-to-many, this limitation restricts the approach to a small subset of EBS. Although PCM supports only one-to-one connectors, the authors do not provide any details explaining this new connector type and its semantics in terms of blocking method invocations and handling of return values. The sketched refinement of connectors abstracts the complete transmission system in one black-box component and thus does not allow the specification of detailed resource demands that depend for example on the number of subscribed sinks.

The Chilies approach developed by Kapova [Kapova 11] uses *Higher Order Transformations* (HOTs) to generate refinement transformations that integrate performance completions into the prediction model. Extended feature diagrams are used to control the transformation generation. In these extended feature diagrams, each feature node (e.g., encrypted communication or data compression) contains a QVT-R code snippet. This code snippet is integrated into the refinement transformation if the respective feature is selected. This generation approach makes the assumption that the different features are independent. But, even if the order of encryption and compression might eventually be negligible from a functional point of view, the differences in terms of performance can be significant. In contrast to our approach, which strictly separates platform-independent and platform-specific aspects, the Chillies approach encapsulates all knowledge in HOTs. As already recognised by Kapova, the complexity of developing a HOT for performance completions is very high and developers require expert knowledge in the areas of M2M transformations, performance completions as well as platform-specific details. A detailed evaluation of the applicability of the Chillies approach in terms of effort reduction compared to the manual specification of refinement transformations is not available.

3.2. Performance Prediction Techniques for Event-based Systems

In the following, we present an overview of existing performance modelling and analysis techniques specialised for EBS including systems based on a centralised MOM as well as distributed environments. A survey of techniques for benchmarking and performance modelling of EBS was published in [Kounev 09b].

Liu et al. [Liu 05a] developed an approach to predict the performance of component-based systems deployed in a Java EE application server. Their approach uses queueing networks to model the system. A lightweight application-independent benchmark is used to derive the resource demands of the application server. In [Liu 05b], they extended their approach for applications using JMS-based communication. However, the workloads considered in their approach do not include multiple message exchanges or interaction mixes.

In [Henjes 06b], a mathematical model of the message processing time and throughput of the WebSphereMQ JMS server is presented and validated through measurements. The presented results show that the system throughput is significantly influenced by the number of subscribed sinks and the number of defined filters. Several similar studies using FioranoMQ, ActiveMQ, and BEA WebLogic JMS server were published in [Henjes 06a], [Henjes 07a] and [Henjes 07b], respectively. [Menth 06] presents a detailed analysis of the message waiting time for the FioranoMQ JMS server. All these studies, however, focus only on the event processing within the middleware and neglect the system architecture and the event processing within the system components. Additionally, they consider only the overall message throughput and latency and do not provide any means to analyse complex event-based interactions and message flows.

In [Baldoni 05, Virgillito 03], computational models for Pub/Sub communication are proposed. The transmission system is represented by a set of delay values that are assumed to be known, which is not realistic to expect. Based on this computational model, the authors derive a probabilistic model for the effectiveness of the transmission system in delivering events to a set of the subscribers. Performance metrics such as event processing and transmission times or resource utilisations are not considered.

He et al. [He 07] use probabilistic model checking techniques to analyse Pub/Sub systems. The model describing the transmission system infrastructure is based on probabilistic timed automata. Component behaviours described as state chart diagrams are translated into probabilistic timed automata. The analysis considers the probability of message loss, the average time taken to complete a task and the optimal message buffer sizes.

In [Sachs 09], Sachs et al. present a detailed evaluation of a MOM server using the SPECjms2007 benchmark. With the aim to simplify the development of performance models for EBS, Sachs defined several performance modelling patterns in [Sachs 11] . These patterns map architecture-level characteristics and attributes like *"Pub/Sub with n subscribers"* or *"Queueing Load Balancer"* to *Queueing Petri Net* (QPN) models. Although these patterns reduce the gap between architecture-level specifications and low level prediction models such as QPNs, still expert knowledge is required as the performance model has to be built manually. The applicability of the modelling patterns and the accuracy of the prediction results was demonstrated using the SPECjms2007 benchmark [Sachs 12].

Kounev et al. [Kounev 08] present a methodology for workload characterisation and performance modelling of distributed event-based systems. Based on a workload model, analytical prediction techniques are used to estimate the mean delivery time. For more accurate prediction results, QPN models are used. The approach relies on the availability of monitoring data from the running system and is thus only applicable if a running system implementation is available.

Mühl et al. [Mühl 09] present an analytical model for Pub/Sub systems using hierarchical identity-based routing. The approach only considers the routing table size and the message rate as factors. In [Schröter 10], Schröter et al. refine this approach and extend it with support for additional routing algorithms. However, both approaches do not consider the client's behaviour in their analyses and are targeted only at analysing the performance of the distributed transmission system instead of the system as a whole.

3.3. Concluding Remarks

This chapter provided an overview of related work in the area of modelling event-based interactions at the architecture-level and performance prediction techniques for EBS. Our review of architecture-level modelling approaches ranges from implementation-oriented component models developed by industry, over generic platform-independent ADLs, up to modelling approaches that have been designed to enable QoS evaluation and prediction. As this area of research has been in the focus of several surveys, we focused our review on the support of modelling event-based interactions provided by a selected set of representative approaches. While several approaches provide support for explicitly modelling event ports provided by components, only few of them allow modelling component compositions by connecting different ports. Support for modelling Pub/Sub communication using one or several intermediate event channels is provided by none of the existing approaches.

Several performance prediction approaches based on architecture-level models explicitly address the integration of middleware-specific behaviour and resource demands into the prediction models. They all highlight the significant impact of the employed underlying communication middleware on the system performance. However, due to the lack of modelling support for decoupled Pub/Sub interactions these approaches are limited to systems using direct one-to-one connections between components.

In contrast, prediction approaches explicitly targeted at Pub/Sub systems focus on the transmission system only and neglect the system architecture and the individual behaviour of the interacting components. Given that such approaches use specialised analytical models, applying them in practice requires detailed expert knowledge, which hampers their integration into a general software development process.

4. Modelling Abstractions for Event-Based Interactions

Event-based interactions are used increasingly often to build scalable and loosely-coupled distributed systems in many different industry domains. The application areas of *Event-based Systems* (EBS) range from distributed sensor-based systems up to large-scale business information systems [Hinze 09]. Modelling such systems at the architecture-level requires a set of abstractions to describe event-based interactions between components. As already discussed in Section 3.1, multiple *Architecture Description Language*s (ADLs) for component-based system exist in industry and research. Although some of them contain modelling elements that support the explicit modelling of direct *Point-to-Point* (P2P) interactions between components, none of them provide support for modelling decoupled *Publish/Subscribe* (Pub/Sub) interactions using an intermediate event channel. Pub/Sub interactions are one of the most often used approaches to realise decoupled many-to-many communication in distributed component-based systems. Supporting the modelling of such systems at the architecture-level requires new and more expressive modelling abstractions.

In this chapter, we develop a set of abstractions enabling the modelling of event-based interactions at the architecture-level supporting the specification of direct P2P communication as well as decoupled Pub/Sub communication. With the native support for P2P and Pub/Sub interactions between components, the developed modelling approach enables the modelling of a large set of different EBS that are not supported by existing approaches. After discussing the requirements on an architecture-level modelling approach for event-based interactions in Section 4.1, we present the developed modelling abstractions. We designed the abstractions with the aim to be capable of being integrated into existing ADLs for component-based system. Section 4.3 describes the behavioural semantics of the introduced modelling abstractions. In Section 4.4, we demonstrate the extension of the *Palladio Component Model* (PCM) a representative and mature ADL for component-based systems using the presented modelling abstractions. Finally, in Section 4.5, we conclude with a short summary.

4.1. Relevant System Aspects and Characteristics

In [Koziolek 06], a QoS-driven modelling process for component-based systems is presented based on the general *Component-based Software Engineering* (CBSE) process defined by Cheesman and Daniels [Cheesman 00]. The authors highlight the partitioning of system models into several preferably independent views that reflect the different development roles (component developer, system architect, system deployer and domain expert) as an essential aspect. This partitioning is based on the observation, that components have several instantiation levels [Becker 06b], which are illustrated in Figure 4.1. At the *Type Level, component developers* describe the system components including their provided and required interfaces as well as their internal behaviour. At the *Instance Level, system architects* instantiate components defined at the *Type Level* and connect their provided and required interfaces to compose a system. It is thereby possible to have several instances of the same component as shown Figure 4.1, with `Comp2` and `Comp3` both being instances of `Component Type B`. A second instantiation of components at the *Run-time Level* is performed when deploying the system in the target execution environment. The *system deployer* specifies the available hardware infrastructure and the allocation of component instances to hardware nodes. As a last step in the CBSE process, the *domain expert* describes the usage profile of the system including input parameters passed to services upon invocation.

The modelling of event-based interactions influences all three component instantiation levels described above. Furthermore, it is important not to mix up these levels and roles including their responsibilities and the respective modelling views. In the following, we discuss the characteristics of event-based interactions with the goal to identify the essential characteristics of that need to be captured in architecture-level models for quality evaluations.

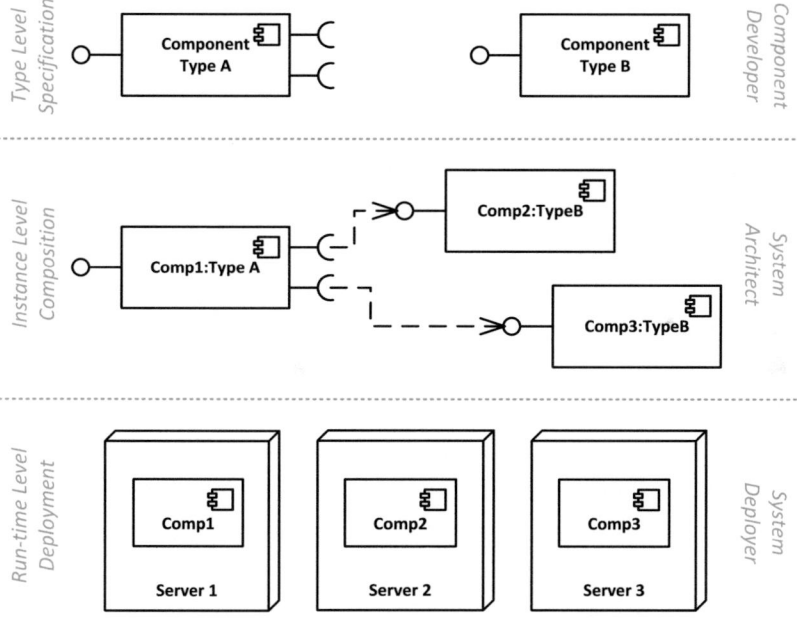

Figure 4.1: Component Instantiation Hierarchy

Events as First Class Entities   In traditional RPC-based distributed systems, components communicate by invoking methods, which are part of interfaces provided by other components [Szyperski 02]. In event-based interactions, the business logic of components is mostly implemented in the form of event handler methods executed when an event is received by a sink. The component emitting the event (the source) and the component receiving it (the sink) must recognise and support the respective type of event, i.e., the event is the common connection point similarly to operational interfaces that are provided or required by components. Thus, in analogy to operational interfaces, the component developer should be able to specify and model "event types" as first class entities and declare the ability of components to emit or to receive specific event types.

Separation of Modelling Aspects   The loose coupling of components combined with the increased system flexibility and adaptability is one of the main benefits promised by event-based interactions. This flexibility and adaptability needs to be taken into account when defining modelling abstractions. Thus, the specification of system components and the specification of their connections should be strictly separated. The specification of components should include the definition of supported events as well as a specification of the event handling behaviour for event sinks. The specification of the event handling behaviour must be done in a way such that it is independent of the number of connected sources or sinks. Only if component internals and the composition of components are specified independently, the connections between components can be changed by the architect without requiring any adaptations of the components themselves. Likewise, changes of the component's behaviour have no influence on the system's architecture. This separation is one of the basic concepts of component-based development.

In addition to the different components a system consists of, the implementation of the transmission system and its internal architecture has a significant impact on the system behaviour [Sachs 09]. Thus, these influences need to be taken into account in prediction techniques for EBS. However, when modelling a system at design-time, platform-specific details should ideally be abstracted at the architecture-level and modelled separately in a dedicated platform-specific model serving as additional input to prediction techniques.

Architecture-Level Abstractions The categorisation schema, introduced in Section 2.1.1, covers general design aspects and distinguishing attributes of EBS addressing both architecture-level characteristics as well as implementation details and run-time behaviour. In the following, we discuss the relevance of these characteristics from the perspective of architecture-level models for quantitative system evaluations.

- **Event Model** The characterisation schema differentiates three types of events, namely notifications, messages, and typed events. Their main differentiating characteristic is the payload of the event and its accessibility from the transaction system's point of view. The content of the payload is an important factor since it may influence the behaviour of the event-handling components. Therefore, architecture-level models for quantitative system evaluations should support modelling events both in terms of their types and possible payloads. The latter includes the definition of the payload's structure in the form of simple unstructured data types for messages, or complex object types for typed events, as well as the possibility to specify the instantiation and value assignment for emitted events. At the architecture-level, *Complex Events* can be seen as notifications with predefined semantics defined by the corresponding event matching patterns, and thus they can be modelled in a similar fashion to notifications. In *Complex Event Pro-*

cessing (CEP) systems, these patterns cover a large part of the system's business logic and their evaluation typically consumes a significant amount of computational resources. Thus, in CEP systems, the design of the event processing algorithms and the pattern language plays a critical role [Gal 10] and in many scenarios they would be the dominating factor determining the overall system behaviour, as opposed to the components emitting and receiving events. Therefore, modelling CEP systems would possibly require a different approach compared to modelling component-based systems with event-based interactions, as done in the context of this thesis.

- **Delivery & Subscription Model** In the P2P delivery model, when a source emits an event, the latter is put in a queue associated with the respective sink. The queue decouples the execution threads of the source and the sink. This decoupling is an essential aspect of event-based communication that differentiates it from *Remote Procedure Call* (RPC)-style interactions. However, from the architecture point of view, the queue can be abstracted and integrated into the P2P connector between the source and the sink. The Pub-/Sub delivery model provides a higher decoupling of sources and sinks by introducing intermediate event channels. In contrast to P2P connections, channel-based Pub/Sub requires an additional model element representing the transmission system's event channel, to which sources and sinks are connected. As discussed in Section 2.1.1, channel-based subscriptions are often used to enforce a logical grouping of events and thus they are an important element for structuring the event space of EBS. For example in distributed sensor-based systems, event channels can be used to realise a geographical grouping of sensors and the events they produce, respectively. Furthermore, the use of an explicit intermediate channel element improves clarity and reduces the modelling effort since connecting n sources with m sinks requires overall $n + m$ connectors, n connections from the sources to the intermediate element and m connectors from the intermediate element to the sinks, instead of $n * m$ direct connections to connect each source with all receiving sinks. The definition of a dedicated subscription element simplifies the distinction of P2P and Pub/Sub communication at the architecture-level. Not all EBS are based on the Pub/Sub model, thus our modelling approach should provide elements that support both types of delivery models. The existence of typed events is a prerequisite for modelling type-based subscriptions. The intermediate channel element can be associated with a certain event type allowing the architect to connect/subscribe a sink to a typed channel and thus to a certain event type.

Content-based subscriptions enable a more fine-grained specification of the events of interest for each sink. Thus, modelling content-based subscriptions requires the possibility to specify filtering rules referring to the event's structure and content individually for each sink. Furthermore, content-based subscription capabilities are often combined with channel- or type-based subscription mechanisms as for example realised in *Java Message Service* (JMS) [Hapner 02] by combining topics with individual message selectors. Architecture-level models should support a grouping of events based on their channel or type combined with the specification of individual filtering rules for each sink. Hierarchical subscriptions allow sinks to subscribe to multiple channels or event types by means of only one subscription to a channel or type defined on a higher hierarchical level. Thus, hierarchical subscriptions increase the system complexity by introducing complex inheritance hierarchies in a similar way as in *object-oriented* (OO) systems [Sheldon 02]. For this reason, for the sake of simplicity, inheritance is often avoided at the architecture-level. The *Unified Modeling Language* (UML), as one prominent example, supports inheritance only in modelling artefacts closely related to the implementation like class diagrams and not in architecture-level modelling artefacts such as component diagrams. Similarly, an easy to use and intuitive modelling approach for quantitative evaluation should avoid the explicit modelling of inheritance at the architecture-level.

- **Interaction Types** As already described as part of the categorisation schema, interactions between components in EBS can have different types depending on the number of participating components. We identified the following interaction types: *one-to-one*, *one-to-many*, *many-to-one*, and *many-to-many*, which differ in the number of sources and sinks that participate in an interaction. Modelling event-based interactions in realistic systems requires support for modelling all the different interaction types. many-to-many interactions are the most complex interaction type and comprise the other types, since neither the number of sources nor the number of sinks is limited. By explicitly supporting the modelling of many-to-many connections at the architecture-level, the architect can use the same model elements for modelling all the previously mentioned interaction types.

- **Degree of Decoupling** The decoupling of sources and sinks and their respective control flows is realised within and supported by the transmission system. Since the decoupling and asynchronous communication between components is an inherent characteristic of event-based interactions, an explicit modelling of event-based connections at the architecture-level is sufficient and does not require an additional modelling of the asynchronous behaviour. Although at the architecture-level, the asynchronous behaviour is specified only implicitly by event-based connections, considering them within the prediction techniques is very important.

- **QoS Model** The different characteristics covered by the QoS model dimension of our characterisation schema have in common that they focus on the run-time behaviour of the system. For example, the realisation of reliable delivery requires different types of persistence and synchronisation techniques within the transmission system. Similarly to the attributes of reliable delivery, the characteristic timeliness/performance cover quality guarantees ensured by the transmission system itself and not by the architecture. From the architecture's point of view, the transmission techniques are transparent and therefore should only be reflected within the platform-specific model describing the transmission system's internals.

  Security and trustworthiness capabilities can either be explicitly implemented as part of the system architecture by including for example explicit authentification and encryption components or they can be transparently provided by the transmission system. In the case of an explicit design, the different components need to be modelled within the system architecture similarly to functional components. If encryption and authentication are taken care of by the transmission system, the connections between sinks, sources and the transmission system might be annotated similarly to the way this is done for reliability attributes. However, usual implementation details should not be part of the architecture-level abstractions and should be included in a platform-specific model describing the transmission system.

- **Transmission System Architecture** As mentioned multiple times, architecture-level prediction models should be decoupled from the implementation and deployment details of the underlying transmission system. However, the latter can have a significant impact on the system's performance and resource utilisation. Thus, these influences should be reflected when evaluating the whole system, but modelling the transmission system's architecture and behaviour should be done as part of the platform-specific middleware model.

Based on the presented overview of the characteristics and aspects of event-based interactions in component-based systems relevant to quantitative system properties, we derive the following requirements on an ADL supporting the modelling of event-based interactions in component-based systems at the architecture-level:

R-1 Separation of modelling concerns

The ADL should provide dedicated and independent views to model the components including their internal behaviour, the component's connections within the system architecture, the deployment of the system, and finally the use and workload of the system.

R-2 Events as first class entities

Similarly to interfaces, events should be modelled as first class entities. Components, or more specifically their source and sink ports, should refer to a common event type definitions, similarly to the way provided and required interfaces refer to a common interface specification.

R-3 Modelling the payload of events

The ADL should support the definition of different event types including the possibility to model their payload and to assign values when instantiating an event.

R-4 Differentiation between P2P and Pub/Sub connections

The ADL should be able to differentiate between P2P delivery and the more decoupled Pub/Sub communication using event channels.

R-5 Specification of sink-specific filtering rules

To reflect content-based subscriptions and event filtering, the ADL should support the definition of filtering rules individually for each sink.

R-6 Abstraction from the communication middleware

The performance influences induced by the communication middleware should be reflected in the system's evaluation, however, modelled independently and separately from the system architecture.

4.2. Core Modelling Abstractions

Based on the presented requirements that should be satisfied by an ADL for component-based EBS, we developed a set of modelling abstractions for describing event-based interactions in architecture-level models for quantitative system evaluations. We developed the modelling abstractions with the aim to be independent of a concrete ADL and thus being applicable to extend different existing ADLs for component-based systems. However, we have to assume the following basic modelling support provided by an ADL for component-based systems to serve as *base ADL* being extended with the developed modelling abstraction:

- Support for specifying data types.

- Support for specifying components and interfaces as first class entities including additional elements to define the provided and required relationships between components and interfaces.

- Support for modelling the different component instantiation levels (type, instance, and run-time) illustrated in Figure 4.1 including the composition of components in terms of connecting provided and required ports.

- Explicit specification of a component's behaviour as sequence of activities. Applying the prediction techniques developed in Chapter 5 additionally requires the support of branches and forks for modelling asynchronous and parallel executions.

Integrating the developed modelling abstractions into a *base ADL*, which provides the listed modelling support, results in an *extended ADL* that provides explicit support for modelling events as first class entities, specifying event ports of a component, connecting components using direct P2P-based connectors as well as decoupled Pub/Sub connections with intermediate event channels, and finally explicitly specifying the deployment of components and event channels. Since the developed modelling abstractions only reference elements defined within the *base ADL* and do not require any modifications of existing elements, the resulting *extended ADL* combines the expressiveness of the *base ADL* with the additional support for event-based interactions. Thus, the *extended ADL* supports the modelling of purely RPC-based and purely event-based systems, but also systems that include a mixture of RPC-based and event-based interactions.

To reflect the different roles in the CBSE process, we grouped the developed modelling abstractions into different views each supporting an individual modelling aspect. The *Events and Components* view provides elements to specify the different events used in the system combined with elements to define communication ports used by components to emit or receive the respective events. The *Behaviour* view provides elements that component developers use to model the internal behaviour of components. This includes the specification of dedicated actions to instantiate and emit events as well as elements to model event handling mechanisms that process events received through sink ports. The *Composition* view enables architects to instantiate components in the context of a system and connect emitting and receiving event ports to describe the flow of events. Finally, the *Deployment* view allows to assign the different system elements to hardware nodes.

Beside the definition of the abstract syntax for each view, the following sections additionally introduce a concrete graphical syntax. We use a running example based on the order management in a supermarket scenario, as depicted in Figure 4.2, to illustrate the graphical syntax and to describe the behavioural semantics of the introduced elements. The exemplary scenario contains a central *order management system*, which receives messages from two *cash desks* informing about products that have been sold and from the *goods receiving department* acknowledging the receipt of ordered products. While the goods receiving department has only one central system to register received shipments resulting in

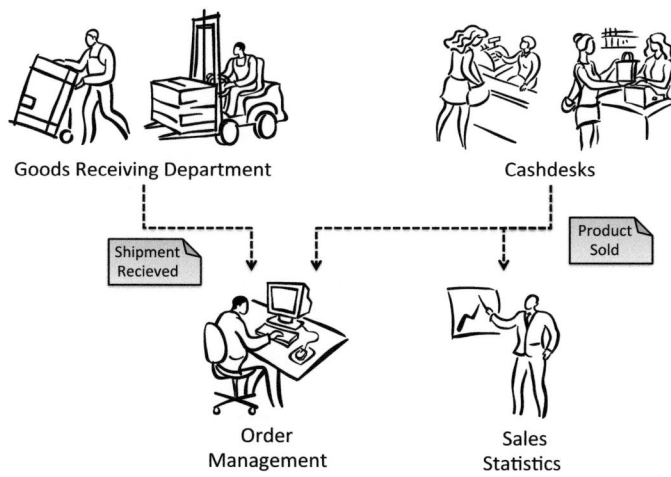

Figure 4.2: Exemplary Supermarket Scenario

only one event source, the supermarket is equipped with several cash desks each acting as an individual event source. The messages about sold products emitted by the *cash desks* are additionally consumed by a *sales statistics system.*

In the following sections, we introduce individually for each view the abstract syntax before demonstrating the concrete syntax in the context of this running example.

4.2.1. Events and Components

In component-based systems, interfaces describe the contract between two components. In the case of synchronous RPC-style communication, the contract consists of a set of method signatures, which describe operations that are required by one component and provided by another one. In the case of event-based iterations, the contract does not include a set

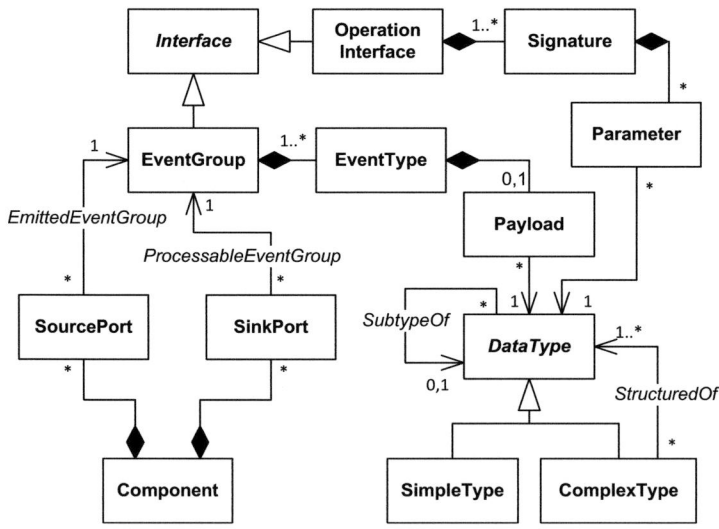

Figure 4.3: Events and Components

of operations but rather a set of event types that can be emitted by one component and received and processed by another.

As shown in Figure 4.3, we define a new model element `EventGroup` as a first class entity within the meta-model. In analogy to interfaces consisting of signatures, the `EventGroup` consists of one or more `Event-Types`. In order to enable the modelling of the payload for typed events or messages, the `EventType` contains an optional element `Payload`, which is associated with the abstract `DataType` element. This abstract element represents the concepts for modelling data types provided by the *base ADL*. When integrating the presented modelling constructs in an existing ADL, the respective meta-model elements provided by the *base ADL* for specifying data types should be used. The sketched modelling of data types illustrated in Figure 4.3 is a simplified abstraction. Usually, a `DataType` can be defined either as a `SimpleType` or a `Complex-Type`, where the latter itself consists of a set of `DataTypes`. Furthermore, the `SubtypeOf` relation allows specifying inheritance hierarchies among data types.

The `EventGroup` represents the contract between components that can either create and emit events of the respective group or that can receive and process them. In order to specify the ability of a component to emit or process events of a certain `EventGroup`, the `Component` element contains a `SourcePort` or `SinkPort` element for each supported `EventGroup`. The number of `SourcePort` and `SinkPort` elements defined for a `Component` is not limited and it is even possible to have multiple ports defined for the same `EventGroup`, which for example would make sense if the respective component provides different event handlers for the same types of events, or the component emits the same type of events on different ports.

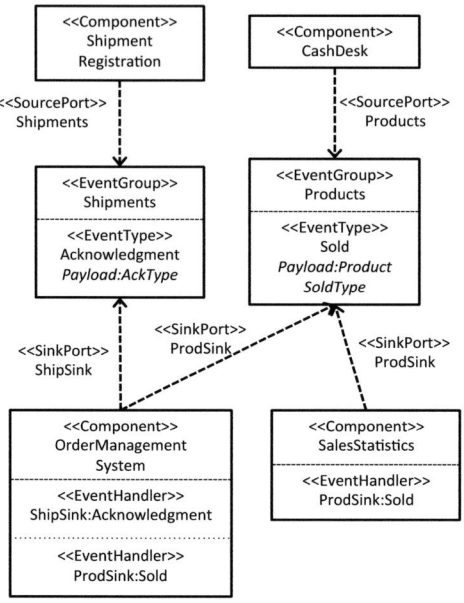

Figure 4.4: Events and Component View of the Supermarket Scenario

Figure 4.4 depicts the events and components view of the exemplary supermarket scenario using a graphical syntax[1]. The view defines two EventGroups, namely *Shipments* and *Products* and the four components, *ShipmentRegistration, CashDesk, OrderManagementSystem,* and *SalesStatistics,* which represent the different systems participating in the scenario. Both EventGroups contain an EventType, which itself includes a Payload with a specified DataType. The *ShipmentRegistration* component defines a SourcePort *Shipments,* which is illustrated as an arrow connecting the Component with the EventGroup. In a similar fashion, the *CashDesk* Component defines a SourcePort connected with the *Products* EventGroup. The *OrderManagementSys-*

---

[1]When describing the exemplary supermarket scenario, we use an *italic* font for element instances and a typewriter font in the case of referring to meta-model elements

tem `Component`, contains two `SinkPorts`, one connected with the *Shipments* `EventGroup` called *ShipSink* and the otherone connected with the `EventGroup` *Products* and named *ProdSink*. In analogy to `SourceRoles`, `SinkRoles` are represented by arrows connecting the `Component` with the respective `EventGroup`. As both `EventGroups` contain one `EventType`, the *OrderManagementSystem* contains two `EventHandlers`. Each `EventHandler`, lists the `EventType` and the `SinkPort` it is responsible for. The *SalesStatistics* `Component` consumes events of the *Products* `EventGroup` and thus contains only one `SinkPort` and the respective `EventHandler`.

The specification of event instantiations and the processing of events within a component is part of the *Behaviour* view described in the next section.

4.2.2. Behaviour

The meta-model extensions presented above cover only the static aspects of components. To model the dynamic aspects, we define new modelling elements to reflect the creation and publishing of events by source components as well as their processing in receiving sink components. As already mentioned, we assume, that the *base ADL* provides support for modelling the behaviour of a component as a sequence of activities. Two examples for such behavioural specifications are activity diagrams, which are part of UML, or the *Resource Demanding Service Effect Specification* (RD-SEFF) language of PCM, which we introduced in Section 2.4. In Figure 4.5, these individual actions provided by the *base ADL* are represented by the abstract `BehaviourElement`, which is contained in a `BehaviourDescription`.

To model the instantiation of an event, we define the new modelling element `EventEmission` as a specialisation of the generic `BehaviourElement`. It references the `SourcePort` through which the event should be published as well as the `EventType` of the event.

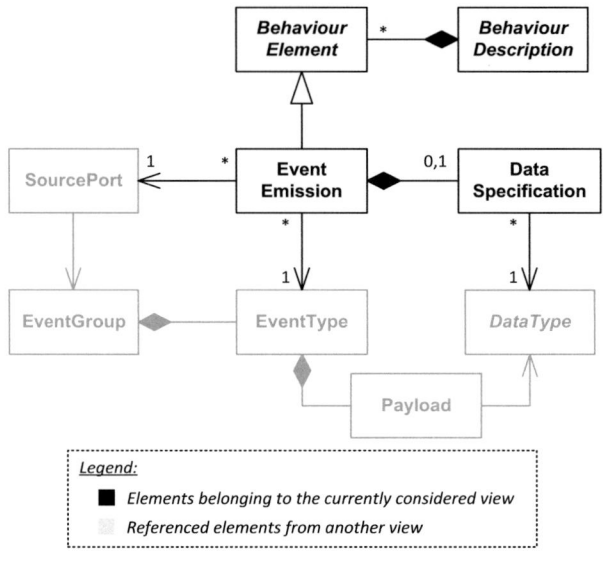

Figure 4.5: Instantiation and Emission of an Event

The `EventType` must be part of the `EventGroup` associated with the `SourcePort`, which can be enforced through an *Object Constraint Language* (OCL) constraint. To specify the payload of the published event, the `EventEmission` can include a `ValueSpecification`. Although the `DataType` of the `Payload` can be uniquely identified by navigating from the `EventEmission` to the associated `EventType`, we define a direct reference between `DataType` and `ValueSpecification` since the `ValueSpecification` element represents a concept, we assume to already exist in the *base ADL* for specifying the value of parameters in operation calls. When modelling operations with more than one parameter, the parameter and the respective `DataType` cannot be uniquely derived. The additional association between `ValueSpecification` and `DataType` ensures, that the `DataType` of the variable the value is assigned to can always be derived.

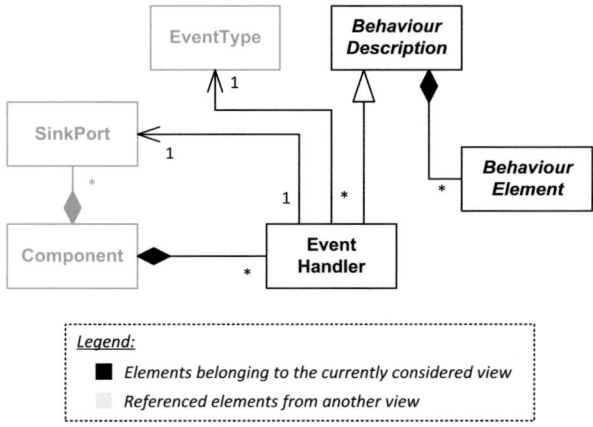

Figure 4.6: Modelling of Event Handling Behaviour

To model the event processing within a sink component, we introduce the new modelling element `EventHandler`. The `EventHandler` is a subtype of the abstract `BehaviourDescription`, which as already mentioned previously represents the concept for modelling component behaviour already existing in the *base ADL*. Reusing this concept allows for modelling an `EventHandler` in the same way the behaviour of provided component services is specified. As illustrated in Figure 4.6, `Components` can contain several `EventHandlers`, each of them associated with exactly one `SinkPort` and a respective `EventType` (from the `SinkPort`'s `EventGroup`).

The presented modelling abstractions for behavioural modelling use the concepts provided by the *base ADL* as foundation and extend them with an additional action for instantiating events. Instead of defining a new graphical syntax for this single element, we propose to use the concrete syntax provided by the *base ADL* and use a representation similar to the action that describes the method invocation and parameter instantiation.

121

With the new modelling elements introduced so far, it is possible to model components and events as well as to define source and sink ports provided by components. Furthermore, the introduced elements allow the specification of the component behaviour when events are emitted through source ports and received through sink ports. Events are modelled as first class entities (requirement R-2) and support the specification of their payload (requirement R-3). Since the specification of components and their behaviour aspects does not contain any references to elements describing the instantiation and composition of components, the specification of components and their event ports is as requested in requirement R-1 independent of their composition within the system architecture.

4.2.3. Composition

In the *Composition* view, system architects define the system architecture by instantiating components and connecting their provided and required interfaces as well as their source and sink ports, respectively. The instantiation of components is modelled using the `CompositionInstance` element, which references the respective `Component` that is instantiated. To connect the event sources and sinks, we developed abstractions to specify direct P2P connections as well as Pub/Sub connections using an intermediate event channel (requirement R-4), which are introduced in the following sections.

P2P Connections

Figure 4.7 illustrates the modelling elements introduced for defining direct P2P connections between source and sink ports of component instances. A `P2PConnector` includes two associations, the `ConnectedSourcePort` and the `ConnectedSinkPort`, referencing the respective `SourcePort` and `SinkPort`, that are connected. Since it is

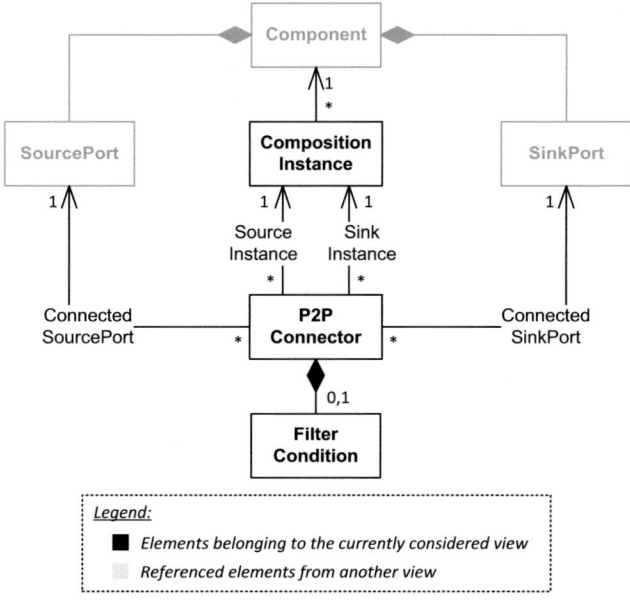

Figure 4.7: Modelling of P2P Connections

possible to have several independent instances of the same component in the systems, the associations to the SourcePort and SinkPort do not provide enough information to determine which specific component instances are involved. For this reason, the P2PConnector contains two additional associations to the CompositionInstance element, the SourceInstance association referencing the component instance emitting events and the SinkInstance association referencing the component instance receiving the events. An additional OCL constraint ensures that the Components associated with the CompositionInstances referenced by SourceInstance and SinkInstance, respectively, are the same Components as the ones referenced by the SourcePort and SinkPort. The *-cardinalities of the associations allow several P2PConnectors starting at one event source to be connected to several independent event sinks or several `P2PConnectors` starting at different sources to be connected to the same sink.

To enable the specification of sink-specific filtering rules (requirement R-5), each `P2PConnector` contains an optional `FilterCondition` element. With our modelling abstractions, we aim on the extension of existing ADLs not on the development of a completely new meta-model. For this reason, the latter is a placeholder to integrate an existing expression language. JMS for example provides a language to specify rules like the expressions "`NumberOfOrders > 1`" or "`age >= 15 AND age <= 19`" as part of message selectors [Hapner 02]. PCM, as a representative ADL for component-based systems provides the so-called *Stochastic Expression* (StoEx) language. In addition to value-based filtering rules like "`event.BYTESIZE <= 1000`", which filters out large messages, or "`event.TYPE == ERROR`", which selects only error messages, PCM's StoEx language supports probabilistic expressions, e.g., 80% of the generated events should be forwarded to the sink. Probabilistic filters enable modelling unreliable event processing as well as abstracting from concrete value dependencies or load balancing strategies.

Pub/Sub Connections

In contrast to direct P2P connections between sources and sinks as presented in the previous section, Pub/Sub connections decouple sources and sinks by introducing an intermediate element, the channel, as described in Section 2.1. In addition to the decoupling aspect, channels allow to structure event-based interactions by grouping logically related events, sources and sinks. To model the channels, we introduce a new modelling element, the `EventChannel` as part of the *Composition* view. Each `EventChannel` is associated with exactly one `Event-Group` ensuring that only compatible sources and sinks are connected

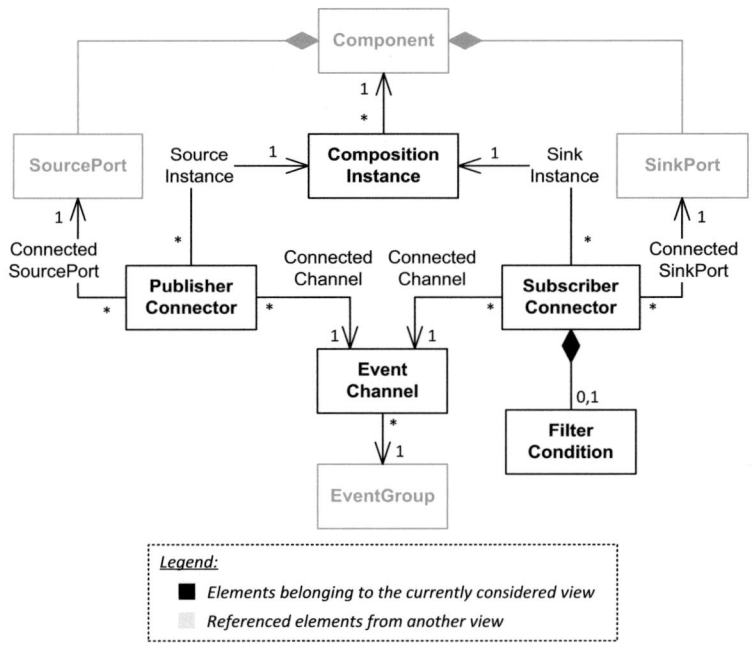

Figure 4.8: Modelling of Pub/Sub Connections

to the channel. We define two dedicated connectors to connect sources
and sinks with an `EventChannel`.

As illustrated in Figure 4.8, a `PublisherConnector` contains a reference to exactly one `CompositionInstance` representing a component and one `SourcePort` of the respective component. This tuple of elements unambiguously identifies the source of the event similarly to the `P2PConnector`. However, instead of directly referencing
a receiving `CompositionInstance` and a respective `SinkPort`, the
`PublisherConnector` is connected with the `EventChannel` used
to publish the event. The cardinalities of the associations ensure that
each `PublisherConnector` connects exactly one `SourcePort` of a
`CompositionInstance` with one `EventChannel`. Nevertheless, it

is possible to connect several sources to one channel or to connect one source to several channels by defining a separate `PublisherConnector` for each connection.

Similarly to the `PublisherConnector`, the `SubscriberConnector` contains a reference to a `CompositionInstance` and one `SinkPort` of the respective component. These associations allow to identify the target of the event. Additionally, the `SubscriberConnector` is associated with the `EventChannel` acting as a source of the subscribed events. As previously, each `SubscriberConnector` connects exactly one `EventChannel` with a `SinkPort` of a `CompositionInstance` while at the same time it is possible to have multiple `SubscriberConnectors` associated with a given channel or sink. In contrast to the `PublisherConnector`, the `SubscriberConnector` can contain an additional `FilterCondition` element to specify individual filtering rules for each sink (requirement R-5) as already described in the context of `P2PConnectors` in the previous section.

The *Composition* view of the exemplary supermarket scenario is depicted in Figure 4.9. In this view, `ComponentInstances` are represented by graphical symbols similar to UML components. Each `ComponentInstance` has an individual name extended with the name of the associated `Component`. The `SourcePorts` defined for the corresponding `Component` are represented by small triangles connected with the `ComponentInstance`. In a similar fashion, `SinkPorts` are illustrated as quadrates with a cut triangle. In our exemplary scenario, we use a `P2PConnector` to directly connect the *Shipments* port of the `ComponentInstance` *SR* with the *ShipSink* port of the *OMS* `ComponentInstance`. The communication between the two *CashDesk* instances and the event consuming *OMS* and *Statistics* `ComponentInstances` is modelled as Pub/Sub interaction using an `EventChannel` named *ProductChannel*. Channels are graphically represented by a diamond. `SubscriberConnectors` and `PublisherConnec-`

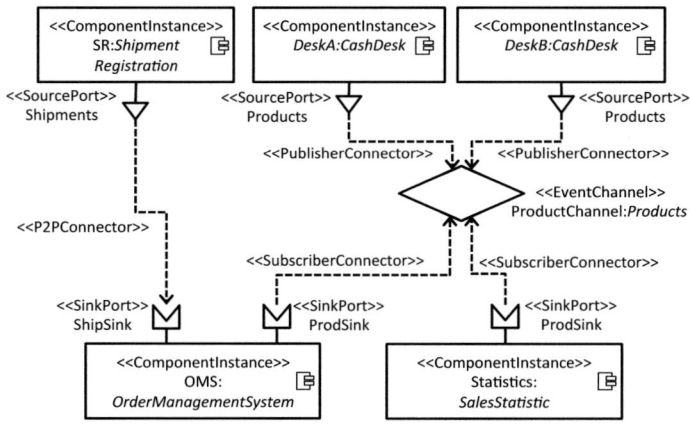

Figure 4.9: Composition View of the Supermarket Scenario

tors illustrated as arrows connect the SinkPorts and SourcePort of the particular ComponentInstance with the *ProductChannel*. Sink specific filtering rules are attributes of SubscriberConnectors and P2PConnectors respectively. For the sake of clearance, they are not represented in the graphical syntax but listed and editable in the attribute list of the respective connector.

4.2.4. Deployment

In the *Deployment* view, the CompositionInstances and EventChannels defined as part of the *Composition* view, are assigned to hardware nodes. CompositionInstances and EventChannels can be deployed individually on different hardware nodes represented by DeploymentContainer elements. In the meta-model, this is reflected by the abstract DeployableEntity element, of which EventChannel and CompositionInstance are subtypes. The explicit deployment of EventChannels on hardware nodes allows to specify the responsible server for each channel that provides the re-

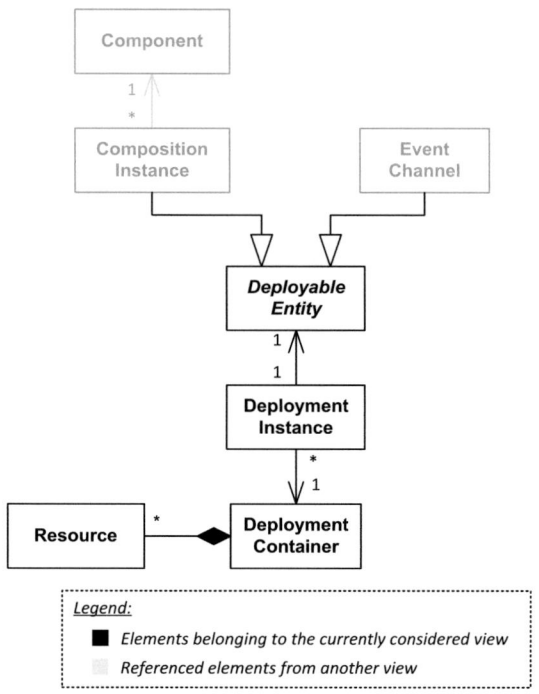

Figure 4.10: Deployment of Components and Event Channels

sources required for routing and delivering the events sent over the channel. Although the presented modelling elements do not include any platform-specific processing behaviour and resource demands (requirement R-6), the explicit deployment of EventChannels allows to later integrate such information in platform-specific models referring to the respective DeploymentContainer. As illustrated in Figure 4.10, each DeploymentInstances refers to exactly one DeployableEntity. To specify the mapping of a DeployableEntity to a hardware node, the DeploymentInstance includes a reference to exactly one DeploymentContainer. The DeploymentContainer itself contains

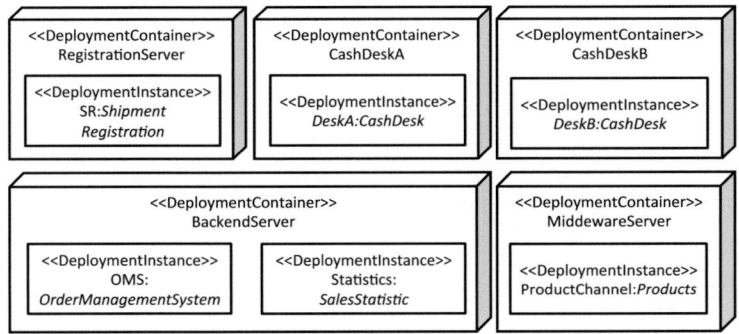

Figure 4.11: Deployment View of the Supermarket Scenario

Resources that abstract hardware resources like CPU, main memory or hard disks. The hardware infrastructure is further modelled by means of the specific modelling elements provided for this purpose by the considered ADL used as a basis.

The presented modelling abstractions for specifying the deployment of components and event channels extend the concepts provided by the *base ADL*. As EventChannels are deployed similarly to ComponentInstances, the graphical representation should be similar as well. Figure 4.11 illustrates the deployment of the different components of the supermarket example. The hardware environment consists of several servers represented by different DeploymentContainers. The *ShipmentRegistration* component is running on a separate server located at the goods receiving department. The central backend sever hosts both the order management and the sales statistics system. For each cash desk an individual DeploymentContainer is specified hosting the respective instance of the *CashDesk* component. Finally, the EventChannel is deployed on a separate *MiddlewareServer*.

4.3. Behavioural Semantics

In this section, we provide a description of the behavioural semantics of the presented meta-model elements for modelling event-based interactions in component-based architecture models using the supermarket scenario as illustrating example. For a formal specification, we refer to Chapter 5 (especially Section 5.4), which describes a transformation into a refined model based on the original PCM. Combined with the formal specification of PCM's behavioural semantics presented in [Koziolek 08a], the provided transformation among other things serves as a formal specification of the behavioural semantics of the modelling abstractions introduced in the previous section.

Figure 4.12(a) shows a UML sequence diagram illustrating the P2P interaction between the shipment registration system *SR* and the order management system *OR* of our exemplary supermarket scenario. *SR* initialises the *Acknowledgement* event within an `EmitEventAction` associated with a `SourcePort` contained in the corresponding *ShipmentRegistration* `Component`. After initialising the event it is sent to the connected `SinkPort` and the execution of *SR* immediately continues.

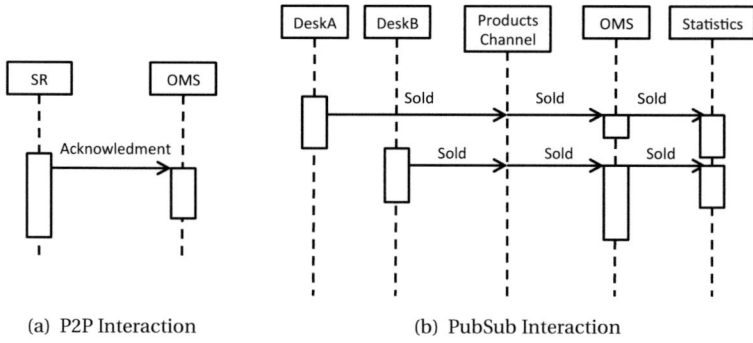

(a) P2P Interaction   (b) PubSub Interaction

Figure 4.12: Behavioural Semantics

As soon as the event is received at the connected `SinkPort`, the optional `FilterCondition` contained in the connector is evaluated. If it evaluates to true the `EventHandler` associated with the `SinkPort` that received the message is executed. Since the execution of *SR* immediately continuos after emitting the event, the `EventHandler` of *OR* is executed in parallel. In the case of several sinks connected with one source using a `P2PConnector`, the event is sent to all sinks in parallel.

Figure 4.12(b) illustrates the communication between the two cash desks *DeskA* and *DeskB* and the receiving *OMS* and *Statistics* systems. Similarly to `P2PConnectors`, the events are initialised within the source components and emitted through the `SourcePort`, while the execution of the components immediately continues. As depicted in Figure 4.12(b), the event is sent to the `EventChannel` the `SourcePort` is connected to, which in our supermarket example is the *ProductsChannel*. When an `EventChannel` receives an event, it replicates the event for each connected `SinkPort` and immediately forwards the events to them in parallel. The optional `FilterCondition` contained in each `SubscriberConnection` is evaluated when an event is received by a sink component similarly to the use of `P2PConnectors`. If the evaluation results in true, the `EventHandler` contained in the component and associated with the particular `EventType` and `SinkRole` is executed.

The presented behavioural semantics presented above assume an optimal "zero-delay" processing and transmission of events, which from an architecture point of view is acceptable. However, from the performance point of view, the transmission system induces several platform-specific delays, which should be considered when evaluating the performance of an EBS. Chapter 5 provides more detail on the event processing within a transmission system, and presents the platform-aware prediction technique that combines architecture-level modelling using the presented modelling abstractions with detailed performance prediction techniques.

4.4. Integration into the Palladio Component Model

In Section 4.2, we presented a set of generic meta-model elements enabling the modelling of event-based interactions at the architecture-level. The defined modelling abstractions are independent of a concrete ADL and are designed to be integrated into different ADLs for component-based systems. In the following, we demonstrate the integration and implementation of these elements into the *Palladio Component Model* (PCM), which was described in Section 2.4. PCM was selected as a representative example given its maturity and extensive tool support. For a detailed specification and description of the PCM meta-model elements, we refer the reader to [Reussner 11].

4.4.1. Repository

As described in Section 2.4, the *PCM Repository* contains interface and component specifications including the behavioural descriptions for each component and provided interface. We extended the repository meta-model to allow the definition of event groups and event types, the specification of the different component ports as well as the behavioural aspects for creating and processing events.

Events

In analogy to the generic modelling abstractions, we extended PCM with the new meta-model elements `EventGroup` and `EventType`, which are illustrated in Figure 4.13. `EventGroup` is a specialisation of the abstract `Interface` element, which is also the base class for `OperationInterfaces`. The `Interface` itself is a specialisation of `Name-`

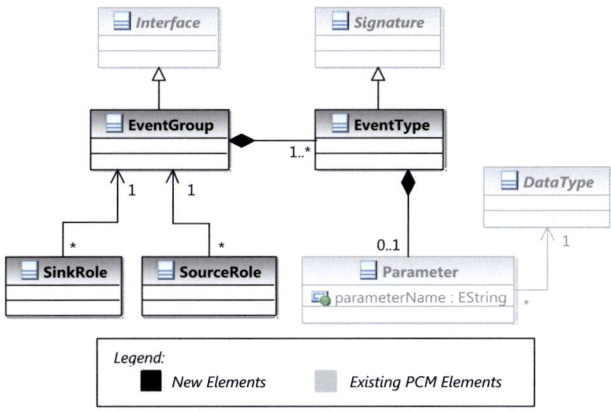

Figure 4.13: EventGroup and EventType in PCM

dEntity, which contains an attribute Name. The latter can be used to assign names to OperationInterfaces and EventGroups.

An EventGroup contains at least one EventType. The Event-Type element is a specialisation of the abstract Signature element and it is the counterpart to OperationSignatures in RPC-based communication. In contrast to OperationSignatures that contain a set of Parameters representing input variables and an optional reference to a DataType describing the return parameter, EventTypes reference only one Parameter describing the payload of the event. We use the PCM element Parameter to exploit the existing capabilities of PCM to describe different DataTypes combined with the specification of behaviour and performance relevant variable characteristics. PCM provides three different elements to describe simple and complex data types namely PrimitiveDataType, CollectionDataType, and CompositeDataType, as sub-classes of the DataType element. Depending on the specific scenario, the performance relevant characteristics of an event vary from a single property such as the sender ID to a complex structure describing the event content. For example, a system might be influenced only by the sender ID stored as a string in an event or a filter might analyse the event content in detail to decide whether any further processing is necessary. Integrating the existing `Parameter` and `DataType` elements into the specification of `EventTypes` provides the flexibility to support all these cases.

Ports

In PCM, interfaces provided or required by a component are modelled using the concept of `Provided-` and `RequiredRoles`. As illustrated in Figure 4.14, the abstract `ProvidedRole` element is contained by the abstract `InterfaceProvidingEntity` while the `RequiredRole` element is part of an `InterfaceRequiringEntity`. These entity types are combined within the abstract `InterfaceProvidingRequiringEntity` using multiple inheritance. The complete inheritance hierarchy, which ends with the `BasicComponent` as a first non-abstract element, was introduced in PCM, to support the component type hierarchy described in [Becker 08a].

For modelling RPC-based communication, PCM provides two specialised roles namely `OperationProvidedRole` and `OperationRequiredRole`, both associated with an `OperationInterface` and defined as sub-classes of `ProvidedRole` and `RequiredRole`, respectively. In analogy to `OperationInterfaces` and the belonging roles, we define the new elements `SourceRole` and `SinkRole` supporting the specification of source and sink ports as described in the generic modelling abstraction. We defined the `SinkRole` as specialisation of `ProvidedRole`, since the event handling behaviour offered by a component and associated with a `SinkRole` provides functionality that can be invoked by other components through emitting an event. Similar to, functionality provided through `OperationProvidedRoles`, functionality provided in form of event handlers can be executed by other components but need not. The `SourceRole` is a spe-

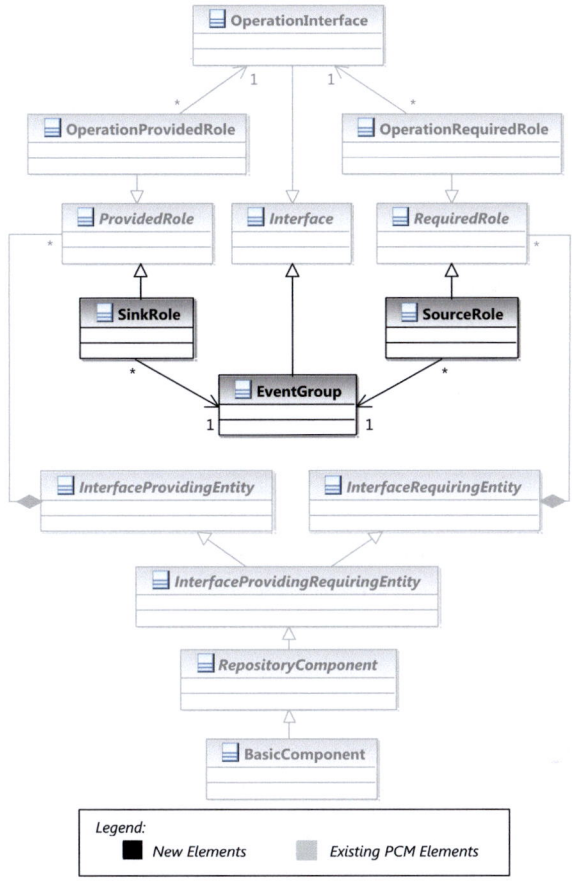

Figure 4.14: Source and Sink Roles

cialisation of the RequiredRole, as events that are emitted by one of
the components through a SourceRole require at least one receiver
that process the event to not being obsolete. Both roles have in common
that they include a reference to exactly one EventGroup containing the
EventTypes emitted or processed by the component.

Behaviour

With RD-SEFF, PCM provides a language to describe the behaviour of components supporting the modelling of complex control and data flows. In the following, we extend the RD-SEFF meta-model with new elements to describe the instantiation and emission of events. Furthermore, we integrate behavioural descriptions to describe the event handling behaviour associated with sink ports.

As depicted in Figure 4.15, our extensions introduce the `EmitEventAction` as a sub-class of `AbstractAction`, which is the base class of all actions a `ResourceDemandingBehaviour` consists of.

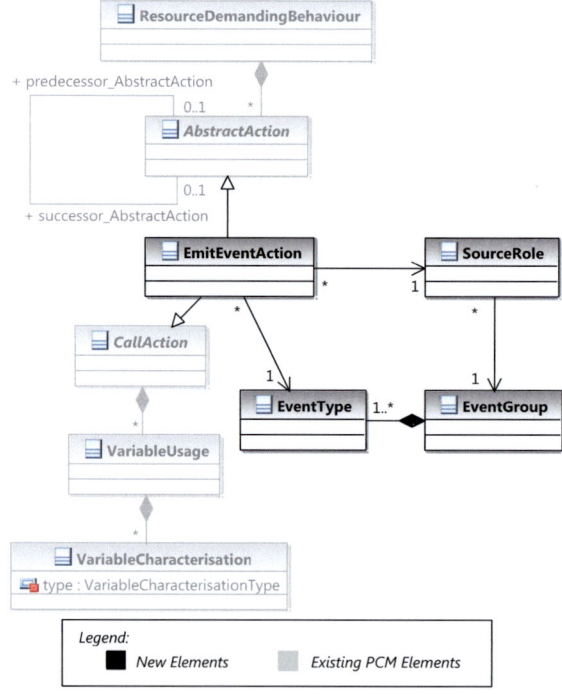

Figure 4.15: Emit Event Action

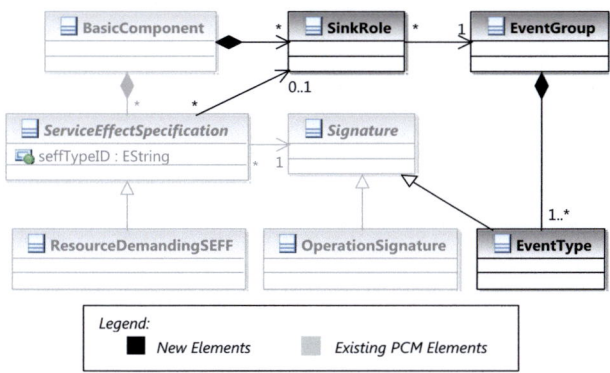

Figure 4.16: Event Handling

Furthermore, EmitEventAction is a specialisation of the abstract CallAction, which subsumes all elements that involve an instantiation and value assignment for variables and parameters. CallActions can include multiple VariableUsages, which themselves can include multiple VariableCharacterisations. Each VariableCharacterisation contains a StoEx expression encapsulated as a string in the PCMRandomVariable element to define the value assignment. For more details on the value specification, we refer to [Reussner 11].

Each EmitEventAction contains a reference to the Source-Role that should be used to publish the event. Additionally, the EmitEventAction references the concrete EventType that is instantiated within the VariableUsage and VariableCharacterisation. An OCL constraint ensures that the EventType referenced by the EmitEventAction is contained in the EventGroup referenced by the SourceRole.

The event handling behaviour is modelled in a similar fashion to the way the behaviour of provided operations is specified through the RD-SEFF language. We exploit the existing abstract ServiceEffect-Specification combined with its specialisation the ResourceDe-

`mandingSEFF`. As depicted in Figure 4.16, each `ServiceEffect-Specification` contains a reference to a `Signature` element identifying the entity whose behaviour is modelled. As the `EventType` is defined as a sub-class of the generic and abstract `Signature` element, a `ServiceEffectSpecification` can be associated either to an `OperationSignature` (when modelling the behaviour of a provided service) or to an `EventType` (when modelling the behaviour of an event handler). PCM in its original version is based on the assumption that a component provides an `OperationInterface` only once. In order to allow components to provide different event handlers for the same `EventType` respectively contain several `SourceRoles` associated with the same `EventGroup`, we define an optional association connecting a `ServiceEffectSpecification` with a `SinkRole`. This additional association ensures that the event handler can always be uniquely identified based on the tuple `SinkRole` and `EventType`.

4.4.2. System

In PCM, the *System* model is used to describe the instantiation and composition of components specified within the *Repository* model. The meta-model provides elements to instantiate components namely the `AssemblyContexts` as well as different `Connectors` used to connect the different ports provided and required by components. Based on our generic modelling approach presented in Section 4.2, we define three new specialisations of the generic `Connector` element: `AssemblyEventConnectors` for specifying direct P2P connectors and `EventChannelSourceConnectors` respectively `EventChannelSinkConnectors` for specifying Pub/Sub connections with an intermediate channel.

As illustrated in Figure 4.17, each `AssemblyEventConnector` contains references to exactly one `SourceRole` and one `SinkRole`. While the number of roles per connector is limited, the same `SinkRole` or

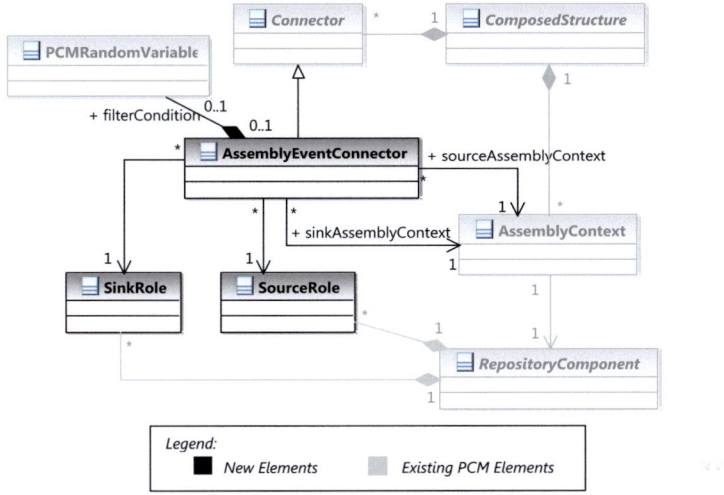

Figure 4.17: P2P Connector

`SourceRole` can be referenced by multiple `AssemblyEventConnectors` resulting in an implicit modelling of many-to-many connections. `AssemblyEventConnectors` include two references to `AssemblyContexts` representing the source and sink component instances, respectively. Given that each component can have multiple ports, both the `AssemblyContexts` and the `Source-` and `SinkRoles` must be specified to provide sufficient information to clearly identify the communicating endpoints.

The specification of sink specific filtering rules is realised by extending the `AssemblyEventConnector` with an optional `PCMRandom-Variable` as `filterCondition` that allows to specify a boolean expression using the StoEx language. Such expressions can include comparison operators to specify value dependent filtering rules but also support the inclusion of probabilistic expressions. For more details on the StoEx language and grammar, we refer the reader to [Reussner 11].

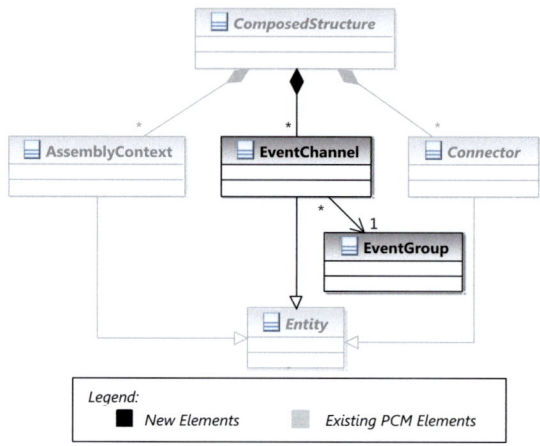

Figure 4.18: Event Channel

For modelling Pub/Sub interactions, we introduce the new `EventChannel` element. As illustrated in Figure 4.18, the `EventChannel`, similarly to `AssemblyContexts` and `Connectors`, is defined as a sub-class of `Entity` and is contained in a `ComposedStructure` representing a composite component or the complete system. Each `EventChannel` is associated with exactly one `EventGroup` to ensure that only compatible `Source-` and `SinkRoles` associated with the same `EventGroup` are connected.

Figure 4.19 illustrates the realisation of the `EventChannelSource-Connector`. It connects a source with an `EventChannel` and thus contains, in analogy to the `AssemblyEventConnectors`, one reference to a `SourceRole` and one reference to an `AssemblyContext` to uniquely identify the component instance and its source port. Additionally, the `EventChannelSourceConnector` refers to the `EventChannel` used to publish the event. Each event published to a channel is forwarded to all sink instances connected to the channel. Similarly to `EventChannelSourceConnectors`, `EventChan-`

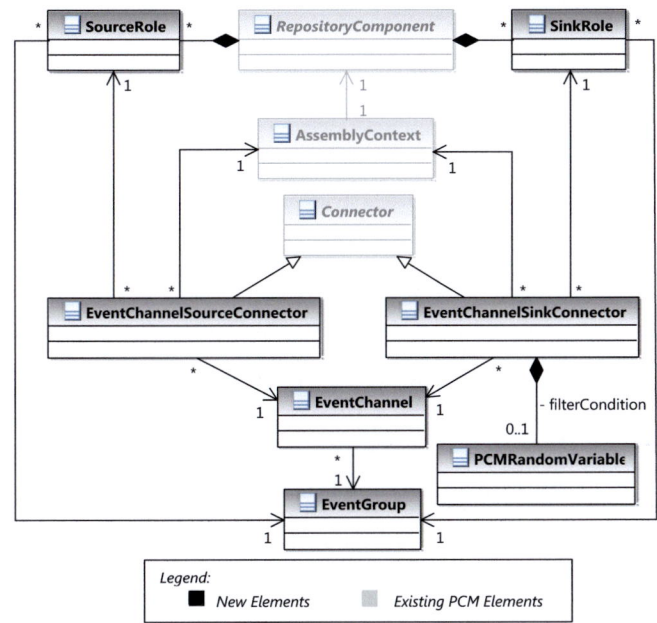

Figure 4.19: Pub/Sub Connectors

nelSinkConnectors contain a reference to an EventChannel, an AssemblyContext, and a SinkPort. In analogy to AssemblyEventConnectors, EventChannelSinkConnectors contain an optional PCMRandomVariable allowing to specify value dependent or probabilistic filtering rules individually for each sink.

4.4.3. Allocation

In PCM, AllocationContexts describe the run-time instances of components. Each AssemblyContext is associated with exactly one AllocationContext and vice versa. PCM does not contain an abstract element representing all deployable entities such as the DeployableEntity, used in the generic modelling abstractions. Since intro-

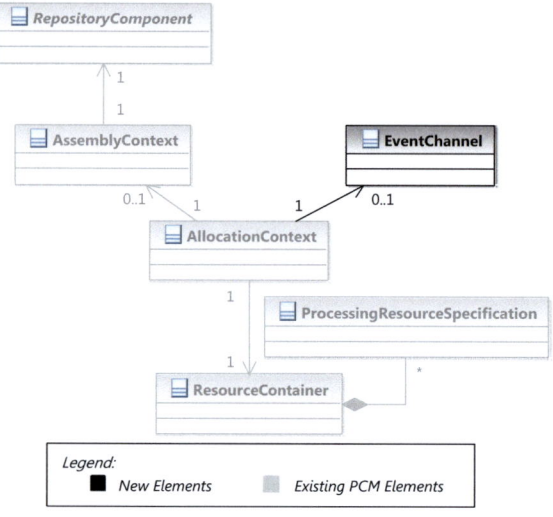

Figure 4.20: Allocation Model

ducing such an element into the original PCM, would result in significant changes of existing elements as well as their inheritance hierarchies and associations, we slightly deviated from the general modelling abstractions. Instead of introducing an abstract element, we extended the AllocationContext element to contain an association either to an AssemblyContext or to an EventChannel. We changed the cardinality of the association between AssemblyContext and AllocationContext from "1" to "0,1" and added a new association allowing to connect AllocationContexts with EventChannels. An OCL constraint ensures that an AllocationContext is always associated with either an AssemblyContext or an EventChannel. In PCM, each AllocationContext is additionally associated with a ResourceContainer representing the hardware node that the respective component instance or the event channel should be deployed on. To specify the different resources provided by the node, the Re-

`sourceContainer` contains a `ProcessingResourceSpecifi-`
`cation` for each offered resource.

4.5. Concluding Remarks

In this chapter, we introduced a set of abstractions that enable the modelling of event-based interactions at the architecture-level. The abstractions provide explicit support for both direct P2P connections between components and decoupled many-to-many interactions based on the Pub/Sub paradigm using an intermediate event channel and thus cover a large set of different EBS. The modelling concepts have been developed with the goal to be independent of a concrete ADL and enable the extension of multiple existing ADLs for component-based systems with an explicit support for modelling event-based interactions at the architecture-level. We demonstrated the extension of an existing ADL with the developed modelling abstractions using PCM as a representative example of a mature ADL for component-based systems.

The contributions presented in this chapter enable the modelling of event-based interactions at the architecture-level and constitute the basis for the platform-aware analysis method presented in the next chapter.

5. Analysis Method based on Model-to-Model Transformations

The modelling abstractions introduced in the previous chapter enable architects to model event-based interactions at the architecture-level. To enable detailed quality evaluations based on the models, this chapter introduces a two-step refinement transformation approach. Since the implementation and behaviour of the employe transmission system has a significant influence on the end-to-end system performance [Sachs 09], the goal of our transformation is to supper platform-independent modelling of the system at the architecture-level while at the same time enabling a detailed platform-aware performance prediction by automatically integrating platform-specific details into the models.

As a novelty to existing refinement approaches (e.g., [Woodside 95], [Kapova 11]), our two-step transformation strictly separates the platform-independent refinement of event-based interactions and the integration of platform-specific details. This strict separation eases the evaluation of different transmission system solutions in terms of their influence on the system performance since varying the underlying platform does not require any adaptation of the architecture-level models. In a similar fashion, the platform-specific models describing the transmission system are defined once independent of the system architecture and can be reused in the context of different systems.

In order to derive a platform-specific model that integrates platform-specific details about the behaviour of the underlying transmission system, the architecture-level model is refined by applying the developed two-step refinement transformation as depicted in Figure 5.1. The pre-

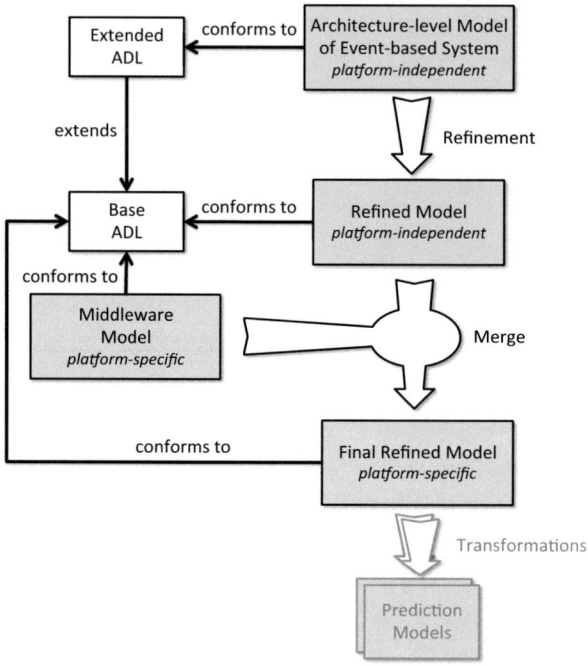

Figure 5.1: Transformation Overview

sented transformation approach is an extension of the merge approach defined in the "*Model-Driven Architecture* (MDA) *Guide*" [OMG 03]. The architecture model is first refined by integrating a platform-independent event processing chain. This refinement step substitutes the event-based connections between components with a chain of components representing the different event processing stages inside the transmission system. Using the resulting refined model as a basis, the next step of the transformation integrates platform-specific components specified in a separate middleware model. These components capture the performance relevant influence factors of the employed transmission system. Since all elements that have been introduced by applying the extensions presented in the previous chapter are substituted with the detailed event-processing chain, the resulting final model serves as input for different existing prediction techniques, that have been implemented for the original base *Architecture Description Language* (ADL).

In the following, we first describe the generic event processing chain that provides a skeleton to integrate platform-specific components representing the different event processing activities within the transmission system. Second, we provide an exemplary description of the two-step transformation explaining the refinement of the model as well as the merging with the middleware model. Finally, in Section 5.4, we provide a formal specification of the complete transformation.

5.1. Generic Event Processing Chain

The generic event processing chain, illustrated in Figure 5.2, consists of six processing stages that are common for *Event-based Systems* (EBS). The execution of the different stages is distributed among the involved source and sink components and the transmission system. Given that the processing chain is defined to be platform-independent, it does not

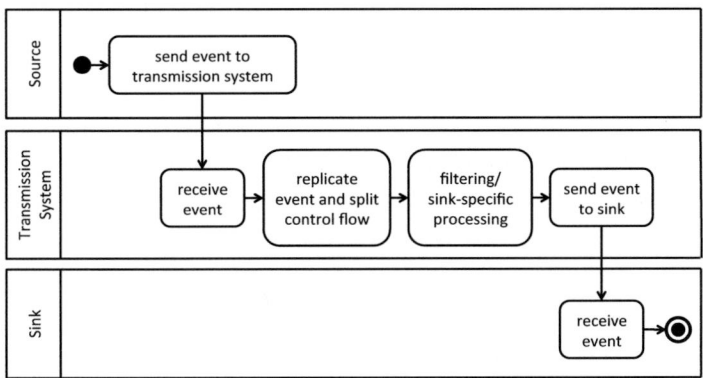

Figure 5.2: Generic Event Processing Chain

include any concrete resource demanding behaviour, however, it provides placeholders to integrate such platform-specific behaviour that is
executed as part of the various stages. The first stage, *send event to transmission system* performed on the source side, includes the communication activities to send the event to the transmission system. This stage
is usually performed within a local library, which encapsulates the communication and includes activities like marshalling, compression, or encryption on the source side. In the parallel *receive event* stage, the event
is received by the transmission system, which includes the communication with the source component as well as possibly additional activities
like for example the de-marshalling required to acknowledge the correct
receipt of the event.

Asynchronous many-to-many communication between components
is one of the main characteristics of event-based interactions. In the
generic event processing chain, this behaviour is reflected by the *replicate event and split control flow* processing stage. While providing a
cloned instance of the event to each connected sink, the control flow
between sources and sinks is decoupled and the cloned events are forwarded to the sinks in parallel as illustrated in Figure 5.3. The remaining
activities of the event processing chain are executed in parallel and independently for each connected sink.

After splitting the control flow, the generic event processing chain contains the *filtering/sink-specific processing* based on the filtering conditions defined within the connectors. If the event matches the defined
filtering conditions for a given sink, the event is further processed. Otherwise, the event processing for the respective sink is terminated. In addition to the filtering, which is considered as platform-independent logic,
the filtering stage allows to integrate additional platform-specific processing like for example data conversion, deserialization, or decompres-
sion. Such platform-specific activities are described as part of the mid-

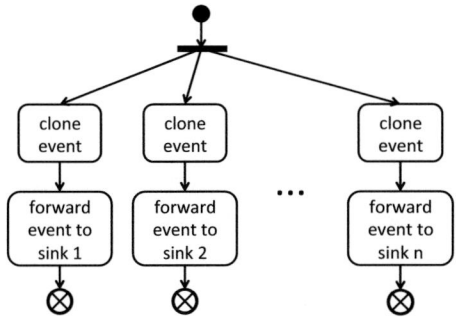

Figure 5.3: Replicate Event and Split Control Flow Step

dleware model which is later integrated when deriving the final platform-specific model.

In analogy to the communication between sources and the transmission system, which is reflected by the first two stages of the event processing chain, the communication between the transmission system and sinks is split into two stages. The *send event to sink* stage encapsulates the communication aspects the transmission system is responsible for while allowing the integration of platform-specific marshalling or serialisation operations. The *receive event* stage is the counterpart stage on the sink side usually executed in parallel by a local library encapsulating the communication with the transmission system.

The presented platform-independent event processing chain is the foundation for the platform-independent refinement transformation presented in the following section.

5.2. Platform-independent Refinement

The platform-independent refinement, which is the first step of our two-step transformation, substitutes event-based interactions modelled at the architecture-level with a chain of components. Each of these components represents exactly one of the presented processing stages. In the following, we present an exemplary transformation of source and sink components to illustrate our approach before providing a formal specification in Section 5.4.

Point-to-Point (P2P) and *Publish/Subscribe* (Pub/Sub) interactions are modelled differently at the architecture-level. In the first case, direct connectors betweens sources and sinks are used while in the second case sources and sinks are connected through intermediary event channels. In the following, we first present a detailed description of the refinement of Pub/Sub connections followed by an description of the differences in case of direct P2P connectors.

5.2.1. Refinement of Publish/Subscribe Connectors

Figure 5.4 presents an overview of the refinement of two source component connected with two sinks using an `EventChannel` with `Publisher-` and `SubscriberConnectors`, respectively. However, before transforming the connectors, the transformation generates an `OperationInterface` for each `EventGroup` including an `OperationSignature` for each `EventType`, with the event itself defined as input parameter.

The `SourcePort` as part of component A is replaced by a port requiring this `OperationInterface` resulting in a synchronous call initiating the event processing chain. This port is connected with the provided operational port of the newly generated *SourcePort*[1] component, which represents the local library that encapsulates the communication with the transmission system. The *SourcePort* component is always deployed on the same node as the source component itself. In a similar fashion, component B is modified and connected with a second instance of the *SourcePort* component.

---

[1] In the following description of the refinement transformation, we use an *italic* font when referring to components of the generic event processing chain and a `typewriter` font in case of meta-model and model elements

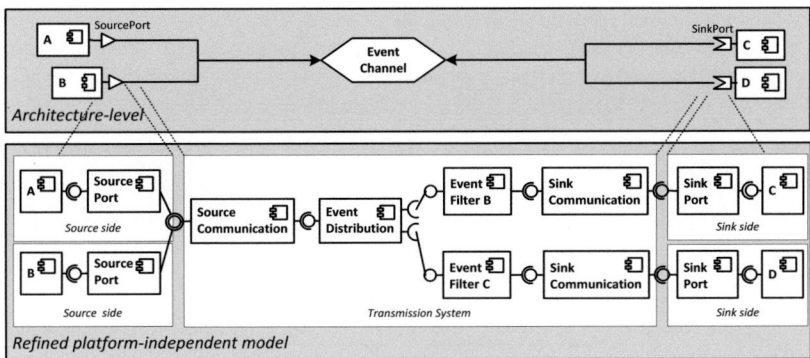

Figure 5.4: Refinement of Event Channels

The `EventChannel` and the corresponding `Publisher-` and `Sub-scriberConnectors` are transformed into a chain of components. The *SourceCommunication* component as first component inside the transmission system receives the emitted events from all *SourcePort* components. The *SourceCommunication* component provides a skeleton to integrate platform specific-components describing the resource demands for receiving and processing the event.

The following *EventDistribution* component is responsible for replicating the event and splitting the control flow for each sink connected with the channel. It forwards the event by calling the provided interface of the sink-specific *EventFilter* component. The generated *EventDistribution* component contains an individual required port of the `OperationInterface` representing the `EventGroup` for each of these sinks. To realise the asynchronous and decoupled behaviour of event-based interactions, the behaviour description of the *EventDistribution* component makes use of an asynchronous fork. This is illustrated in Figure 5.5 using *Palladio Component Model* (PCM) as an example meta-model where a `ForkAction` is defined in the respective *Resource Demanding Service Effect Specification* (RD-SEFF) containing a separate `ForkBehaviour`

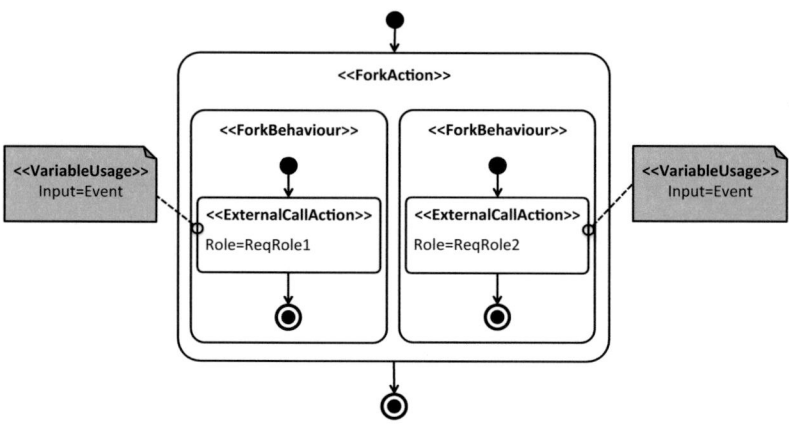

Figure 5.5: Fork-Based Event Splitting

for each sink. Each of these behaviours contains an action to call the next component through the required port that has been integrated for the respective sink component.

The *EventFilter* component, which is generated individually for each sink connected with the channel, is connected with the sink-specific required operational port of the *EventDistribution* component. The *Event-Filter* component encapsulates the sink-specific filtering rule for the respective sink. `SubscriberConnectors` as well as `P2PConnectors` contain an optional sink-specific filtering rule in form of a boolean expression. In contrast to the other components, which directly call the next component in the chain of responsibility, the *EventFilter* component includes a branch using the boolean expression contained in the connector as guard. Thanks to this guard, the event processing continues with the call of the *SinkCommunication* component only, if the filtering rules evaluates to `TRUE`, otherwise the event processing for this specific sink is terminated.

Similarly to the *SourceCommunication* component, the *SinkCommunication* provides a skeleton to integrate relevant resource demanding behaviour of the transmission system when communicating with the respective sink.

In analogy to the transformation of `SourcePorts`, each `SinkPort` is replaced by a provided operational port and an additional instance of the *SinkPort* component. This component is the counterpart of the *SinkCommunication* component and abstracts the local library of the sink component and its local resource demanding behaviour at the sink side. In addition to the provided operational interface, the sink component is modified to handle the incoming operation calls of the transmission system when events are delivered. The existing behavioural descriptions specifying the `EventHandlers` are linked with the `Signature` representing the `EventType` and the operational required port that has been generated to substitute the `SinkPort`. Since the event is handed over as a parameter of the signature, it can be accessed in a similar fashion compared to accessing the event within an `EventHandler`. For this reason, no further modifications of the behavioural descriptions are required.

`EventChannels` are explicitly deployed by defining a `DeploymentInstance`, which connects an `EventChannel` with exactly one `ResourceContainer`. In analogy to this deployment, the different components representing the transmission system, i.e., the *SourceCommunication, EventDistribution, EventFilter* and *SinkCommunication* components, that have been generated and instantiated when transforming the `EventChannel` are deployed on the same `ResourceContainer`. The *SourcePort* component is always deployed on the same `ResourceContainer`, the source component is running on. In a similar fashion, the *SinkPort* component is deployed on the `ResourceContainer` the respective sink component is running on.

5.2.2. Refinement of Point-to-Point Connectors

The transformation of P2P connections is quite similar to the processing of Pub/Sub connections and varies only in the instantiation and deployment of components. Figure 5.6 illustrates the transformation of a source component connected through P2PConnectors with two sink components.

In contrast to the transformation of Pub/Sub connections, which instantiate the event processing chain once for each EventChannel, the transformation of P2P connections generates an instance of the event processing chain for each source component. The SourcePort of the source component is substituted with a required port referencing the OperationInterface representing the EventGroup. This required port is connected with a new instance of the *SourcePort* component respectively its provided port. Similarly to the processing of Pub/Sub connections, the *SourcePort* component is connected with *SourceCommunication* component, which itself invokes an instance of the *EventDistribution* component. The *EventDistribution* contains an individual required operational port for each sink connected with the SourcePort using a P2PConnector. For each P2PConnector an individual *EventFilter*

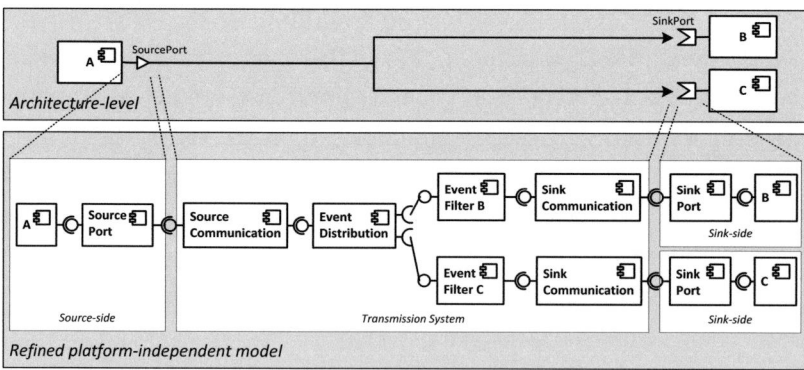

Figure 5.6: Refinement of a Source with Point-to-Point Connectors

component is generated encapsulating the branch with the `EventFil-teringCondition` contained in the connector as guard. In analogy to Pub/Sub connections, the event processing chain is completed with an instances of the *SinkCommuncation* and *SinkPort* components.

Similar to the case of Pub/Sub connections, the *SourcePort* and *SinkPort* components are deployed on the same `ResourceContainers` hosting the source and sink component respectively. To support peer-to-peer-based as well as centralised middleware systems, the components representing the transmission system are deployed differently depending on the existence of a central `ResourceContainer` hosting the middleware named "Middleware". If the `ResourceEnvironment` contains such a `ResourceContainer`, the components belonging to the transmission system, i.e., *SourceCommunication, EventDistribution, EventFilter* and *SinkCommunication*, are deployed on this node otherwise they are deployed on the `ResourceContainer` hosting the source component.

5.3. Merging with Platform-specific Middleware Components

From a modelling point of view, the general event-based connections between components and the specific middleware used for the technical implementation are at two different abstraction levels. For this reasons, we separate the platform-specific behaviour and resource demands of a middleware implementation using a dedicated middleware model. As a result of this separation, changes of the system architecture to evaluate different design alternatives do not require any adaptation of the middleware model. Additionally, variations of the middleware with the aim to evaluate different middleware products and their influence on the performance of the system do not require changes of the architecture model.

The middleware model contains platform-specific components describing the behaviour and resource demands of the middleware for

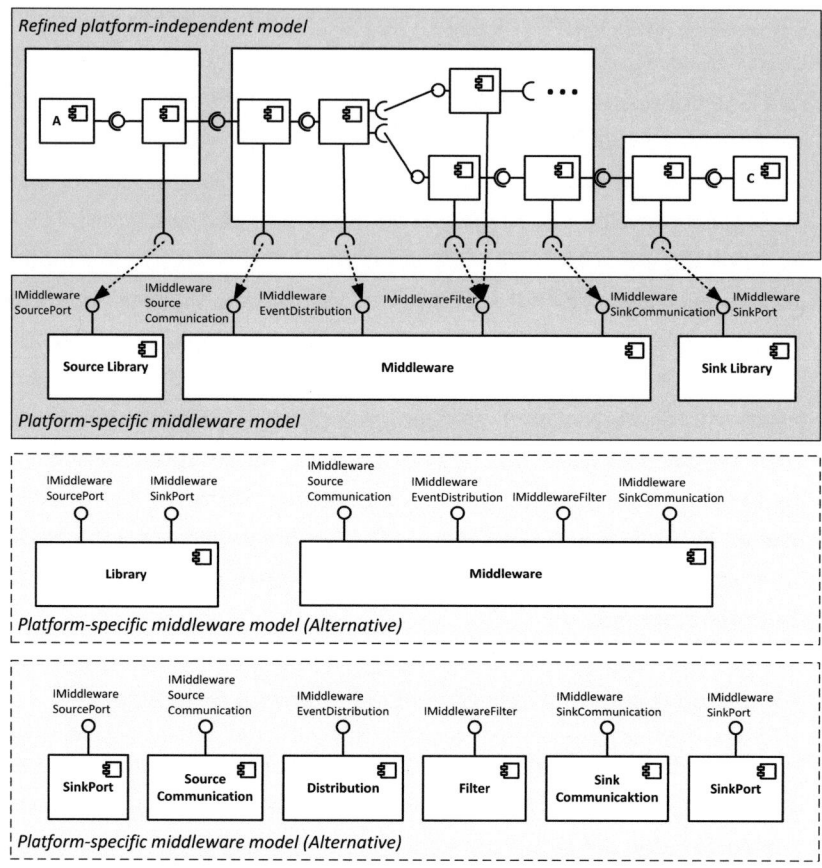

Figure 5.7: Examples of Middleware Models and their Weaving

executing the different event processing steps. To enable the integration of the platform-specific components, their specifications have to conform to the *base ADL* used as basis for integrating the modelling abstractions for event-based interactions. The middleware model includes six predefined operational interfaces namely IMiddleware-SourcePort, IMiddlewareSourceCommunication, IMiddlewareEventDistribution, IMiddlewareFilter, IMiddlewareSinkCommunication, and IMiddlewareSinkPort. Each interface contains a signature having a similar name as the interface and containing one input parameter representing the processed event. As one example, the operation defined as part of the IMiddlewareSour-cePort interface is named handleSourcePort. The definition of individual interfaces for each operation allows a variable modelling of the middleware. The middleware model can contain a dedicated component for each interface but also allows to specify only one component providing all interfaces and every variation between these two options. Figure 5.7 illustrates possible variations.

The integration of the platform-specific components into the platform-independent event processing chain follows the transformation process depicted in Figure 5.8. The first step is the identification and localisation of the components providing the different middleware interfaces. As a next step, the components representing the platform-independent event processing are extended to invoke the platform-specific middleware component providing the respective middleware interface. This extension includes the integration of a new required oper-

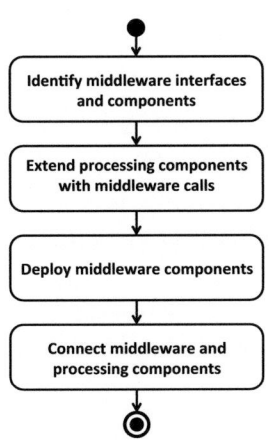

Figure 5.8: Middleware Weaving Process

ational port into the event processing component. Furthermore, the behavioural specification of the component is extended with an additional action to initially invoke the middleware component before continuing the event processing by calling the next component in the event processing chain. The third step generates the deployment specification for the different platform-specific middleware components. All components are instantiated and deployed to the same `ResourceContainer` the respective platform-independent component is deployed to. The transformation ensures that each `ResourceContainer` contains only one instance of each platform-specific component. This instance is shared between the multiple instances of platform-independent components. This deployment of platform-specific middleware components as local singletons enables the consideration of software resources like local thread pools or semaphores used within the middleware or local library shared over different sources or sinks running on the same container. Finally, the merging transformation generates the connectors between the newly generated required operational ports of the platform-independent event processing components with the corresponding provided operational port of the platform-specific middleware component instance on the same resource container. The result of the model merging is the refined platform-specific model that conforms to the *base ADL* and thus can serve as input to multiple existing analysis and prediction techniques defined for the *base ADL*.

5.4. Formalised Transformation Description

While the previous section gave an overview on the developed transformation approach as well as the substitutions and completions performed when executing the transformation based on illustrating examples, this section introduces a formalised representation of the transformation using the extended PCM presented in Section 4.4 as source and

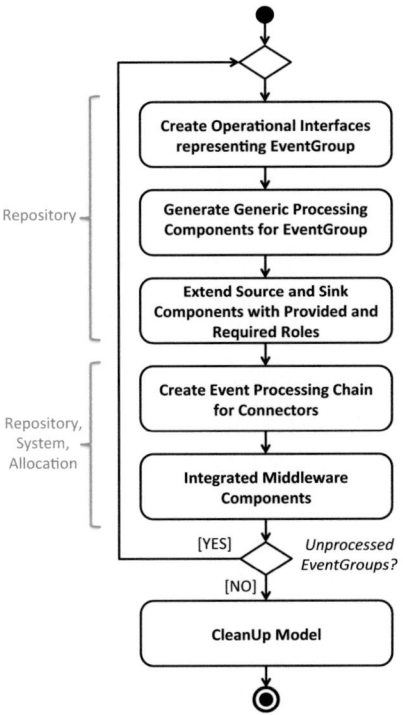

Figure 5.9: Transformation Process Overview

target meta-model. Figure 5.9 presents an overview of the transformation, which consists of several transformation procedures. These procedures cover different transformation aspects ranging from the substitution of `EventGroups` and `EventTypes` in the *Repository Model* over the processing of connectors in the *System Model* up to the individual deployment of generated components as part of the *Allocation Model*.

The transformation iteratively transforms each `EventGroup`. As illustrated in Figure 5.9, it contains a loop iterating over all `Event-Groups`. First of all, an `OperationInterface` representing the `EventGroup` is generated. Based on the generated interface the corresponding event processing components providing and requiring this interface are created and added to the `Respository`. Later these components are instantiated and composed to realise the component chain representing the platform-independent event processing chain. To connect source and sink components with the event processing chain, the components are extended with `Provided-` and `RequiredRoles` referencing the `OperationInterface`. As final step in the processing loop for each `EventGroup`, the connectors, P2P as well as Pub-/Sub, connecting `Source-` and `SinkRoles` associated with the current `EventGroup` are processed and substituted with an instance of the platform-independent processing chain. As last processing step within the loop, the transformation integrates the platform-specific components specified within the middleware model. Finally after processing all `EventGroups`, the model is cleaned up and all event-related elements that have been substituted and refined in the previous steps are removed.

In the following, we present a detailed specification of the developed transformation steps based on *MOdel transformation LAnguage* (MOLA), a formalised transformation language, which we already introduced in Section 2.2.3. In contrast to other graph-based transformation languages with control-flow annotations like Henshin [Arendt 10] or Story Diagrams [von Detten 12], MOLA is the only one providing an explicit *foreach* loop construct. MOLA combines a strict formalisation that can be directly compiled into executable model-to-model transformations [Sostaks 10] with an intuitive graphical representation [Kalnins 04]. These characteristics of MOLA, which were the reason why we selected it, have been confirmed by the tool evaluation and comparison presented in [Rose 12].

5.4.1. Main Transformation Loop

Figure 5.10 illustrates the main procedure, which is the starting point of the refinement transformation. It includes the main loop iterating over all `EventGroups`, as described in the transformation overview presented in the introduction of this section. In addition to the mapping rules that generate an `OperationInterface` that later substi-

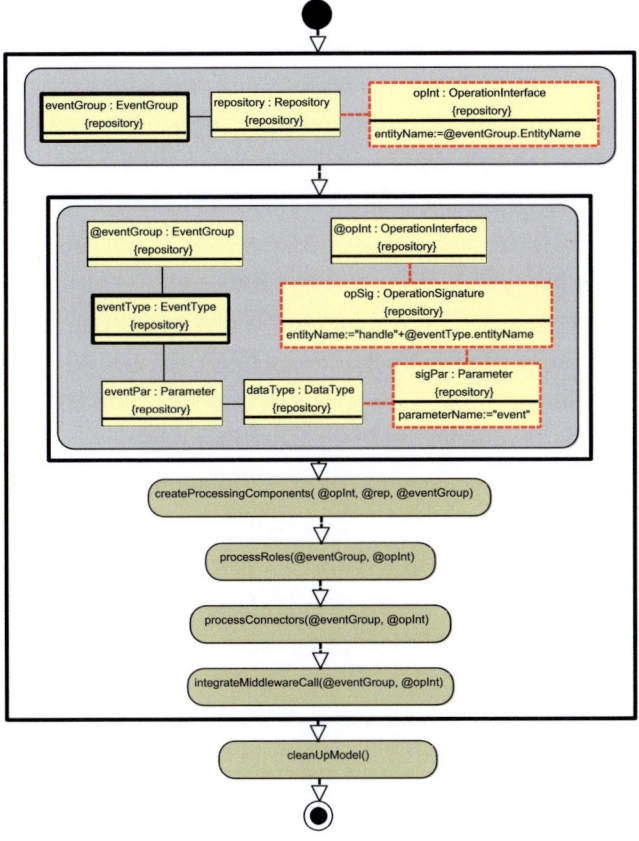

Figure 5.10: Main Procedure `Transformation`

tutes the `EventGroup`, the procedure contains several procedure calls, each representing one of the transformation steps presented above.

The control flow starts with a loop including a mapping rule that specifies the iteration over all `EventGroups` contained in a `Repository`. The mapping rule creates an `OperationInterface` belonging to the same `Repository` for each `EventGroup`. The attribute `Entity-Name` of this newly created `OperationInterface` is initialised using the `EntityName` of the `EventGroup`. Following the interface generation, a nested foreach loop iterates over all `EventTypes` contained in the `EventGroup`. The included matching rule creates an `OperationSignature` for each `EventType`. The generated `OperationSignature` contains a `Parameter` with the attribute `parameterName` set to `"event"`. This `Parameter` references the `DataType` originally associated with the `EventType`. After generating the complete `OperationInterface` for an `EventGroup`, the subprocedures responsible for generating the processing components, extending the components with additional `OperationProvided-` and `OperationRequiredRoles`, processing of the different connectors, and finally integrating the platform-specific middleware components are executed. All these procedures have in common, that they receive the current `EventGroup` and the newly generated `OperationInterface` as input parameter. After iterating over all `EventGroups`, the procedure for cleaning up the model is executed. The following subsections provide a detailed description of the different procedures.

5.4.2. Generation of Processing Components

The procedure `createProcessingComponents` generates the `BasicComponents` that represent *SourcePort, SourceCommunication, SinkCommunication* and *SinkPort* for the given `EventGroup`. The structure and the contained RD-SEFFs of the *EventDistribution* component depend on the number of connected sinks and thus are generated

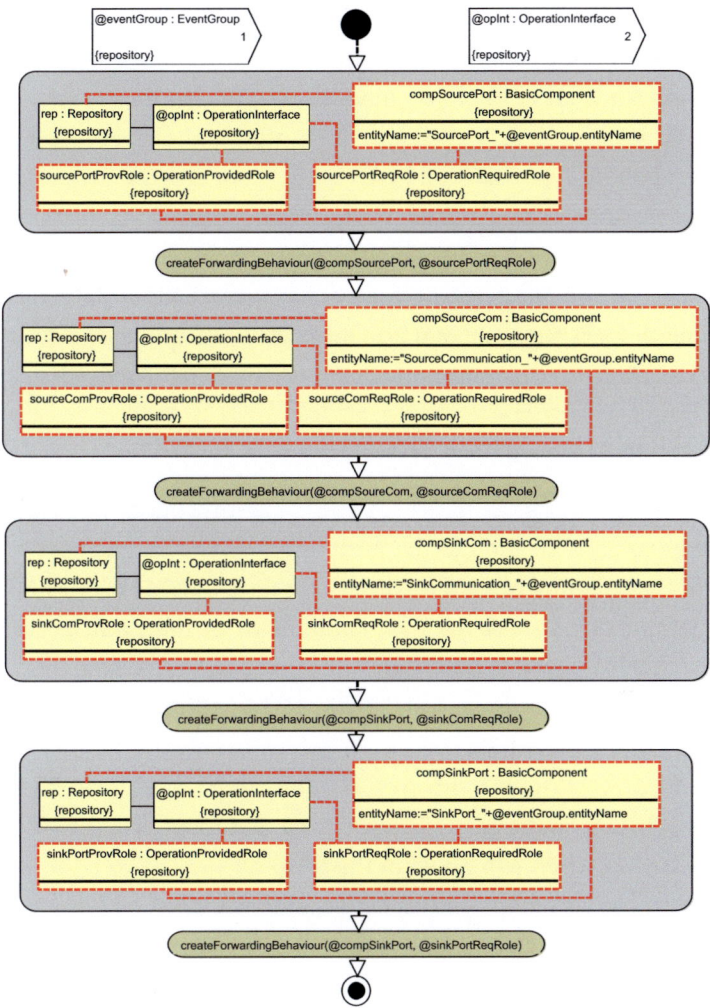

Figure 5.11: Procedure `createProcessingComponents`

when processing the connectors. Since the *EventFilter* components encapsulates the sink-specific filtering rules contained in the connectors, it is also individually generated when processing the connectors.

The procedure, as illustrated in Figure 5.11, contains a dedicated mapping rule for each of the four components. Within these rules, a new `BasicComponent` is created and the attribute `entityName` is set to the component type followed by an underscore and the `entityName` of the `EventGroup`. For each component, an `OperationProvidedRole` and an `OperationRequiredRole` associated with the `OperationInterface opInt` received as second input parameter are generated. Each mapping rule is followed by a call of the `createForwardingBehaviour` sub-procedure described in the following.

Generation of Forwarding Behaviours

The `createForwardingBehaviour` sub-procedure generates the behavioural specification in the form of RD-SEFFs for each service respectively signature offered by the component handed over as first input parameter. To call the next component in the event processing chain, each RD-SEFF contains an `ExternalCallAction` connected with the `OperationRequiredRole` of the component, which is the second input parameter.

Figure 5.12 illustrates the `createForwardingBehaviour` procedure, which includes a foreach loop iterating over all `OperationSignatures` contained in the `OperationInterface` associated with the `OperationRequiredRole` received as second input parameter. Within this loop, a new `ResourceDemandingSEFF` referencing the current `OperationSignature` is added to the component. Each `ResourceDemandingSEFF` consists of a `StartAction`, an `ExternalCallAction` and finally a `StopAction`. These actions are interconnected using the predecessor respectively successor associations defined for all `AbstractActions`. The generated `Exter-`

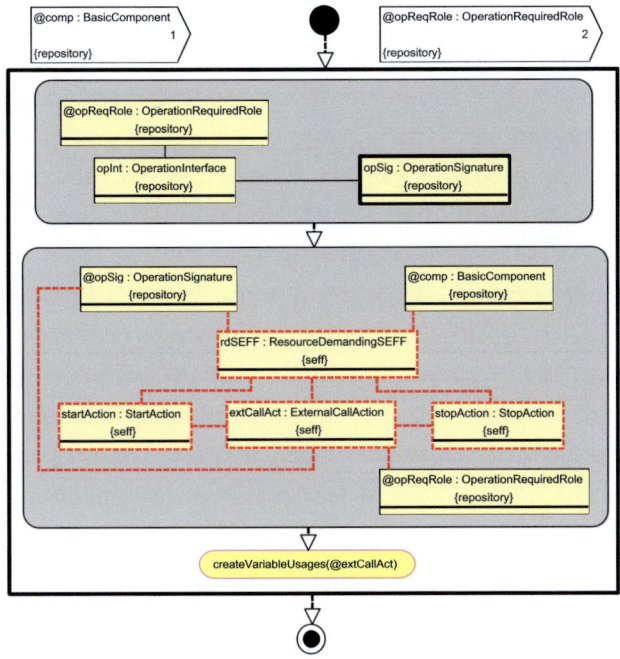

Figure 5.12: Sub-Procedure `createForwardingBehaviour`

`nalCallAction` is associated with the current `OperationSigna-`
`ture` and the `OperationRequiredRole` received as input parameter, which is the connection point to the next component in the event
processing chain. The loop ends with the execution of the procedure
`createVariableUsages`, which extends the `ExternalCallAc-`
`tion` handed over as parameter with `VariableUsages` and `Vari-`
`ableCharacterisations` required to forward the event's content as
part of the operation call.

Generation of Variable Usages and Characterisations

As already described, the *"event"* parameter of the `OperationSigna-`
`ture` represents the event that is forwarded. As PCM does not sup-

port a direct forwarding of parameters, an explicit value assignment using `VariableUsages` and `VariableCharacterisations` is required. In case of a `SimpleDataType`, the `ExternalCallAction` contains only one `VariableUsage` with the name of the parameter, while for `CompositeDataTypes`, a dedicated `VariableUsage` for each `DataType` used as part of the `CompositeDataType` is required. Each `VariableUsage` contains at least one `VariableCharacterisation` referencing one of the five predefined `CharacterisationTypes`, STRUCTURE, NUMBER_OF_ELEMENTS, VALUE, BYTE-SIZE, and TYPE. Additionally, each `VariableCharacterisation` contains a `PCMRandomVariable`, which encapsulates a string representing the *Stochastic Expression* (StoEx) to specify the assigned value.

In the case of complex data types, the generation of `VariableUsages` and `-Characterisations` requires a recursive execution. Furthermore, in PCM the addressing of inner data types as well as the definition of stochastic expressions is based on strings. Given that MOLA is a graph transformation language, its support for recursive operations with string handling is limited. However, MOLA provides the possibility, to integrate external procedures, for example written in Java, into the transformation.

Listing 5.1 illustrates the `createVariableUsages` procedure, which is integrated as external procedure into the MOLA transformation. Before calling the recursive sub-method `addUsage`, the procedure initially extracts the data type of the event and sets the namespace to "event", which is the generated name of the parameter as shown in Figure 5.10. Together with a reference to the current `ExternalCallAction`, these variables are handed over to the method `addUsage`. This method initialises a new `VariableUsage` for the current `namespace` and then adds a new `VariableCharacterisation` for each `CharacterisationType`. All `VariableCharacterisations` contain a string representing a StoEx defining the value that should be assigned.

Listing 5.1: Pseudo Code `createVariableUsages`

```
1   createVariableUsages(ExternalCallAction eca){
2       DataType type = eca.getDataTyp
3       Namespace name= new Namespace("event");
4       addUsage(eca,namespace,type);
5   }
6
7   addUsage(ExternalCallAction eca, String namespace,
            DataType type){
8       usage=createUsage(namespace);
9       usage.addChar(Characterisation.STRUCTURE,
10          new StoEx(namespace.toString+".STRUCTURE");
11      usage.addChar(Characterisation.NUMBER_OF_ELEMENTS,
12          new StoEx(namespace.toString+".NUMBER_OF_ELEMENTS
                ");
13      usage.addChar(Characterisation.VALUE,
14          new StoEx(namespace.toString+".VALUE");
15      usage.addChar(Characterisation.BYTESIZE,
16          new StoEx(namespace.toString+".BYTESIZE");
17      usage.addChar(Characterisation.TYPE,
18          new StoEx(namespace.toString+".TYPE");
19      eca.add(usage);
20
21      foreach InnerType it in type{
22          addUsage(eca, namespace.add(it), it.getType)
23      }
24  }
```

This string contains the namespace, which addresses the parameter or one of the included subtypes, extended with the dot-separated name of the `CharacterisationType`. After adding a `VariableUsage` to the `ExternalCallAction`, the `addUsage` method is recursively called for each included subtype represented by an `InnerType` declaration. The namespace is extended to directly address this subtype and handed over together with the data type of the subtype and the `ExternalCallAction`.

5.4.3. Processing of Roles

After generating the generic event processing components, the procedure `ProcessRoles` is responsible to extend source and sink components with additional `OperationRequired-` respectively `OperationProvidedRoles`. Additionally, the procedure adapts the included RD-SEFFs. In case of a source, the `EmitEventAction` is substituted with an `ExternalCallAction` and in case of a sink, the RD-SEFF describing the event handling is connected with the provided `OperationSignature`.

Figure 5.13 depicts the `processRoles` procedure. The first element is a foreach loop iterating over all `SourceRoles` corresponding to the `EventGroup` stored in the input parameter `eventGroup`. An `OperationRequiredRole` referencing the `OperationInterface` received as second input parameter is generated for each `SourceRole` that is connected with a `RepositoryComponent`. After creating the `OperationRequiredRole` two sub-procedures, namely `processEmitActions` and `createSourcePortContexts` are executed. Both receive the current `SourceRole` and the newly created `OperationRequiredRole` as input parameters. We present more details on these two sub-procedures after describing the second loop, which iterates over all `SinkRoles`.

In analogy to the processing of a `SourceRole`, the first rule in the loop extends the `RepositoryComponent` that contains the current `SinkRole` with an additional `OperationProvidedRole`. A second embedded loop iterates over all `EventTypes` that are contained in the `EventGroup` referenced by the current `SinkRole` of the outer loop. The `RepositoryComponent`, this role belongs to, already contains a `ResourceDemandingSEFF` for each `EventType` describing the event handling behaviour. The mapping rule substitutes the link to the `EventGroup` with a link to the `OperationSignature`. The

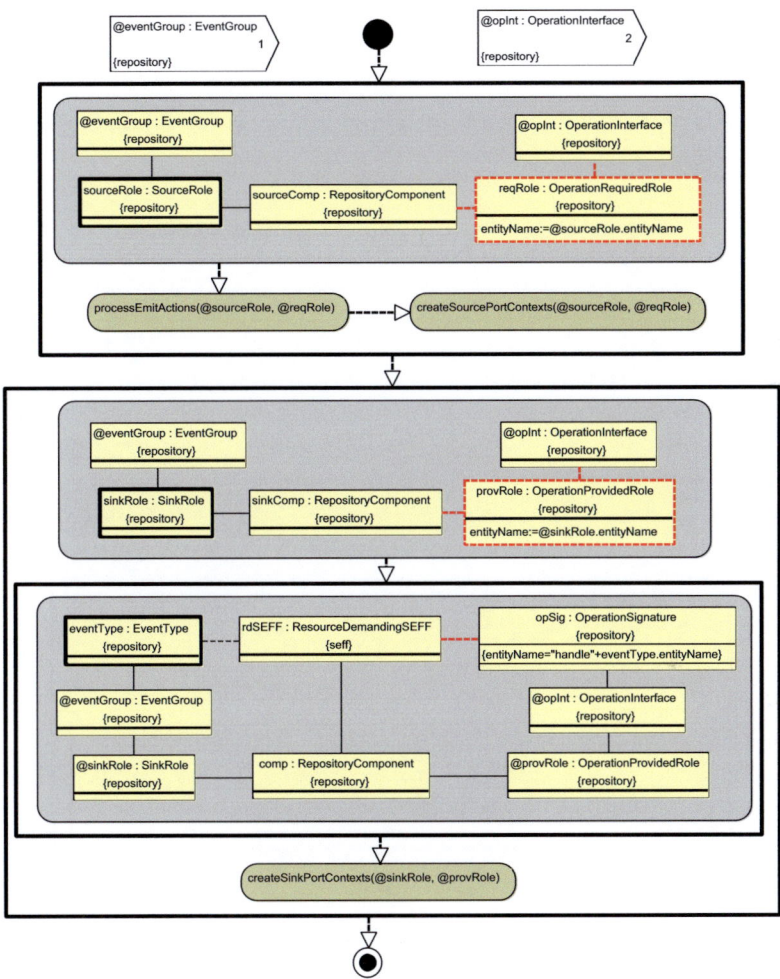

Figure 5.13: Procedure `processRoles`

corresponding signature is identified using the attribute `entityName`, which was set when generating the `OperationInterfaces` for all `EventGroups` in the main procedure of the transformation. As final step in the iteration over all `SinkRoles`, the sub-procedure `createSinkPortContexts` responsible for instantiating and connecting the *SinkPort* and *SinkCommunication* components corresponding to the `EventGroup` is invoked.

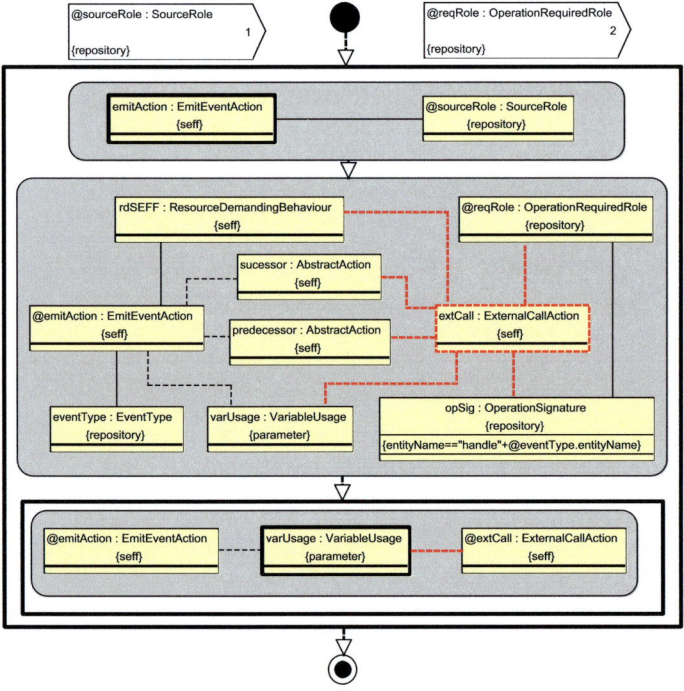

Figure 5.14: Sub-Procedure `processEmitActions`

Processing of Emit Actions

The sub-procedure `processEmitActions`, which is executed after integrating the new `OperationRequiredRole`, substitutes the original `EmitEventActions` with `ExternalCallActions` referring to the `OperationRequiredRole` in order to call the next component in the event processing chain.

As shown in Figure 5.14, the transformation iterates over all `EmitEventActions` associated with the input parameter `sourceRole`. For each `EmitEventAction`, the transformation creates an `ExternalCallAction`. The new action substitutes the `EmitEventAction` in the control flow by transferring the references to the succeeding and preceding `AbstractAction`. Additionally, the new action is connected with the input parameter `reqRole` and the `OperationSignature` that represents the `EventType` associated with the original `EmitEventAction`. Again, the `OperationSignature` is identified using the attribute `entityName`. In a final embedded loop, all `VariableUsages` contained in the `EmitEventAction` are transferred to the `ExternalCallAction`.

Generate Context Elements for Sources and Sinks

The two procedures `createSourcePortContexts` and `createSinkPortContexts` encapsulate the instantiation of the *SourcePort* respectively *SinkPort* components and their connection with the source or sink component. The structure of both transformation procedures is similar. They differ only in the platform-independent component that is instantiated. For this reason, we use the `createSourcePortContexts` procedure as an example for both procedures and show the `createSinkPortContexts` procedure in Appendix A.1.

As illustrated in Figure 5.15, the procedure contains a loop iterating over all `AssemblyContexts` belonging to the `RepositoryCompo-`

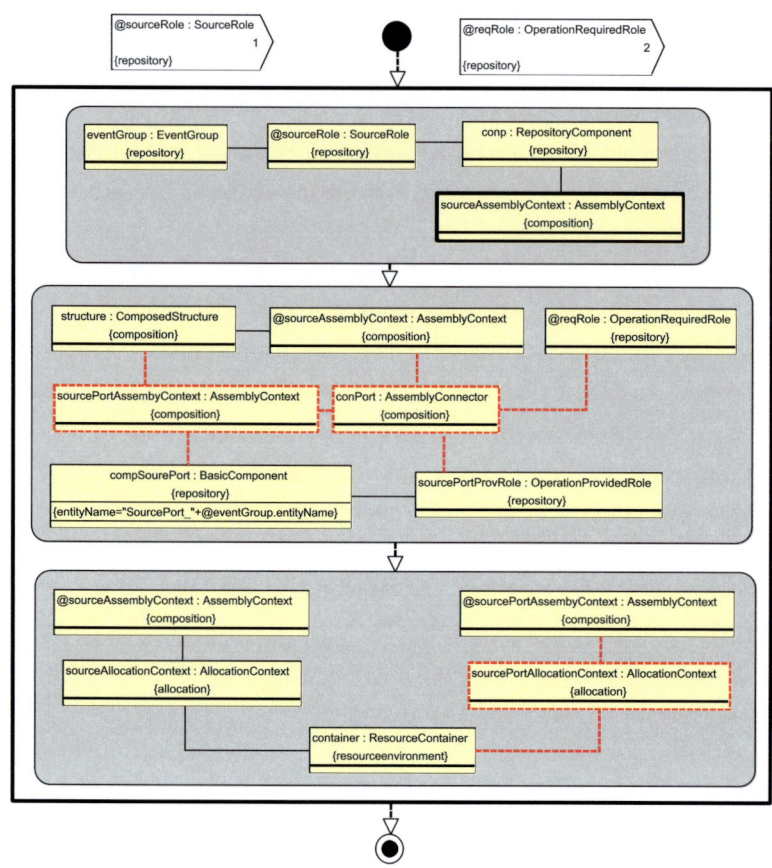

Figure 5.15: Sub-Procedure `createSourcePortContexts`

nent that belongs to the `SourceRole` received as input parameter. In the second rule, the `BasicComponent` representing the *SourcePort* component is identified using a constraint on the attribute `entity-Name`, which exploits the generation pattern for component names used in the `createProcessingComponents` procedure. The constraint selects the component with the string `"SourcePort_"` concatenated with the name of the `EventGroup` referenced by the input parameter `sourceRole`. Additionally, the rule generates a new `Assembly-Context` associated with the identified `BasicComponent`. A newly created `AssemblyConnector` connects the `OperationRequire-dRole` and the current `AssemblyContext` of the source component with the generated `AssemblyContext` representing the *SourcePort* component and its provided role.

As a final step within the loop, the created `sourcePortAssembly-Context` is deployed in the same `ResourceContainer` as the source component itself. The mapping rule creates a new `AllocationCon-text` that on the one hand references the `sourcePortAllocation-Context` and on the other hand the `ResourceContainer` associated with the `AllocationContext` of the `sourceAssemblyContext`. After integrating the *Source-* and *SinkPort* components and connecting them with the operational interfaces, the main transformation continues with the processing of connectors.

5.4.4. Transformation of Event Channels and Connectors

The transformation of event channels generates an *EventDistribution* component skeleton for each event channel. This skeleton contains only the provided interface together with an initial RD-SEFF. The provided interface is connected with the *SourceCommunication* component, which itself is later connected with the *SourcePort* components belonging to the connected event source. Afterwards, the channel-specific *EventDistribution* component is extended with a dedicated `OperationRequire-dRole` and an additional `ForkBehaviour` for each event sink connected with the channel. Finally, the connector-specific *EventFilter* component is generated and connected.

Figure 5.16 depicts the `processChannelsandConnectors` procedure. It consists of one main loop that iterates over all `EventChannels` associated with the current `EventGroup`. For each `EventChannel`, a new *EventDistribution* component is created and

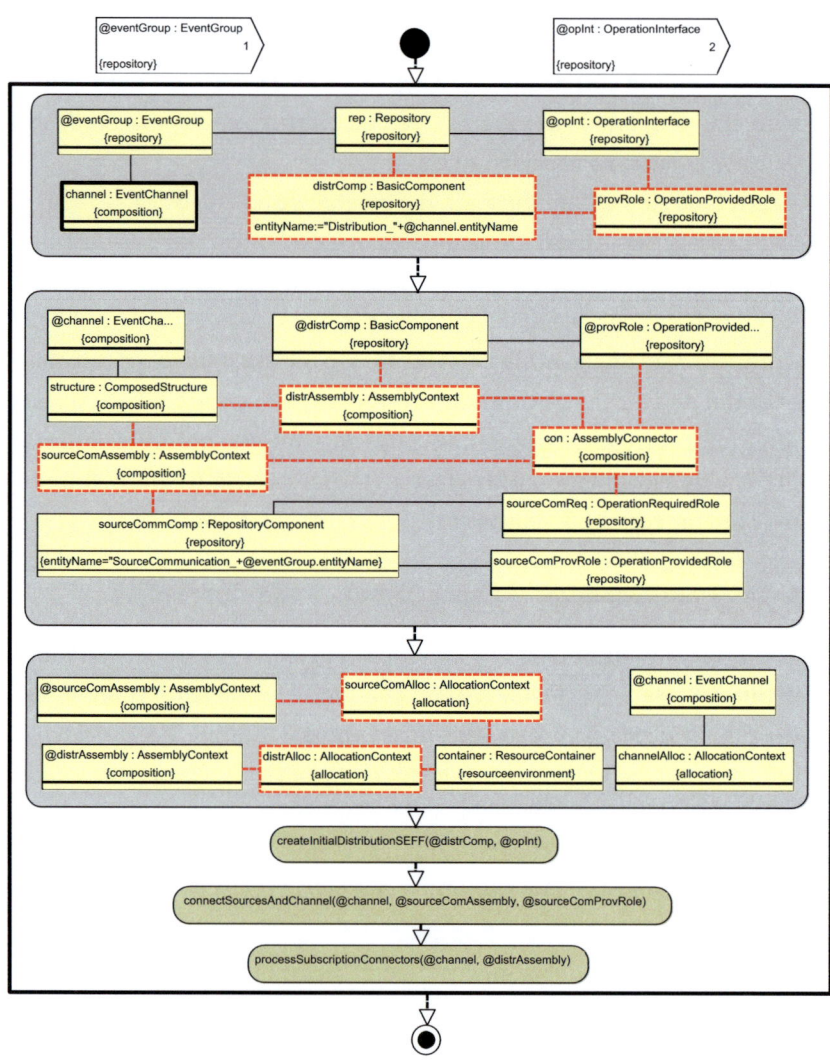

Figure 5.16: Procedure `processChannelsandConnectors`

added to the `Repository`, in which the `EventGroup` received as input parameter is defined. As the number of required interfaces and the internal behaviour depends on the number of connected sinks, the *EventDistribution* component is individually generated for each channel. For this reason, the attribute `entityName` is set to the type of the component `"Distribution_"` extended with the `entityName` of the `EventChannel` and not the `EventGroup` as done in the `createProcessingComponents` procedure. Furthermore, the rule extends the component with an `OperationProvidedRole` associated with `OperationInterface` representing the `EventGroup`.

The second mapping rule generates two `AssemblyContexts` namely `distrAssembly` and `sourceComAssembly` that are associated with the currently generated *EventDistribution* component and respectively with the *SourceCommunication* component. Again, a constraint on the `entityName` is used to identify the respective *SourceCommunication* component. Both `AssemblyContexts` are added to the `ComposedStructure` that contains the current `EventChannel`. A new `AssemblyConnector` connects these new `AssemblyContexts` and the `OperationProvided-` respectively `OperationRequiredRoles` of the respective components.

The third rule creates two `AllocationContexts` to specify the deployment of the newly created `AssemblyContexts` on the `ResourceContainer` referenced by the `AllocationContext` belonging to the current `EventChannel`.

After executing the sub-procedure `createInitialDistributionSEFF`, which integrates an initial RD-SEFF into the *EventDistribution* component, the `connectSourceWithSourceCommunication` procedure connects all event sources and the corresponding *SourcePort* components with the *SourceCommunication* component. The sub-procedure `processSubscriptionConnectors` is executed to complete the chain of event processing component by introducing the *EventFilter* and *SinkCommunication* components and connecting them with the corresponding *SinkPort* component. The following sub-sections provide a detailed description of these sub-procedures.

Generation of an initial RD-SEFF

The sub-procedure `createInitialDistributionSEFF` (illustrated in Figure 5.17) iterates over all `OperationSignatures` that are contained in the `OperationInterface` received as input parameter `opInt`. For each `OperationSignature`, a new `ResourceDemandingBehaviour` is created, added to the component `comp`, and finally associated with the current `OperationSignature`. All generated `ResourceDemandingBehaviours` contain a `StartAction`, a `ForkAction` and a `StopAction` that are connected using the `predecessor` and `successor` associations. The `ForkAction` provides a container for `ForkBehaviours` generated later when processing the connectors between channels and sinks.

Connecting Sources with Source Communication Components

The aim of the sub-procedure `connectSourceWithSourceCommunication` is the connection of the newly instantiated *SourceCommunication* component and respectively its `AssemblyContexts` with the `AssemblyContext` of the *SourcePort* and the respective `OperationProvidedRole`.

As illustrated in Figure 5.18, the procedure starts with a pure mapping rule. The aim of this rule is to identify the `AssemblyContext` of the *SourcePort* component that belongs to the `AssemblyContext` of the source component received as input. To identify the `AssemblyContext` of the *SourcePort* component, the rule follows the already existing `AssemblyConnector` between the `AssemblyContexts` of the event source and the corresponding *SourcePort* component. This connector has already been created when executing the `pro-cessRoles` procedure. Exploiting the reference between `Alloca-tionContext` and `BasicComponent`, the `OperationRequire-dRole` of the *SourcePort* component to be connected with the `Op-erationProvidedRole` of the *SourceCommunication* component is identified. This mapping is unique, as the event processing components with exception of the *EventDistribution* component contain exactly one `OperationProvided-` and one `OperationRequiredRole`.

The second and last rule creates a new `AssemblyConnector` that connects the identified `OperationProvidedRole` of the *SourcePort* component and the respective `AssemblyContext` with the `Opera-tionProvidedRole` and `AssemblyContext` of the *SourceCommu-nication* component received as input parameters.

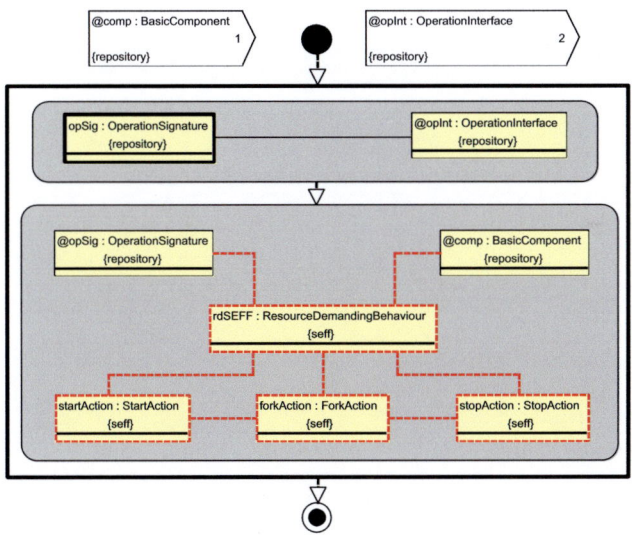

Figure 5.17: Sub-Procedure `createInitialDistributionSEFF`

Transforming Subscription Connectors

The transformation of the connectors between a channel and sinks is more complex compared to the connectors between sources and the channel. In addition to the pure identification and composition of `AssemblyContexts`, this transformation procedure adapts and extends the *EventDistribution* component depending on the number of connected sinks. Furthermore, it generates connector- respectively sink-specific *EventFilter* components. For this reason, the procedure `processSubscriptionConnector`, illustrated in Figure 5.19, contains several sub-procedures responsible for the different aspects.

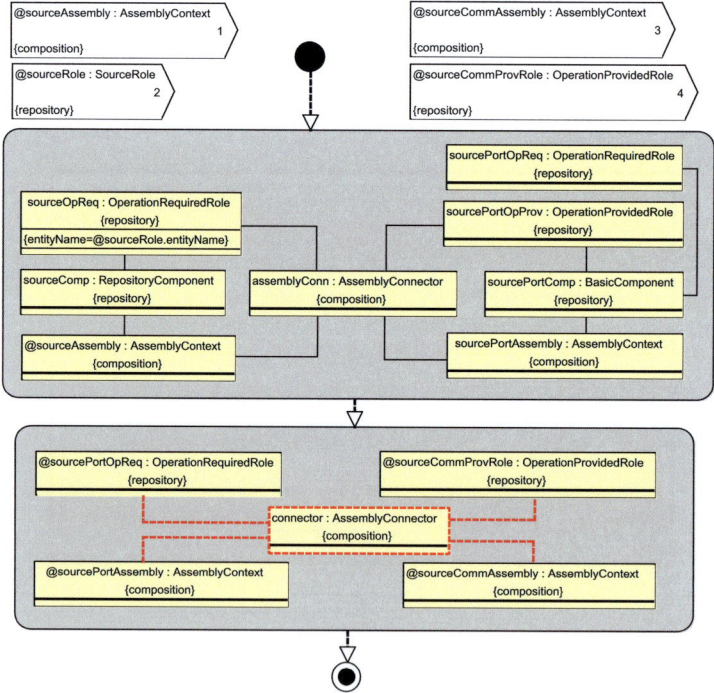

Figure 5.18: Sub-Procedure `connectSourceWithSourceCommunication`

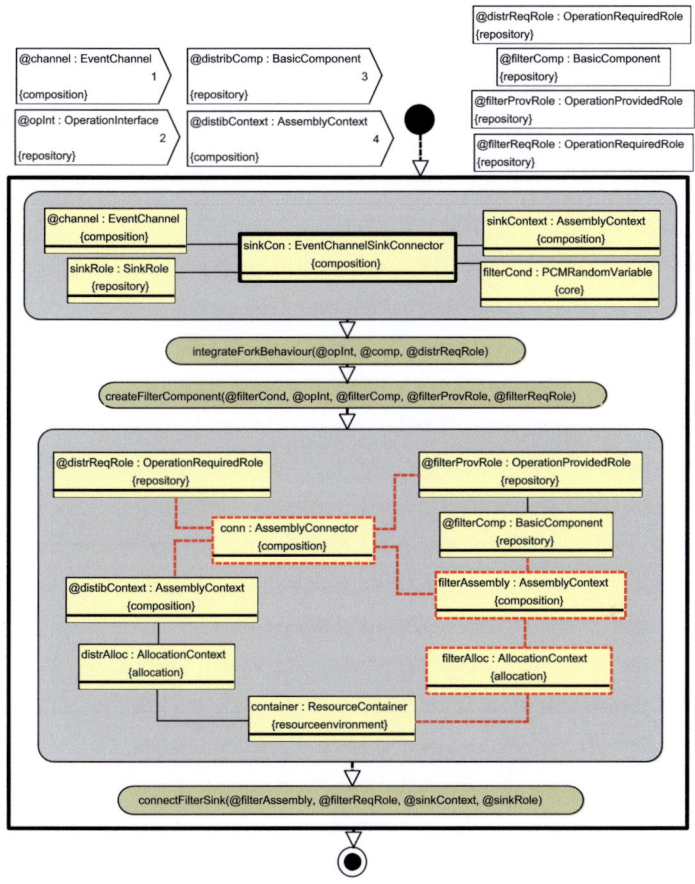

Figure 5.19: Sub-Procedure `processSubscriptionConnector`

The procedure `processSubscriptionConnector` has four input parameters: the current `EventChannel` and the `OperationInterface` representing the corresponding `EventGroup` as well as the *EventDistribution* component and its `AssemblyContext`. The last two have been generated within the first rules of the `processChannelsandConnectors` procedure. In addition to these parameters, the procedure contains four internal variables that are used as IN-OUT parameters to return elements generated within sub-procedures. These variables are the `OperationRequiredRole` (`distrReqRole`) that is added to the *EventDistribution* component and the generated *EventFilter* component (`filterComp`) including its `OperationProvidedRole` (`filterProvRole`) and `OperationRequiredRole` (`filterReqRole`).

The control flow iterates over all `EventChannelSinkConnectors` connected to the current `EventChannel`. The first mapping rule identifies the `AssemblyContext` and `SinkRole` referenced by the `EventChannelSinkConnectors` as well as the `PCMRandomVariable` that contains the filter condition. For each `EventChannelSinkConnector` the `integrateForkBehaviour` procedure extends the *EventDistribution* component handed over as parameter with a new `OperationRequiredRole`, which is returned using the IN-OUT parameter `distrReqRole`. Furthermore, the procedure integrates a new `ForkBehaviour` into the already existing `ForkAction`. In the following, we first describe the remaining parts of the `processSubscriptionConnector` procedure, before providing more details on the different sub-procedures. After extending the *EventDistribution* component, the sub-procedure `createFilterComponent` generates the connector-specific *EventFilter* component based on the interface and the filter condition handed over as IN parameters and returns the created component itself and the required and provided roles using the

IN-OUT parameters `filterComp`, `filterProvRole`, and `filter-ReqRole`.

The following rule instantiates the created *EventFilter* component by creating a new `AssemblyContext` associated with the `BasicComponent` returned and stored in the variable `filterComp`. A new `AssemblyConnector` connects this context and the belonging `OperationProvidedRole` with the `AssemblyContext` and the `OperationRequiredRole` of the *EventDistribution* component. While the `AssemblyContext` is one of the input parameters, the `OperationRequiredRole` is returned by the `integrateForkBehaviour` procedure and stored in the variable `distrReqRole`. Furthermore, the rule creates an `AllocationContext` connected with the new `AssemblyContext` of the *EventFilter* component. This `AllocationContext` references the same `ResourceContainer` associated with the `AllocationContext` belonging to the *EventDistribution* component.

As last operation in this procedure, the sub-procedure `connectFilterSink` is executed. It is responsible for completing the connections between the different components in the event processing chain and finally connecting the component chain with the *Sink* component. The `AssemblyContext` and `OperationRequiredRole` of the *EventFilter* component together with the `AllocationContext` and `SinkRole` of the *Sink* component referenced by the `EventChannelSinkConnector` are input parameters of this sub-procedure.

Integration of Fork Behaviours

The sub-procedure `integrateForkBehaviour` consists of two processing steps. First, the component is extended with an additional `OperationRequiredInterface`, which is later used to connect the sink component and the intermediate components of the event processing chain, respectively. Second, the RD-SEFFs and the contained

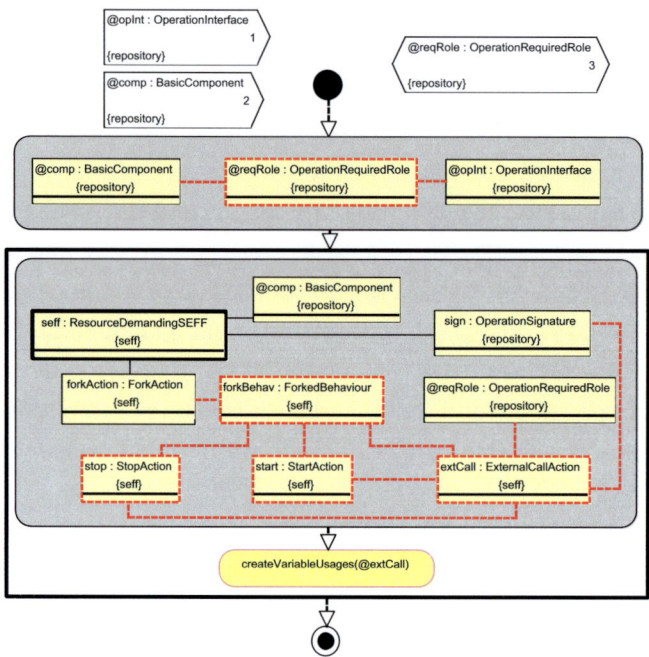

Figure 5.20: Sub-Procedure `integrateForkBehaviour`

`ForkActions` are extended with an additional `ForkBehaviour` to split the control flow independently for each connected `Sink`.

The first rule of the procedure (see Figure 5.20), generates a new `OperationRequiredRole` that connects the `BasicComponent comp` with the `OperationInterface opInt`, both received as input parameter. The IN-OUT parameter `reqRole` is used to store the newly created `OperationRequiredRole` and return it to the calling `processSubscriptionConnector` procedure.

After generating the `OperationRequiredRole`, a loop iterates over all `ResourceDemandingSEFFs` belonging to the `BasicComponent` received as input. Each `ResourceDemandingSEFF` is associated with exactly one `OperationSignature`, which is identified within this rule. As the `ResourceDemandingSEFF`s are the result of the already explained procedure `createInitialDistribution-SEFF`, it is known that each behaviour contains exactly one `ForkAction`. This `ForkAction` is extended with an additional `ForkedBehaviour` that contains a `StartAction`, an `ExternalCallAction`, and a `StopAction` connected via the successor and predecessor associations. The `ExternalCallAction` contains a reference to the newly created `OperationRequiredRole` and the `OperationSignature` that corresponds to the current `ResourceDemandingSEFF`. Although the `ResourceDemandingSEFF` references the provided signature, the required signature is identical as the respective provided and required interfaces are identical. As a final step in the loop, the external procedure `createVariableUsages`, described in Section 5.4.2, is used to generate the `VariableUsages` and `VariableCharacterisations` required to forward the event's content.

Generation of Filter Components

The `createFilterComponent` sub-procedure generates individual *EventFilter* components for a given interface and filter condition specified as StoEx. Both are defined as input parameters namely `opInt` and `filterCondition`. To return the generated `BasicComponent` as well as included roles, the procedure defines the IN-OUT parameters `component`, `provRole`, and `reqRole`. A `BranchAction` with an integrated `GuardedBranchTransition` realises the filtering. Encapsulating the forwarding `ExternalCallAction` within a `GuardedBranchTransition` with the filter condition as guard ensures that the event is forwarded only if the condition evaluates to true.

The transformation procedure, depicted in Figure 5.21, starts with the generation of a new `BasicComponent` belonging to the same `Repository` the interface `opInt` is contained in. The component is extended with an `OperationProvidedRole` and an `Oper-`

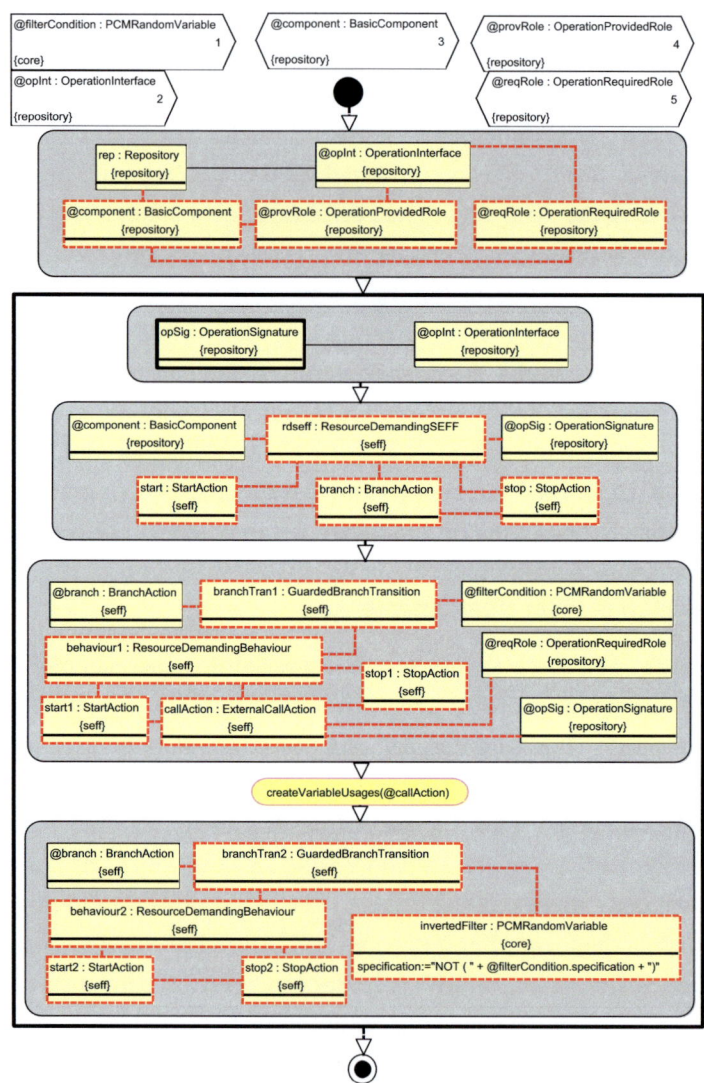

Figure 5.21: Sub-Procedure `createFilterComponent`

`ationRequiredRole` both associated with the `OperationInter-face` `opInt`. Following this first rule, a loop iterates over all `OperationSignatures` belonging to `opInt`.

The loop contains several rules to define the loop variable, create the initial RD-SEFF and finally to integrate the `GuardedBranchTransitions` into the `BranchAction`. Furthermore, the loop includes a call of the already described procedure `createVariableUsages`.

After defining the iteration over all `OperationSignatures` contained in `opInt`, the second rule extends `component` with a `ResourceDemandingSEFF` associated with the current `OperationSignature`. Furthermore, it integrates a `StartAction`, a `BranchAction`, and a `StopAction` (all connected using the predecessor and successor relations) into the `ResourceDemandingSEFF`. The next rule generates a `GuardedBranchTransition` and integrates it into the `BranchAction`. The `filterCondition` that contains the `PCMRandomVariable` received as one of the input parameters is assigned as guard. The `GuardedBranchTransition` contains a `ResourceDemandingBehaviour` that, in analogy to the forwarding behaviours generated in the `createForwardingBehaviour` procedure, contains a `StartAction`, an `ExternalCallAction`, and finally a `StopAction`. The `ExternalCallAction` is associated with `opSig`, the current `OperationSignature`, and `reqRole`, the `OperationRequiredRole` generated as part of the second rule. The following call of the already introduced external procedure `createVariableUsages` generates the `VariableUsages` and `VariableCharacterisations` required to forward the event payload.

The behavioural semantics of PCM [Reussner 11] specifies that exactly one `BranchTransition` within a `BranchAction` is executed. As PCM does not provide an explicit *ELSE* construct, the last rule generates a second `GuardedBranchTransition` with the inverted condition using the `NOT` operator provided by the StoEx language. As illustrated in

Figure 5.21, a new `PCMRandomVariable` is instantiated and assigned to the `GuardedBranchTransition`. The attribute `Specification`, which contains the string representation of the StoEx, is set to the specification of the `filterCondition` surrounded by the `NOT` operator and the belonging brackets. The `GuardedBranchTransition` contains an "empty" `ResourceDemandingBehaviour` that contains only a `Start-` and `StopAction`. These two `GuardedBranchTransitions` ensure that always one `ResourceDemandingBehaviour` is executed. The `ResourceDemandingBehaviour` that includes the `ExternalCallAction` to the next component in the event processing chain is executed only if the `filterCondition` evaluates to true. Otherwise, the second behaviour is executed and the control flow terminates with the final `StopAction`.

Connecting the Filter Components

`connectFilterSink` is the last sub-procedure called within the `processSubscriptionConnectors` procedure and thus also the final sub-procedure of the complete `processChannelsandConnectors` procedure. It instantiates and integrates the *EventFilter* and *SinkCommunication* components to complete the chain of event processing components.

The transformation procedure, shown in Figure 5.22, has four input parameters. These parameters are the `AssemblyContext` (`filterContext`) and the `OperationRequiredRole` of the *EventFilter* component (`filterReqRole`) as well as the `AssemblyContext` (`sinkContext`) and the `SinkRole` (`sinkRole`) belonging to the sink addressed by the connector. The control flow of the transformation starts with a rule that identifies the `EventGroup` associated with the `sinkRole` parameter.

The second rule identifies the `BasicComponent` that represents the *SinkCommunication* component belonging to the `EventGroup` iden-

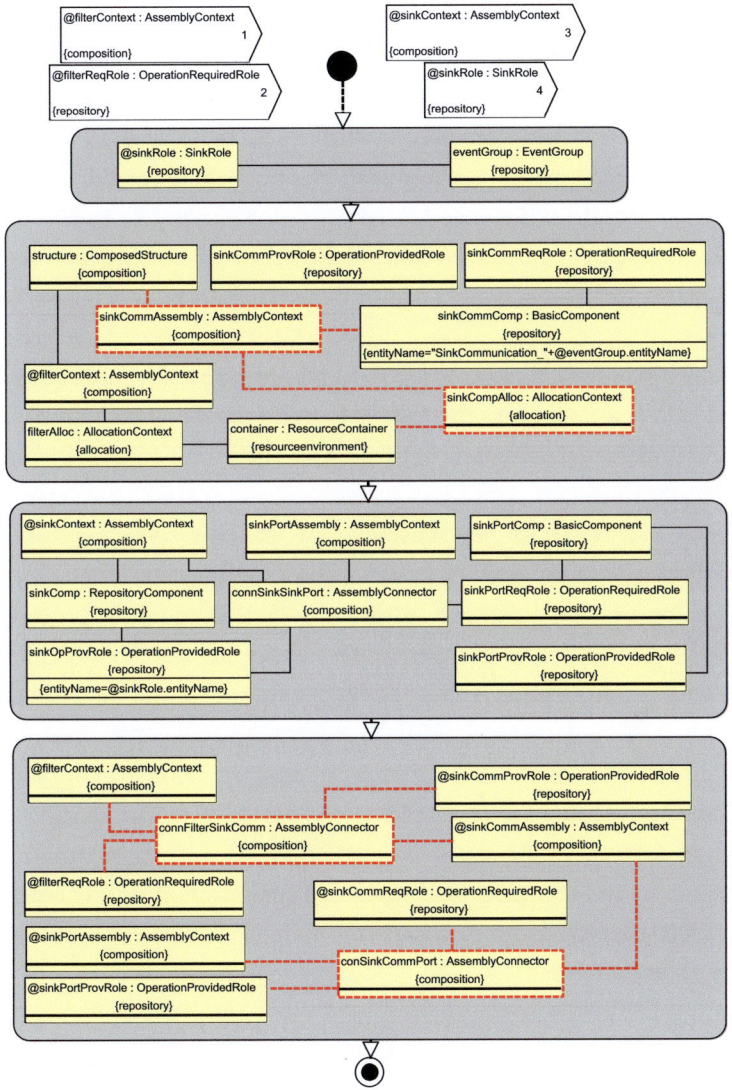

Figure 5.22: Sub-Procedure `connectFilterSink`

tified in the previous rule. Again we use the generated value of the attribute `EntityName` to identify the matching *SinkCommunication* component. Additionally, the rule creates an `AssemblyContext` associated with the identified component. The created `AssemblyContext` is added to the `ComposedStructure`, the `AssemblyContext` of the *EventFilter* component received as input belongs to. Furthermore, a new `AllocationContext` is generated. This context connects the new `AssemblyContext` with the `ResourceContainer` that is also referenced by the `AllocationContext` belonging to `filterContext`.

Similarly to the `processPublishingConnectors` procedure, the third rule is a pure mapping rule to identify the `AssemblyContext` of the *SinkPort* component belonging to the sink component represented by the input parameter `sinkContext`. Using the input parameter `sinkContext` as starting point, the corresponding `RepositoryComponent` and its `OperationProvidedRole` are identified using the `entityName` attribute, which is equal to the `entityName` of the `sinkPort` parameter. Following the already existing `AssemblyConnector`, the `sinkPortAssembly` and the respective `sinkPortReqRole` are located. Based on these elements, the rule derives the `BasicComponent` that represents the *SinkPort* component and the corresponding `OperationProvidedRole`. The identified elements are used in the last rule to instantiate the *SinkCommunication* component and complete the processing chain by connecting both the *EventFilter* as well as the *SinkPort* component with the *SinkCommunication* component.

In the final rule, two new `AssemblyConnectors` are generated. The first one (`connFilterSinkComm`) connects the `filterContext` and the `filterReqRole` representing the *EventFilter* component with the *SinkCommunication* component represented by the `sinkCommAssembly` and the `sinkCommProvRole`. The second one

connects `sinkCommAssembly` and the respective `OperationRe-`
`quiredRole` (`sinkCommReqRole`) with the `AssemblyContext`
and the `OperationProvidedRole` of the *SinkPort* component. Both
have been identified within the previous mapping rule. With this last
`AssemblyConnector`, the event processing from source to sink components is completed and finalised.

5.4.5. Transformation of Point-to-Point Connectors

The processing of P2P connectors has several commonalities with the
processing of Pub/Sub connections and thus it reuses several sub-
procedures. In contrast to the channel-based communication, the event
processing chain is not generated for each channel but rather for each
event source. For this reason, the transformation iterates as depicted
in Figure 5.23 over all `AssemblyContexts` belonging to a `Repos-`
`itoryComponent` that contains a `SourcePort` associated with the
`EventGroup` received as input parameter `eventGroup`.

The first rule generates a new *EventDistribution* component
(`distrComp`) for each `sourceAssembly`. The new component is extended with an `OperationProvidedRole` associated with the `Op-`
`erationInterface` received as second input parameter and representing the `EventGroup`. Additionally, the transformation creates
a new `AssemblyContext` referencing the generated `BasicCompo-`
`nent` as part of the `ComposedStructure` that the `sourceAssem-`
`bly` corresponds to. In analogy to the processing of Pub/Sub connectors, the already introduced sub-procedure `createInitialDistri-`
`butionSEFF` integrates a stub of the behavioural description into the
component.

The second rule identifies the `BasicComponent` representing the
SourceCommunication component belonging to the current `Event-`
`Group` using the attribute `entityName`. A new `AssemblyCon-`
`text` associated with this `BasicComponent` is added to the `Com-`

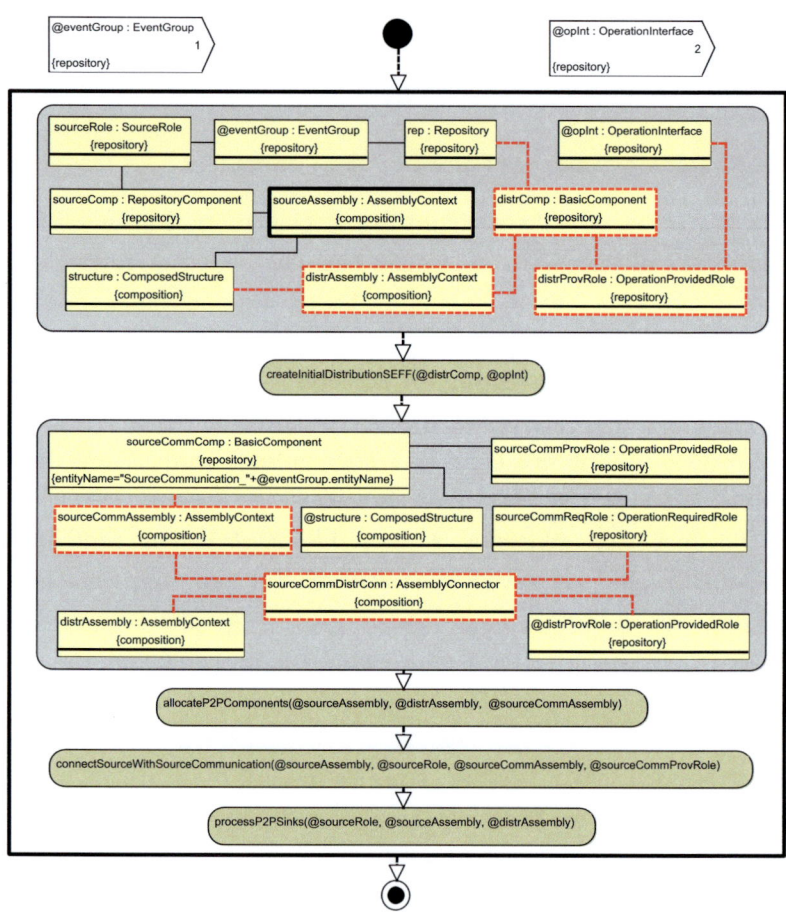

Figure 5.23: Sub-Procedure `processP2PConnectors`

`posedStructure` `structure`, which was already identified as part of the previous rule. Furthermore, the rule generates a new `Assem-blyConnector` connecting the two `AssemblyContexts` and their `OperationRequired-` and `OperationProvidedRole`.

Finally, the three sub-procedures `allocateP2PComponents`, `connectSourceWithSourceCommunication`, and `process-P2PSink` are executed. While the second one has already been used and explained in the context of the `processChannelsAndConnec-tors` procedure, the following sub-sections provide a description of the two remaining procedures.

Allocation of Components

For channel-based connections, the deployment of middleware components is explicitly specified by defining an `AllocationContext` for each `EventChannel`. In contrast, P2P connections are direct connections between the source and sink component without any intermediate elements. Peer-to-peer systems, which lack a central transmission system are mostly limited to P2P connections. In this case, the transmission system is deployed together with the components. However, in order to also support P2P connections in centralised and server-based systems, the transformation introduces an implicit deployment specification. If a central middleware server is defined within the *Resource Environment*, the components representing the transmission system are deployed on this container. Otherwise, the `allocateP2PComponents` allocates the components on the same `ResourceContainer` that hosts the source component.

For this reason the `allocateP2PComponents` procedure, illustrated in Figure 5.24, starts with a rule to check if a `ResourceCon-tainer` fullfilling the constraint `entityName="Middleware"` exists. If the rule can be matched, which means that such a `Resource-Container` exists, the left execution path is taken and the identified

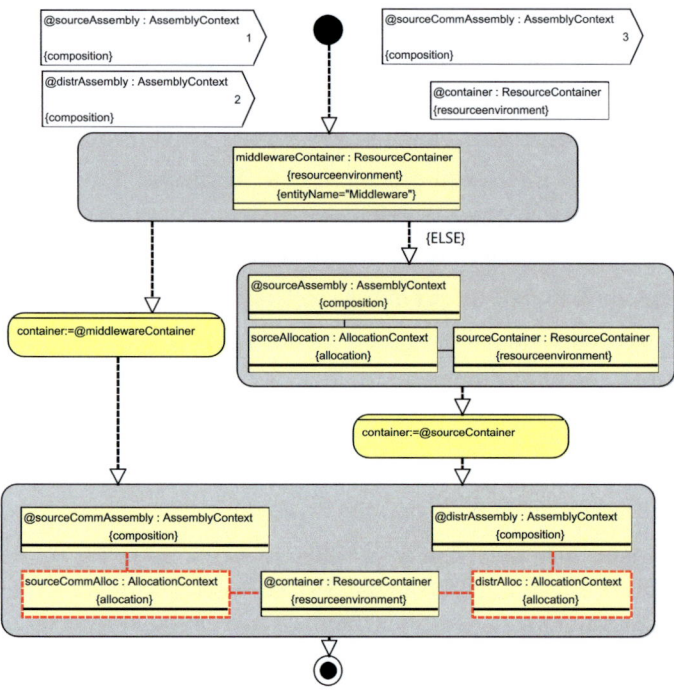

Figure 5.24: Sub-Procedure `allocateP2PComponents`

`ResourceContainer` is stored in the internal variable `container`. Otherwise, the right path is taken and an additional rule identifies the `ResourceContainer`, that the event source is deployed on, and then stored in the variable `container`.

As a last rule merging the two execution paths, two new `AllocationContexts` are generated to connect the `AssemblyContexts` of the *EventDistribution* and the *SourceCommunication* components with the `ResourceContainer` stored in the variable `container`.

Transformation of Sinks

Similarly to the `processSubscriptionConnector` procedure, the `processP2PSinks` procedure completes the component chain. It differs only in few aspects. In contrast to the `processSubscription-Connector` procedure, which receives the `EventChannel` as input parameter and iterates over all associated `EventChannelSinkConnectors`, the `processP2PSinks` receives an `AssemblyContext` and a `SourceRole` representing the event source as input and iterates over all `AssemblyEventConnectors` associated with this element tuple.

In analogy to the `processSubscriptionConnector` procedure, the two sub-procedures `integrateForkBehaviour` and `createFilterComponent` are used to extend the *EventDistribution* component with an `OperationRequiredRole` for each connected sink and to generate the sink-specific *EventFilter* component.

The following rule generates an `AssemblyContext` associated with the *EventFilter* component returned by the `createFilterComponent` procedure. This new `AssemblyContext` belongs to the `ComposedStructure` that the `AssemblyContext` of the *EventDistribution* component is contained in. A new `Assembly-Connector` connects these two `AssemblyContexts` and their `OperationProvided-` and respectively `OperationRequiredRoles`. Furthermore, the rule creates a new `AllocationContext` in order to deploy the `AssemblyContext` of the *EventFilter* component on the same `ResourceContainer` as the *EventDistribution* component.

The last rule is again an exclusive mapping rule to identify the `AssemblyContext` and `SinkRole` referenced by the `AssemblyEventConnector`. Both elements together with the `AssemblyContext` of the *EventFilter* component and the respective `OperationProvide-`

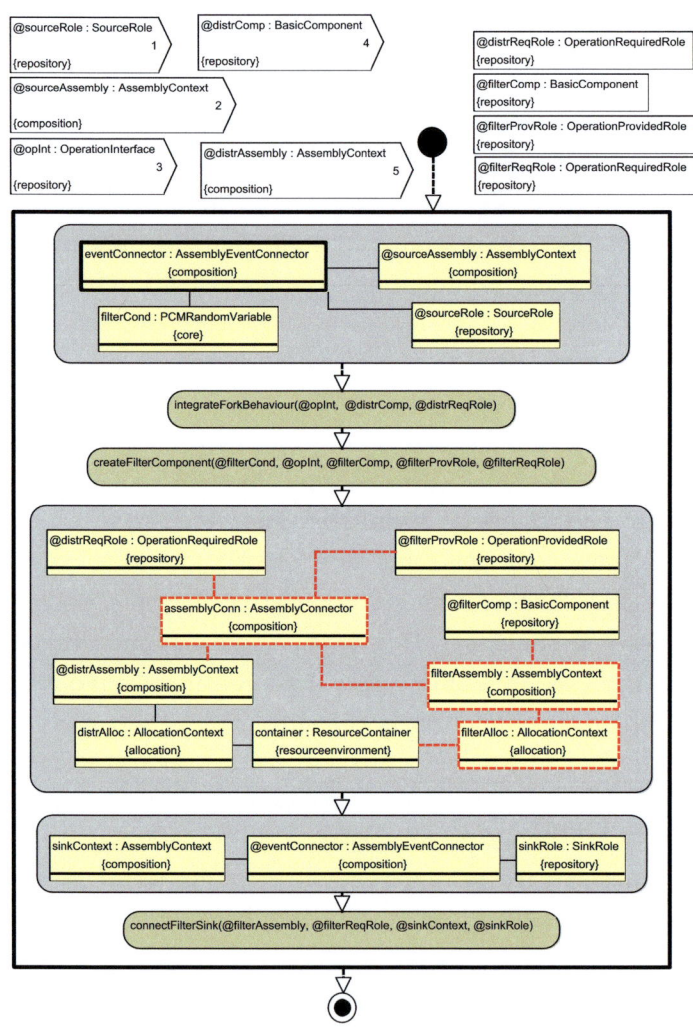

Figure 5.25: Sub-Procedure `processP2PSinks`

`dRole` are forwarded to the `connectFilterSink` procedure. As explained in Section 5.4.4, the `connectFilterSink` procedure instantiates the *SinkCommunication* component and connects the remaining component instances completing the event processing chain.

5.4.6. Integration of Middleware Components

The integration of middleware-specific components follows the process described in Section 5.3. The `integrateMiddlewareComponents` procedure, depicted in Figure 5.26, sequentially extends the different event processing components that correspond to an `EventGroup`. The transformation procedure integrates an additional middleware call into the RD-SEFFs of the event processing components. Furthermore, it integrates and deploys the platform-specific components. The procedure is invoked within the loop of the main procedure and thus executed individually for each `EventGroup`. It receives the generated `OperationInterface` representing the `EventGroup` as input parameter. This information enables the identification of the event processing components in the model as all of them have in common that they provide and require this interface.

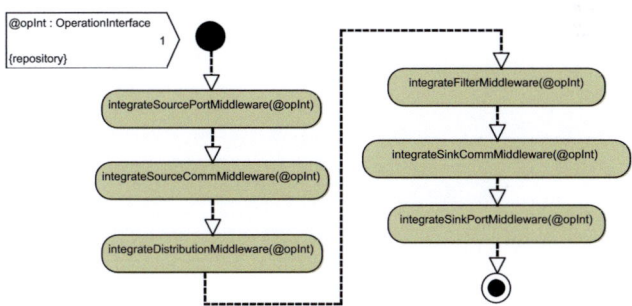

Figure 5.26: Sub-Procedure `integrateMiddlewareComponents`

The component-specific procedures, called within the `inte-grateMiddlewareComponents` procedure, have a similar structure and differ only in the mapping rules that identify the different components. For this reason, we select two sub-procedures, namely `integrateSourcePortMiddleware` and `integrate-DistributionMiddleware`, which we describe here as representative examples and refer to Appendix A.2 for the presentation of the remaining procedures.

Integration of Source Port Middleware

The procedure `integrateSourcePortMiddleware`, shown in Figure 5.27, serves as a representative example for the procedures `integrateSourceComMiddleware, integrateSinkCommMid-`

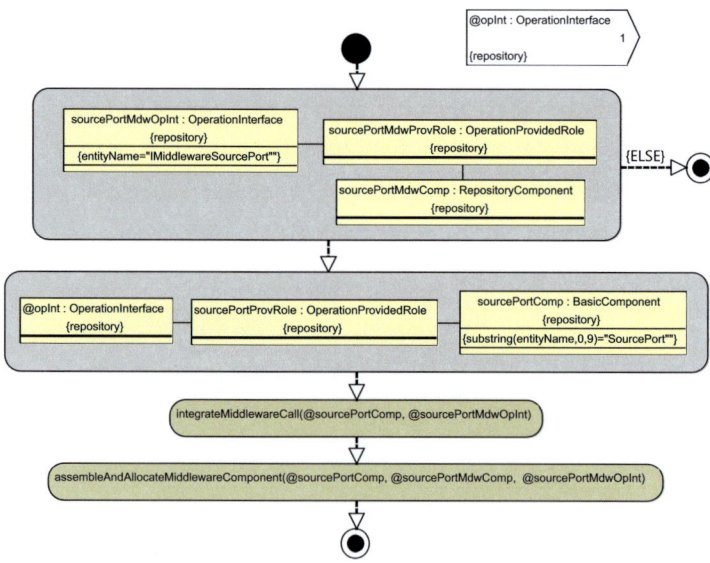

Figure 5.27: Sub-Procedure `integrateSourcePortMiddleware`

dleware, and `integrateSinkPortMiddleware`. The only differences are the constraints to identify the involved components.

The procedure starts with a mapping rule to query components that contain an `OperationProvidedRole` associated with the `IMiddlewareSourcePort` interface, which is identified based on its `entityName`. If the mapping is successful, which means that a middleware-specific component exists within the repository, the execution of the procedure continues with the next rule. Otherwise, the control flow continues with the *ELSE* branch and terminates. In this case the *SourcePort* component is not extended and the event is directly forwarded to the next event processing component since the middleware model does not contain any platform-specific component for the corresponding event processing stage.

The second rule queries the component that should be extended with the middleware call. The mapping exploits the constraint that the `entityName` of the `BasicComponent` starts with `"SourcePort"` and the fact that the component provides the `OperationInterface` `opInt` representing the `EventGroup`.

The following call of the `integrateMiddlewareCall` procedure hands over the identified *SourcePort* component (`sourcePortComp`) together with the middleware interface (`sourcePortMdwOpInt`). This procedure, which is described in the following section, extends the event processing component with a call of the corresponding platform-specific middleware component. Finally, the `assembleAndAllocateMiddlewareComponent`, which receives the two identified components (`sourcePortComp` and `sourcePortMdwComp`) and the middleware interface `sourcePortMdwOpInt` as input, instantiates, assembles and deploys the components. Both sub-procedures are described in the following.

Extending Event Processing Components with Middleware Calls

The `integrateMiddlewareCall` procedure extends the `Basic-Component` received as input parameter `comp` and its RD-SEFFs. This extension integrates a call of the middleware-specific component as first action into the behavioural specification. This ensures that the middleware-specific behaviour is executed before the event is further processed to the next component.

As depicted in Figure 5.28, the procedure first extends the component `comp` with an `OperationRequiredRole` associated with the `middlewareInterface` received as second input parameter. Following that, a foreach loop iterates over all `ResourcedDemandingSEFFs` contained in the component `comp`.

The following rule generates a new `ExternalCallAction`. To integrate this action as first element in the execution process, the successor respectively predecessor associations between `StartAction` and the first `AbstractAction` element are removed and substituted with an association between the `StartAction` and the new `ExternalCallAction` and a second association connecting the `ExternalCallAction` with the primarily first `AbstractAction`. Furthermore, the new `ExternalCallAction` is associated with the `OperationRequiredRole` created as part of the first rule and the `OperationSignature` contained in the middleware interface `middlewareInterface`. The `OperationInterfaces` that need to be provided by the middleware are predefined. For this reason, it is known that each interface contains exactly one signature and thus the simple mapping of interface and signature is sufficient to identify the correct signature. Additionally, the mapping rule identifies the `Parameter` contained in the `OperationSignature` as input parameter, as this element is required within the next rule.

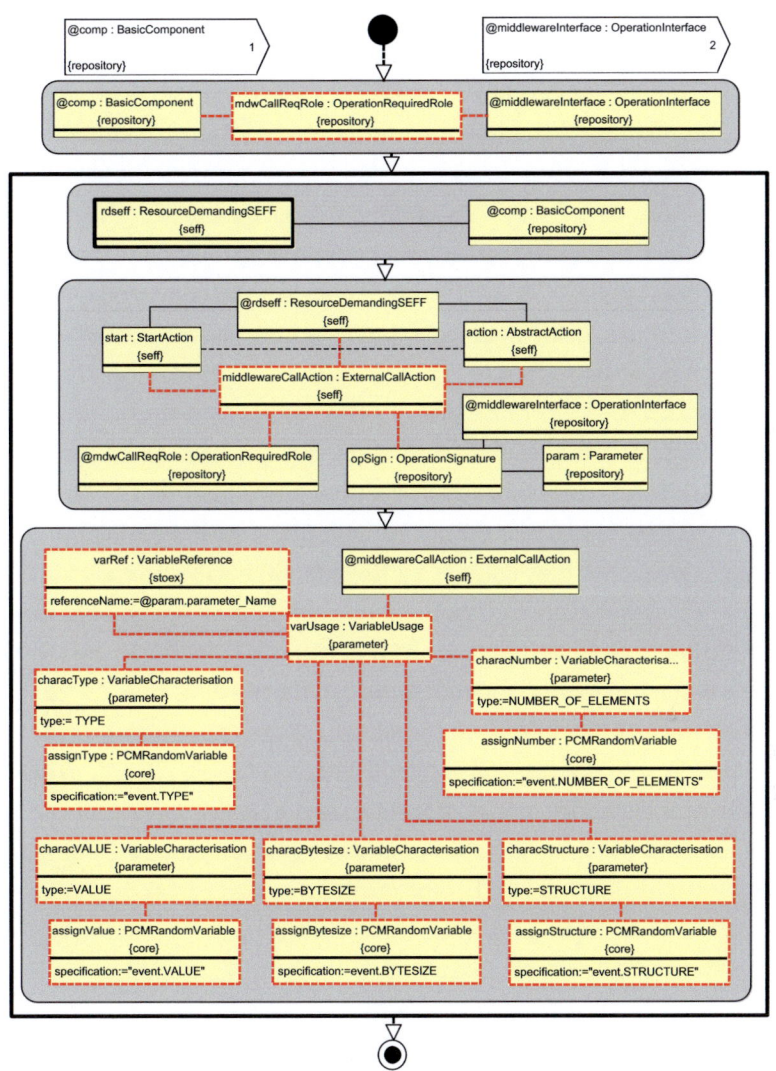

Figure 5.28: Sub-Procedure `integrateMiddlewareCall`

The last rule in the loop generates a `VariableUsage` and some additionally required elements to forward the performance characteristics to the middleware. In contrast to the event forwarding within the event processing components realised by the `createVariableUsages` procedure, this mapping generates only one `VariableUsage` containing the five predefined characteristics TYPE, VALUE, BYTESIZE, STRUCTURE, and NUMBER_OF_ELEMENTS, common for all data types. The middleware model is defined independently of the system model and is reusable for different systems. To enable this, it does not contain any dependencies on system specific data types and uses only generic characteristics common for all data types.

A `VariableReference` added to the `VariableUsage` identifies the `Parameter` that is characterised by the five `VariableCharacterisations`, one for each of the five predefined types. In PCM, `VariableReferences` do not contain direct references to `Parameters`, but rather they contain a string identifying the `Parameter` by name. For this reason, the mapping rule contains an assignment to set the attribute `referenceName` of the `VariableReference` to the name of the `Parameter` identified within the previous rule. All `VariableCharacterisations` contain an assignment, which sets the attribute `type` to the respective type (TYPE, VALUE, BYTESIZE, STRUCTURE, and NUMBER_OF_ELEMENTS), and a `PCMRandomVariable` that contains the value definition as string representation of a StoEx. For each `PCMRandomVariable`, the attribute `specification` is set to the name of the input parameter representing the event and the type of the characterisation separated by a dot. The name of the parameter is always set to `"event"` when generating the `OperationInterfaces`, thus the specification is set to `"event.%CHARACTERISATION_-TYPE%"`, where `%CHARACTERISATION_TYPE%` is substituted with the respective type.

Composition and Allocation of Middleware Components

After extending the event processing component with a middleware call as part of the previous sub-procedure, the `assembleAndAllocateMiddleware` procedure instantiates the middleware components, connects them with the processing components and finally deploys them on hardware resources. It receives the processing component (`comp`), the middleware component (`middlewareComp`), and the `OperationInterface` (`middlewareInterface`) provided by the middleware component as input.

As there might be several `AssemblyContexts` respectively `AllocationContexts` belonging to the same processing component, the procedure iterates over all `AllocationContexts` belonging to the `BasicComponent comp`. This iteration is defined within the first rule of the procedure, which is depicted in Figure 5.29.

The second mapping rule checks the existence of an `Assembly-` and `AllocationContext` belonging to the middleware component `middlewareComp` that are associated with the same `ResourceContainer` as the current `AllocationContext` of `comp`. If the mapping is successful, which means that there is already a deployed instance of the middleware component on the `ResourceContainer`, the execution skips the following rule and continues with the last rule. If the mapping is not successful, the ELSE branch contains a rule that creates a new `Assembly-` and `AllocationContext` associated with `middlewareComp`. The `AllocationContext` references the `ResourceContainer` that the processing component is deployed on.

The last rule, which is executed in any case, generates a new `AssemblyConnector`. This connector connects the `AssemblyContext` of the processing component and the `OperationRequiredRole` generated within the `integrateMiddlewareCall` procedure, with the

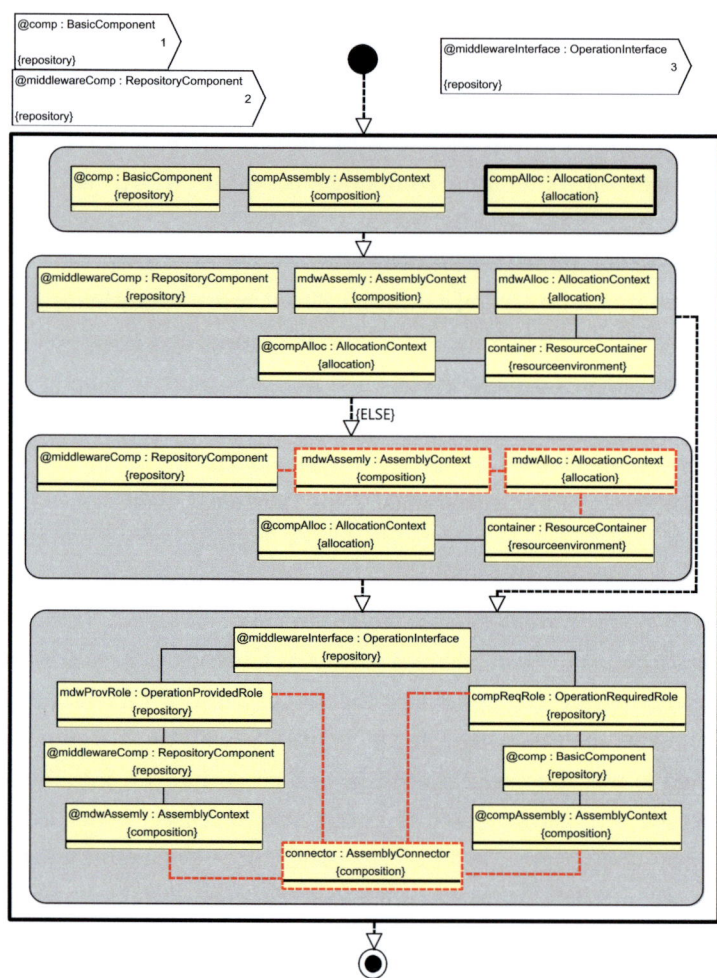

Figure 5.29: Sub-Procedure `assembleAndAllocateMiddleware`

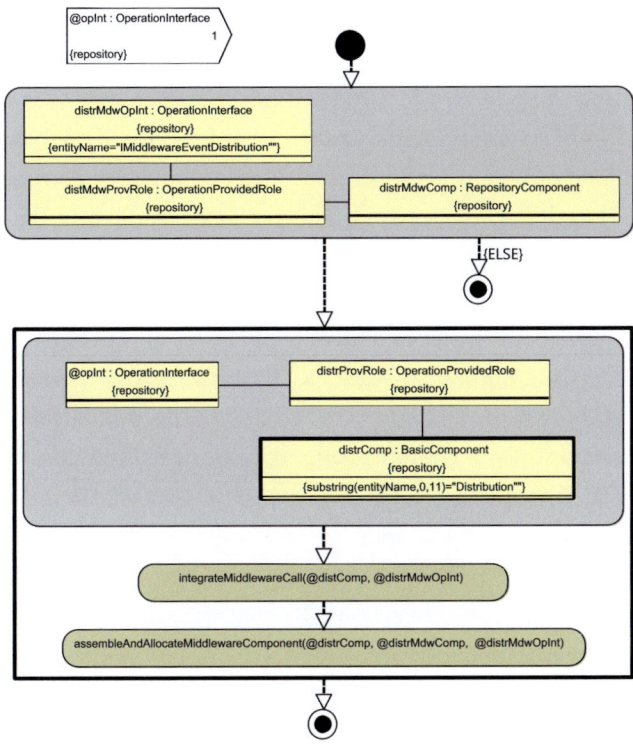

Figure 5.30: Sub-Procedure `integrateDistributionMiddleware`

`AssemblyContext` and the `OperationProvidedRole` of the middleware component associated with `middlewareInterface`.

Integration of Event Distribution Middleware

In analogy to the `integrateSourcePortMiddleware` procedure, the `integrateDistributionMiddleware` procedure (shown in Figure 5.30) and the similar `integrateFilterMiddleware` procedures start with a mapping rule to identify and check the existence of a component providing the middleware interface.

While the transformation or more specifically the `createProcess-`
`ingComponents` procedure generates exactly one `BasicComponent`
representing the *SourcePort, SourceCommunication, SinkCommunica-*
tion, and *SinkPort* components for each `EventGroup`, it might generate
several different `BasicComponents` representing the *EventDistribu-*
tion and *EventFilter* components. This is caused by the fact, that *Event-*
Filter components contain sink-specific filtering rules, and the structure
of the *EventDistribution* components depends on the number of connected sinks, which leads to source-, channel-, or sink-specific components for the same `EventGroup`. For this reason, the two procedures `integrateDistributionMiddleware` and `integrate-`
`FilterMiddleware` contain a loop iterating over all components that
provide the `OperationInterface` `opInt` and whose entityName
starts with `"Distribution_"` or `"Filter_"`. Similarly to the `in-`
`tegrateSourcePortMiddleware` procedure, the two procedures
`integrateMiddlewareCall` and `assembleAndAllocateMid-`
`dleware` are executed to extend the processing component with an additional middleware call and finally connect and deploy the middleware
component.

5.4.7. Cleaning up the Refined Model

After generating the event processing chain and integrating the platform-
specific middleware components based on the procedures explained in
the previous sections, the `cleanUpModel` procedure, shown in Figure 5.31, removes leftover event-related elements. The procedure itself
consists of several foreach loops.

The first three loops iterate over `AssemblyEventConnec-`
`tors`, `EventChannelSourceConnector`, and `EventChan-`
`nelSinkConnector`, respectively. They all have a similar structure starting with a first rule to define the loop variable. The second
rule deletes the current instance stored in the loop variable. After re-

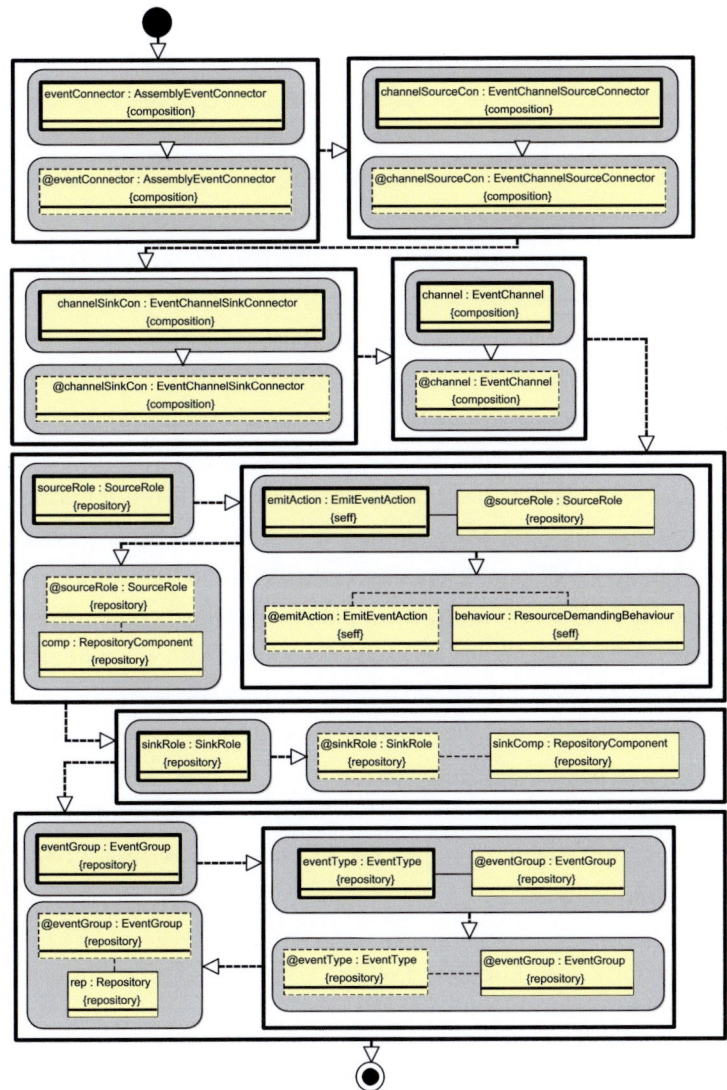

Figure 5.31: Sub-Procedure `cleanUpModel`

moving all event-related connectors, the fourth loop iterates over all `EventChannels`. Again, the first rule defines the loop variable while the second one removes the respective element.

After removing all connectors and channels, the next two loops remove `Source-` and `SinkRoles` belonging to a component. The first one iterates over all `SourceRoles`. After defining the loop variable in the first rule, a second embedded loop iterates over all `EmitEventActions` associated with the current `SourceRole`. The `EmitEventAction` is removed from the `ResourceDemandingBehaviour` it belongs to and completely deleted. After this embedded loop, the current `SourceRole` is detached from the component and deleted. The loop iterating over all `SinkRoles` does not contain any inner loops. It detaches and removes the `SinkRole` from the `RepositoryComponent`.

The last loop iterates over all `EventGroups`. Before removing an `EventGroup` from the `Repository` it is contained in, an embedded loop iterates over all `EventTypes` belonging to the `EventGroup` and removes them. After executing this final procedure all event-related extensions of the meta-model have been removed and substituted with components of the event processing chains based on synchronous `OperationInterfaces`. Furthermore, the middleware-specific components have been integrated into the event processing and all event-related meta-model elements have been removed. The resulting model is now compatible with the original PCM and serves as input to existing prediction techniques.

5.5. Transformation Implementation

MOLA is a formal and executable transformation language accompanied by a transformation engine [Sostaks 10] and a modelling tool [Latvia 12] both supporting the ECore meta-meta-model, which is the basis for defining the PCM meta-model. However, a fully automated integration into the Palladio prediction process was inhibited by the following technical reasons:

- **Namespace conversion** In PCM, the different sub-models and packages have predefined namespaces. The current version of the MOLA-based transformation engine does not support such namespaces and substitutes them with a relative addressing of packages. Compensating this behaviour would requires additional adaptation steps directly manipulating the *XML Metadata Interchange* (XMI)-serialisation of the model before and after executing the transformation to re-substitute the namespaces.

- **Source Code Access** The MOLA tool is publicly available [Latvia 12], however, only as a binary version integrated into a specialised windows version of Eclipse. The tool supports the generation of externally executable transformations. However, due to the missing access to the source code, we were not able to fix the namespace issue within the transformation generators.

- **Long-term support** PCM is built on top of the Eclipse framework with a yearly release cycle. The MOLA project is decoupled from this cycle which might result in version conflicts in future releases of Eclipse and especially the *Eclipse Modeling Framework Project* (EMF), which provides the core model handling and storage functionality.

In order to provide a long-term stable and maintainable implementation of our transformation fulfilling the quality requirements to be integrated into the official PCM release, we selected *QVT Operational Mapping Language* (QVT-O) as implementation language. As described in Section 2.2.4, QVT-O is the operational version of the *Query/View/Transformation* (QVT) standard. The selection of QVT-O for the implementation of our transformation is based on the following criteria. A more detailed evaluation and comparison with *QVT Relations Language* (QVT-R) is presented in [Klatt 10].

- **Native support in Eclipse** The *Eclipse Modeling Project* [Eclipse Foundation 12], which is fully integrated into Eclipse and the surrounding framework, provides native support to execute QVT-O transformations. Therefore, no additional transformation engines are needed.

- **Maintainability** Compared to QVT-R the maintainability of QVT-O transformations especially in the case of inplace transformations is higher. To realise inplace transformations with QVT-R, the model has to be copied using an individually generated copy transformation [Goldschmidt 08] resulting in large sets of generated relations that have to be partially adjusted manually. Furthermore, our experiences gained in student and research projects show that the learning curve for developers who are well versed in modern programming languages and start working with QVT-O grows much faster compared to QVT-R

- **Experience** Within our group, QVT-O has already been successfully applied in several projects that transform PCM models, for example [Ciancone 10, Meier 10, Vogel 12]. The experience show that QVT-O is a mature and stable transformation language.

- **Integration into PCM workflow** The PCM Workflow Engine already provides a QVT-O transformation job, which significantly easies the integration of QVT-O-based transformations into the prediction workflow.

As illustrated in Figure 5.32, the implementation consists of several QVT-O files grouped into 4 *logical* packages. These packages are *logical* as the QVT-O standard does not provide any structuring concepts like

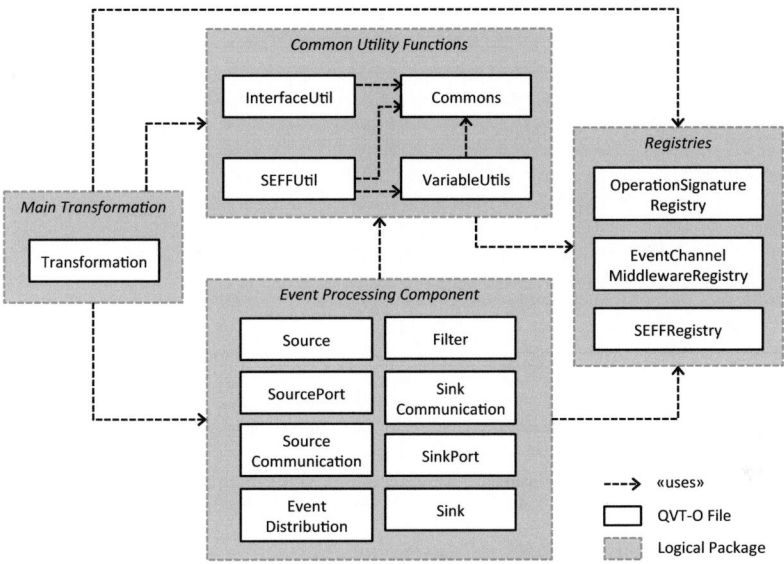

Figure 5.32: Structural Overview of the Implementation

Java packages beyond the separation into different files. The *Main Transformation* packages includes the main procedure of the transformation. While the *Event Processing Component* package contains several operations that are specialised for a certain element type, the *Common Utility Functions* package subsumes general manipulation operations that are used in different contexts and for different elements. Finally, the *Registries* package provides functionality to query and search for different element instances within the model.

In the following, we provide a brief overview of the implementation. For more details, we refer to [Klatt 10] and the documented code, which is part of the official Palladio workbench since release 3.3 [Palladio 12].

Main Transformation The *Main Transformation* package contains only one QVT-O file that contains the main procedure and several query

Listing 5.2: Finder Operations

```
1   query Finder_findAllEventGroups(
2       in allocationModel : PCM_ALLOC) : Set(EventGroup){...}
3   query Finder_findAllSourceRoles(
4       in allocationModel : PCM_ALLOC) : Set(SourceRole){...}
5   query Finder_findAssemblyEventConnectors(
6       in sourceRole : SourceRole,
7       in allocationModel : PCM_ALLOC)
8       : Set(AssemblyEventConnector){...}
9   query Finder_findSystem(
10      in allocationModel : PCM_ALLOC) : System {...}
11  query Finder_findAllocation(
12      in allocationModel : PCM_ALLOC) : Allocation {...}
13  query Finder_findAllocation(
14      in assemblyContext : AssemblyContext,
15      in allocationModel : PCM_ALLOC) : Allocation {...}
16  query Finder_findResourceContainer(
17      in assemblyContext : AssemblyContext,
18      in allocationModel : PCM_ALLOC) : ResourceContainer
            {...}
19  query Finder_findMiddlewareContainer(
20      in allocationModel : PCM_ALLOC) : ResourceContainer
            {...}
21  query Finder_findOperationProvidedRole(
22      in interfaceName : String, in repository : PCM_REP)
23      : OperationProvidedRole {...}
```

operations. The query operations support the identification and selection of meta-model element instances and thus require direct access to the complete source and target models. Although some of these querying operations should, from a semantical point of view, be located in other packages, the current implementation of the QVT-O language does not support the forwarding of complete models to procedures located in external files. We marked these queries, shown in Listing 5.2, with the prefix Finder_ to ease their extraction into separate files as soon as support for this is provided by the QVT-O implementation. All other operations are marked with the prefix Transformation_.

Listing 5.3: Source_transformEmitEventActions

```
1  helper Source_transformEmitEventActions(
2              sourceRole: SourceRole,
3              requiredRole : OperationRequiredRole,
4              availableEmitEventActions : Set(
                  EmitEventAction)) {
5
6  // get the emit event actions currently pointing to the
       source role
7      var emitEventActions := availableEmitEventActions->
8          select(e |  e.sourceRole__EmitEventAction =
               sourceRole and
9                     e.predecessor_AbstractAction <> null and
10                    e.successor_AbstractAction <> null);
11     emitEventActions->forEach(emitEventAction) {
12         Source_createExternalCallAction(emitEventAction,
13                     requiredRole,sourceRole);
14     };
15     return;
16  }
```

Event Processing Components The *Event Processing Components* package includes individual QVT-O libraries, one for each component of the event processing chain as well as the source and sink components. For example, the operations defined in the *Source* library adapt and extend the original source component as described in the previous sections. The helper `Source_transformEmitEventActions()`, shown as an example in Listing 5.3, substitutes `EmitEventActions` with `ExternalCallActions`.

The *Sink* library provides helpers to manipulate components that contain an `EventSinkRole`. This includes the creation of `OperationProvidedRoles` and the assignment of the RD-SEFFs that describe the event handling. In contrast to the other operations, which are all implemented as helpers, the `Sink_createSinkOperationProvidedRole()`, depicted in Listing 5.4, is implemented as a mapping. Mappings have a caching characteristic and thus ensure that only one

Listing 5.4: Sink_createSinkOperationProvidedRole

```
1   mapping Sink_createSinkOperationProvidedRole(
2               sinkComponent : RepositoryComponent,
3               operationInterface : OperationInterface)
4               : OperationProvidedRole {
5       entityName := operationInterface.entityName
6               +'OperationProvidedRole'
7               +Commons_getUniqueElementNameSuffix();
8       providingEntity_ProvidedRole := sinkComponent;
9       providedInterface__OperationProvidedRole :=
                operationInterface;
10  }
```

`OperationProvidedRole` is created for a specific `SinkRole`, even if it is connected to multiple sources.

The remaining libraries in the *Communication Components* generate the platform-independent event processing components. As already described, these `BasicComponents` are equipped with an `OperationRequiredRole` and an `OperationProvidedRole` associated with the `OperationInterface` that replaces the `EventGroup`. All operations have in common that they instantiate and deploy the created `BasicComponents` in the `ComposedStructure` and `Resource-` `Container` provided as parameters.

Common Utility Functions The libraries in the *Common Utility Functions* package include operations for general element modifications. These operations are used by multiple operations from different packages to create or manipulate model elements. The *InterfaceUtil*, *SEFFUtil* and *VariableUtil* libraries provide manipulation operations specialised for interfaces, RD-SEFFs, and variables and their instantiation, respectively.

Registries The *Registries* package includes operations to support a simplified lookup and querying of specific model elements. These registries provide capabilities with advanced usability and expressiveness compared to the caching feature of QVT-O mapping operations. The registries substitute the error-prone string comparison used in the MOLA transformations to identify elements created in previous processing steps.

5.6. Concluding Remarks

In this chapter, we presented the developed prediction approach enabling quantitative system evaluations of component-based systems applying event-based interactions. A two-step refinement transformation combines architecture-level modelling using the abstractions introduced in Chapter 4 and detailed platform-aware *Quality-of-Service* (QoS) prediction. The first step refines the event-based interactions with a detailed platform-independent event processing chain, which acts as skeleton for the integration of platform-specific components in the second step. Since the integrated event-processing chain conforms to the *base ADL*, the refined model serves as input for multiple existing prediction techniques defined for the *base ADL*.

Beside the introduction of the two-step refinement transformation approach, this chapter presented a formalisation of the transformation using the extended version of PCM, described in Section 4.4, as a basis. Finally, we gave a short overview of the implementation of the transformation and its integration into the PCM tool chain. The results presented in this and the previous chapter provide the basis for the evaluation of our approach presented in the next chapter.

6. Validation

The primary goal of the work presented in this thesis is enabling the architecture-level modelling of event-based interactions in component-based systems while providing support for detailed platform-aware performance prediction techniques as a basis for quantitative system evaluation. In order to achieve this goal, Chapter 4 introduced generic modelling abstractions for event-based interactions, which were implemented as an extension of the *Palladio Component Model* (PCM) serving as a representative *Architecture Description Language* (ADL) for component-based systems. Based on these extensions, the two-step refinement transformation presented in Chapter 5 substitutes the event-based interactions with a detailed event processing chain and integrates additional platform-specific components enabling in-depth quantitative system analysis by means of existing prediction techniques.

According to [Böhme 08], prediction models can be validated on various levels. Assuming an existing implementation *(Type 0 validity)*, *Type I* validations focus on metrics, i.e., the comparison of measured and predicted values, and demonstrate that prediction results reflect the observed reality with an acceptable margin of error. *Type II* validations focus on the applicability of the modelling approach and cover the expressiveness of the modelling language to describe representative real-world systems as well as ability of trained users to apply the approach with reasonable effort. *Type III* validations finally aim at demonstrating that the approach has benefits over other competing approaches, which normally is very cost- and time-intensive as it requires to conduct projects multiple times under the same preconditions.. The evaluation goals defined in Section 6.1 focus on Type I and Type II validation of our approach while also considering its Type III validity at the conceptual level.

In order to provide a comprehensive evaluation of our approach, we selected two representative real-world systems from different application domains that cover the major classes of event-based systems. The first case study is based on a traffic monitoring system developed at the University of Cambridge [Bacon 08] and built on top of a distributed peer-to-peer middleware called *Peer-to-peer Implementation of Reconfigurable Architecture for Typed Event Streams* (PIRATES) [Ingram 09b]. The second case study is the official SPECjms2007 benchmark, a supply chain management system representative of real-world industrial applications built on top of a centralised *Message-Oriented Middleware* (MOM). The different interactions exercise a complex transaction mix including *Point-to-Point* (P2P) and *Publish/Subscribe* (Pub/Sub) communication [Sachs 09].

The rest of this chapter is structured as follows: In Section 6.1, we present the goals of our evaluation, which we defined based on the success criteria and application scenarios listed in Chapter 1. The following sections present the detailed evaluation of the developed modelling and prediction approach in the context of the two case studies: The traffic monitoring system in Section 6.2 and the SPECjms2007 benchmark in Section 6.3. Section 6.4 presents two external projects that have already been using the results presented in this thesis including the reported experiences. Finally, in Section 6.5, we summarise and discuss the evaluation results.

6.1. Evaluation Goals

The main goal of this thesis is the development of an integrated methodology and framework supporting the modelling and performance prediction of component-based systems with event-based interactions. To provide a detailed evaluation, this goal is broken down into the following three evaluation goals covering the different success criteria identified in Section 1.3.

6.1.1. Goal 1: Prediction Capabilities

When evaluating prediction techniques, the accuracy of the predicted metrics (Type I validity) is a crucial aspect for their successful application. To evaluate the accuracy of our techniques, we deploy the two case studies in multiple variations in our testbed. We compare performance measurements (processing time and resource utilisation) with measurements taken on the running system for different usage profiles ranging from low load scenarios up to the maximal load that can be processed by the system. When evaluating design time performance prediction techniques, a prediction error of around 35% is typically considered as acceptable [Menascé 04]. In addition to the accuracy, the prediction results should provide enough information allowing an architect to analyse and compare different design and deployment options enabling indepth quantitative system evaluations and architecture improvements. To demonstrate the suitability of the prediction results to serve as a basis for improving the system architecture or for modifying it to accommodate changed requirements, the traffic monitoring case study (Section 6.2) contains different system evolution scenarios covering external factors like workload and hardware changes as well as internal changes like system adaptations and extensions.

6.1.2. Goal 2: Modelling Capabilities

The expressiveness of the developed language enabling the modelling of the different types of event-based interactions is an important aspect for Type II validity. The two case studies we selected represent complementary types of *Event-based Systems* (EBS). The traffic monitoring system is a distributed peer-to-peer system based exclusively on P2P interactions. The SPECjms2007 benchmark is supply chain management system based on a central *Java Message Service* (JMS) server with a complex mixture of both P2P and Pub/Sub interactions with multiple event types. These case studies cover nearly all characteristics of EBS presented in Section 2.1.1 and can thus be seen as representative for most existing EBS.

In addition to the expressiveness, the usability of the language enabling architects to model design alternatives and specify deployment options with low effort is a significant success criteria when applying the approach in realistic scenarios as part of Type II and Type III validations. To analyse this aspect, we evaluate the effort required to perform adaptations of the model instances to reflect different design alternatives or deployment options within the traffic monitoring case study. Furthermore, we compare the modelling effort required when using the original version of PCM and modelling event-based interactions manually using complex workarounds as described in [Rathfelder 10a] against the modelling effort when using the extended PCM version developed as part of this thesis to show the improved usability.

6.1.3. Goal 3: Integration of Modelling and Prediction Aspects

Applying the developed modelling and prediction approach within the software design and development process requires a smooth integration and combination of modelling capabilities for event-based interactions at the architecture-level with detailed analysis and prediction techniques. A high degree of automation reduces the manual effort required to derive the performance model based on architecture-level design models and thus lowers the barrier to integrate model-based prediction techniques into the development process. An empirical study evaluating the applicability of the Palladio approach in comparison to other modelling and prediction approaches has already been conducted [Martens 08a, Martens 08b] and is not in the focus of this thesis. However, the two real-world case studies presented here demonstrate the automated integration of different middleware-specific components implemented as part of the extended PCM-Bench. Furthermore, the traffic monitoring case study shows the integration of the performance prediction techniques into an automated scalability analysis process.

In the following, we present the two case studies including the detailed evaluation results. After these case studies, Section 6.4 gives an overview of two external projects, in which our approach has been applied. FInally, Section 6.5 discusses the evaluation results and presents some concluding remarks.. .

6.2. Traffic Monitoring Case Study

The system under study is a traffic monitoring application based on results from the *Transport Information Monitoring Environment* (TIME) project [Bacon 08] at the University of Cambridge. It consists of multiple distributed components emitting and consuming different types of events. The system is based on the component-based middleware PIRATES [Ingram 09b] introduced in Section 2.1.2. The PIRATES framework encapsulates the communication between components and thus enables easy reconfiguration of component connections and deployment options without affecting the component implementations. After a short introduction of the scenario, we present the different components the traffic monitoring system consists of. In four different scenarios representing different system evolution stages, we demonstrate the application of our approach in the context of evaluating and optimising design alternatives as well as capacity planning. Finally, we perform a detailed evaluation of the prediction accuracy comparing predicted performance metrics with measurements conducted in our testbed for the different scenarios.

6.2.1. Application and Scenario

The application enables monitoring and controlling the traffic in a city like Cambridge. The system monitors passenger cars on streets using license plate recognition techniques. Based on this data, the application detects speeding and is able to calculate the individual toll for each car. An additional functionality provided by the system is the estimation of buses that are near traffic lights when they turn red. This allows city planners to measure the effects on public transport of different light scheduling policies and can contribute to assessing the impact of future alternatives (such as changing the light behaviour based on bus proximity). This application is interesting because it collects and integrates data from different distributed sensors and systems. Furthermore, it contains components with high and varying resource demands like the licence place recognition algorithm. Thanks to the employed event-based middleware, the system architecture is highly adaptable in terms of adding new components or changing the connections between components or their location. Due to the complexity of the system, the influence of adaptations on the overall system performance and utilisation can hardly be anticipated by the architect. In such scenarios, model-based *Quality-of-Service* (QoS) prediction techniques support the architect in evaluating the system as presented in this case study.

Components

The traffic monitoring application consists of 8 different classes of PIRATES components (see Figure 6.1) described below. Due to the use of the PIRATES middleware, it is possible to distribute these components over several computing nodes with redundant instances as well as to centralise them on one node without any changes of the component implementations.

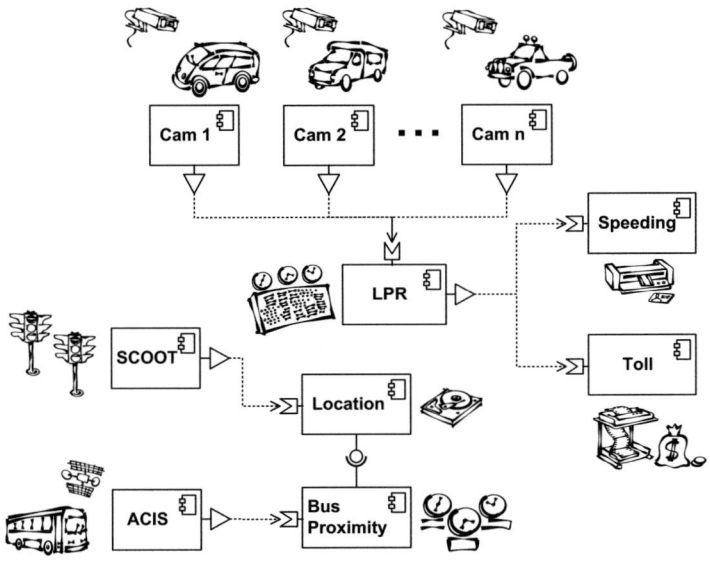

Figure 6.1: Case Study Overview

Lamp Post Mounted Camera (the "Cam component")   As described in [Evans 10], some lamp posts are equipped with cameras. In our extended scenario, these cameras take pictures of each vehicle passing the street. Each camera is connected to a local PIRATES component responsible to publish the taken picture together with position information of the camera and a time stamp. As the cameras have limited computing resources, further processing of the image has to be performed on remote servers.

Licence Plate Recognition (the "LPR component")   The LPR component receives the events emitted by one or more Cam components. The implementation is based on the JavaANPR library [Martinsky 06], which provides algorithms to detect license plate numbers of vehicles. The recognised number together with the timestamp and the location information received from the Cam component is then emitted. This image processing is very resource consuming, so we separated it from any further processing of this data. Combined with the easy system reconfiguration provided by the PIRATES middleware, this allows the distribution of the load over several computing nodes all running an individual instance of the LPR component. Additionally, it is possible to add additional components processing the detected license plate information without any effects on the already existing components.

Speeding Detection (the "Speeding component")   One component receiving the events of detected license plate numbers is the Speeding component. It calculates the speed of a vehicle based on the distance between two cameras and the elapsed time between the two pictures. [Webster 09] reports about the installation of a similar system in London, in which, however, the license plate recognition functionality is tightly coupled with speeding detection functionality as part of a single component. In our system, the separation of license plate recognition and speeding detection into two separate components allows using the information about the observed license plates also in other contexts like for example the toll calculation as described in the following.

Toll Calculation (the "Toll component")   The second component processing the events emitted by the LPR component is the Toll component. Assuming all arterial roads are equipped with Cam components the Toll component calculates the toll fee that must be paid for entering the city. The toll calculation can also be bound to certain roads. The Express Toll Route [etr 10] system installed near Toronto, or the VideoMaut system [ASFINAG 11] operated in Austria, are two examples of systems calculating road fees for frequently used highways based on recognised license plate numbers.

Bus Location Provider (the "ACIS component") The bus location provider uses sensors (in our case, GPS coupled with a proprietary radio network) to note the locations of buses and report them as they change. Such a component produces a stream of events, each containing a bus ID, a location, and the time of the measurement. In the purest instantiation, there is one such component per bus. However, nothing prevents a component reporting on multiple buses' positions, or one component being responsible for all buses. Many intermediate architectures are possible, such as a component per geographic area or a component per bus operator.

Location Storage (the "Location component") The Location component maintains state data for a set of objects like the most recent location that was reported for each of them. The component has no knowledge of what the objects are, each of them is identified only by its name. The input is a stream of events consisting of name/location pairs with timestamps making the ACIS component a suitable event source.

Traffic Light Status Reporter (the "SCOOT component") In the city of Cambridge, the city's traffic lights are controlled by a SCOOT system [Hunt 81], designed to schedule green and red lights so as to optimise use of the road network. As a necessary part of controlling the lights, the system knows whether each light is red or green and can transmit a stream of data derived from vehicle detecting induction loops installed in the roads. The *SCOOT* component is a wrapper of this system. It supplies a source endpoint emitting a stream of events corresponding to light status changes (red to green and green to red), a second source endpoint emitting a stream of events that reflect *SCOOT's* traffic flow data, and two RPC endpoints that allow retrieval of information about a junction (such as its name and its location) as well as links between junctions (the junction the link is attached to, the location of the link's stop line, and so

223

on). While our implementation uses *SCOOT* because that is available to us, another means of detecting junctions' status could be used with no changes to the rest of the system, the SCOOT component provides effective decoupling between the *SCOOT* system and the traffic monitoring application.

Proximity Detector (the "Bus Proximity component") The Bus Proximity component receives a stream of trigger events reflecting when lights turn from green to red. This stream is emitted by the SCOOT component. Upon such a trigger, the SCOOT component's *Remote Procedure Call* (RPC) facility is used to determine the location of the light that just turned red. This is collated with current bus locations collected by the Location component to find which buses are nearby.

6.2.2. Architecture-level Model for Performance Evaluation

The architecture-level model of the traffic monitoring system is based on the extended version of PCM described in Section 4.4. In the following, we present each of the different sub-models that a PCM model instance consists of in a separate section.

Component Repository

As illustrated in Figure 6.2, the *Component Repository* contains one `Ba-sicComponent` for each of the system components presented in the previous section. In order to enable a type-safe composition of the system, we specified four `EventGroups` with overall five `EventTypes` and the `OperationInterface` LinkInfo. This `OperationInter-face` is provided by the SCOOT component and required by the Bus Proximity component. For each component we specified the `Sink-` and `SourceRoles`. To connect the components with the *Usage Model* that specifies the rate of incoming events, we defined additional `Opera-`

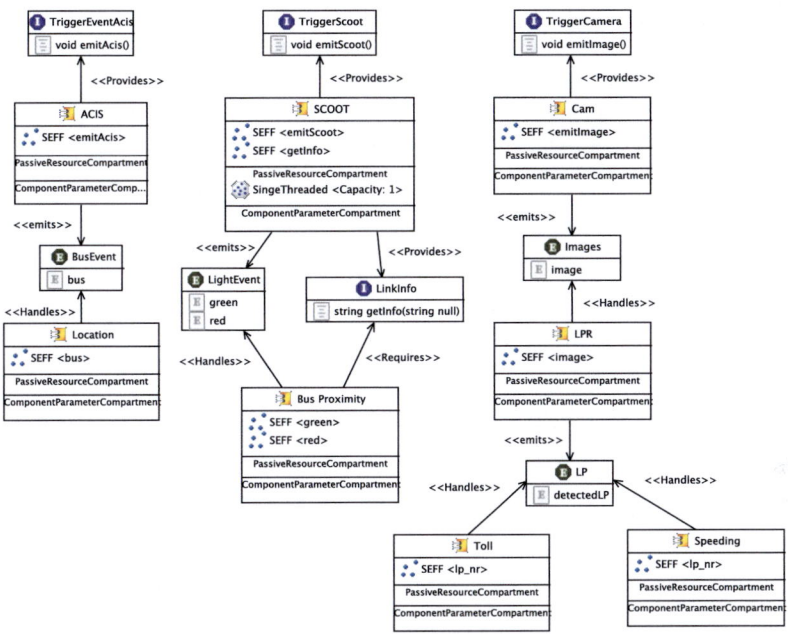

Figure 6.2: Component Repository of the Traffic Monitoring System

tionInterfaces to trigger the event emissions by sources. The *Component Repository* contains one of these trigger interfaces for each of the three components ACIS, SCOOT, and Cam. The SCOOT component contains a PassiveResource used to reflect the single-threaded implementation of the component.

Except for the LPR, the resource demands of the components are nearly constant and independent of the data values included in the event. This allows us to model them as fixed demands in an InternalAction of the respective *Resource Demanding Service Effect Specification* (RD-SEFF). For each component, we measured the internal processing time under low system load to derive the resource demands. Table 6.1 lists the individual resource demands of the components.

Table 6.1: Event Processing Times

Component	ACIS	SCOOT Event	RPC	Location
Processing Time [ms]	35.0	50.0	65.0	40.0

Component	Bus Proximity	Toll	Speeding
Processing Time [ms]	50.0	40.7	50.4

Measurements with different images showed that the resource demands of the LPR component were highly dependent on the content of the image. PCM allows to specify parameter dependencies, however, it is not possible to distinguish the image parameters. Thus, we modelled the resource demand using a probability distribution function. We analysed a set of 100 different images. For each image, we measured the processing time using `System.nanoTime()` required by the recognition algorithm over 200 detection runs. The standard deviation was less than 2% of the mean value for all measurements. The measurements indicate that the processing of images that can be successfully recognised

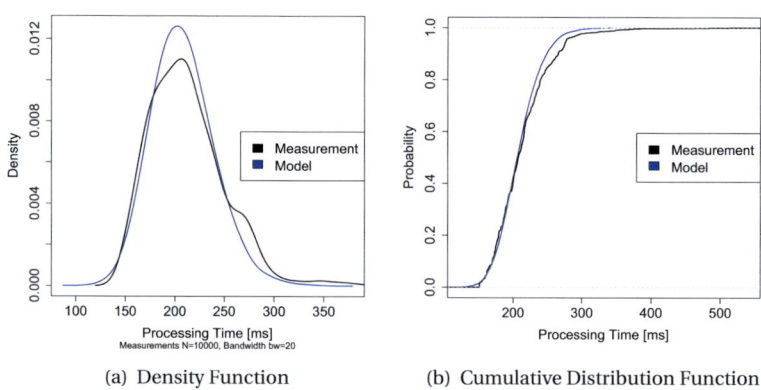

(a) Density Function (b) Cumulative Distribution Function

Figure 6.3: Measured and Predicted Processing Time Distribution

is nearly log-normal distributed ($\mu = 12.2353, \sigma = 0.146403$). Figure 6.3, illustrates the fitted distribution function compared with the measured values. Pictures where no license plate could be detected have a significantly higher but fixed processing time of 1092.4ms.

To represent this behaviour in the RD-SEFF of the LPR component, we used a `BranchAction`. One `BranchBehaviour` contains an `InternalAction` with the fixed demand for undetected images and the other one contains a log-normal distribution $\mathcal{LN}(\mu, \sigma^2)$ with the fitted parameter values $\mu = 12.2353$ and $\sigma = 0.146403$.

Middleware Repository

The PIRATES-specific *Middleware Repository* contains one component representing event sources and one representing event sinks. Both components include a semaphore to model the single threaded behaviour of the PIRATES implementation. Furthermore, the RD-SEFFs include `InternalActions` to represent the resource demands imposed by the PIRATES middleware. We instrumented the PIRATES implementation to measure the processing time in the different event processing steps. In order to derive the CPU demands, we extended the PIRATES framework with several sensors that collect the time spent within the library to communicate with the wrapper and within the wrapper to communicate with the wrapper of the connected component. We ran experiments and measured the time spent in the library and the wrapper under low workload conditions. We took the mean value over more than 10,000 measurements whose variation was negligible. Table 6.2 lists the derived resource demands of the library and the wrapper.

System Model

In this case study, we evaluate different design variations required to support the system's evolution. For this reasons, we need to adapt the *Sys-*

Table 6.2: CPU Demands of PIRATES middleware

Source		Sink	
Library	**Wrapper**	**Library**	**Wrapper**
0.0357 μs	15.2 μs	0.0357 μs	7.73 μs

tem Model for each scenario we analyse. Depending on the scenario, the relevant components are instantiated and the event sources and sinks are connected accordingly. We use only direct P2P connectors, as PIRATES does not support Pub/Sub communication. The *System Model* describes the logical connections between components only and thus it is independent of the components' deployment on different hardware resources.

Deployment Model

According to the deployment option that should be analysed, we use the *Allocation Model* to describe the allocation of components on individual hardware nodes. In our case study, the *ResourceEnvironment* describes our test environment (see Figure 6.4) and consists of 8 `ResourceContainers`, each containing one `ProcessingResource` representing the CPU. We selected processor sharing on 4 cores as `Scheduling-`

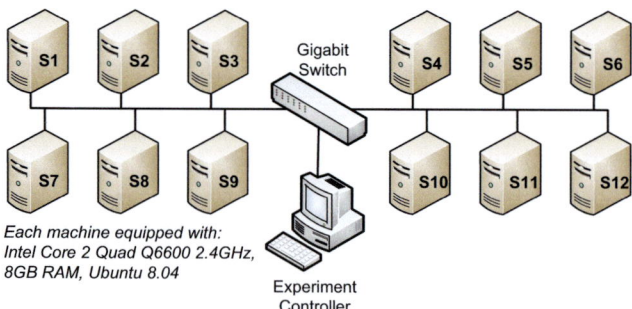

Figure 6.4: Experimental Environment of the Traffic Monitoring System

`Policy`, as all machines in our testbed are equipped with quad-core CPUs. The `ResourceContainers` are connected by a `LinkingResource` with a throughput of 1 GBit/s. The mapping of components to hardware nodes is adjusted according to the individual deployment options in the various scenarios.

Usage Model

The *Usage Model* consists of three different types of behaviours executed in parallel. Two `UsageBehaviours` are used to trigger SCOOT and ACIS to emit events. For both behaviours, we specify an `OpenWorkload` with an exponentially distributed inter-arrival time with a mean value of 200ms. Additionally, we introduce a `UsageBehaviour` for each street equipped with two cameras. In these behaviours, the two calls of the cameras are separated by a `DelayAction`. With this equally distributed delay, we simulate the driving time of a vehicle from the first camera to the second one. Each invocation of the Cam component includes the specification of the image size. Similarly to the other behaviours, we use an exponentially distributed inter-arrival time for the `UsageBehaviour`.

6.2.3. Applicability Demonstration

After introducing the system components and the performance model, we now demonstrate the application of our approach to evaluate different architecture alternatives and deployment options. In the real-world, the requirements on the system, the system itself, and the available hardware infrastructure evolve over time. These changes require to evaluate the system considering different design and deployment options. Finding the maximal processable event rate for a given deployment option or identifying a resource-efficient deployment scenario that still meets all requirements on the event processing times is a complex task. Using

229

performance prediction techniques eases the analysis of performance attributes for different deployment scenarios or event rates, as they remove the need for expensive testing and measurements on real hardware. Our case study consists of four different scenarios that cover most of the changes and evolution stages typical for EBS (e.g., change of the system workload, change of available hardware resources, modification of a component, or introduction of new components). These changes influence the system performance and thus their impacts must be carefully evaluated by the system architect.

In [Rathfelder 11c], we demonstrated the application of an automated model-based performance prediction approach in the context of a capacity planning process. Evaluating EBS requires the analysis of different design variations as well as the evaluation of different load situations. In order to reduce the required effort, we developed an automated model-based scalability analysis process (see Figure 6.5). As input to the process an architecture-level model of the system combined with a specification of the parameter variations (e.g., load or size variations) must be provided. This specification includes the upper and lower bounds as well as the increments of the parameter variations. By means of this specification, the values of model parameters are set. This adapted model is the input to the two-step refinement transformation described in Chapter 5. Depending on the selected prediction technique, this refined model is transformed into one of the supported prediction models, e.g., *Layered Queueing Network* (LQN) or *Queueing Petri Net* (QPN), or directly into

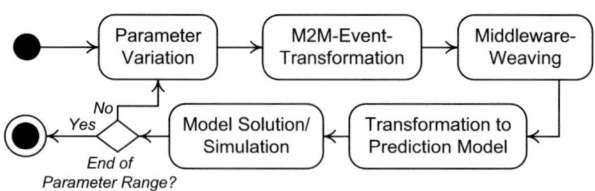

Figure 6.5: Model-based Scalability Analysis Process

a Java-based simulation code. As a last step, the prediction itself is performed by solving the analytical models or running simulations. Once the upper bounds of the considered parameters are reached, the prediction process ends. Otherwise, the process starts again with a new parameter value. In the following scenarios, we apply this automated performance prediction to conduct scalability analysis for each design and deployment option.

Scenario 1 - Throughput Analysis

This scenario, which we use as a basis for all other scenarios, demonstrates the use of our approach to derive the maximal event rate that can be successfully processed by the system without queueing up events. The *System Model* in this case consists of single instances of SCOOT, ACIS, Location, and Bus Proximity. ACIS and SCOOT have a fixed event rate of 5 events per second. Additionally, one street is equipped with two cameras and two instances of the Cam component, which are connected to one LPR component. The detected license plate numbers are processed by the Speeding component. In this scenario, all processing components (i.e. LPR, Speeding, Location, and Bus Proximity) are deployed on one central server, as illustrated in Figure 6.6. The utilisation of this central server is the target performance metric of interest in this scenario.

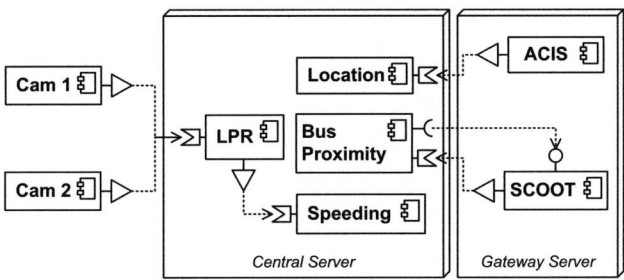

Figure 6.6: Deployment of Scenario 1

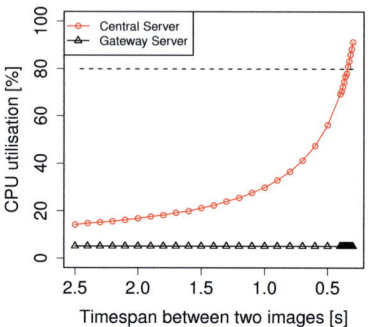

Figure 6.7: Predicted CPU Utilisation in Scenario 1

The Cam components are running on individual computing nodes that are part of the camera systems mounted on the street lights. As part of the *Allocation Model*, we deployed them on a separate node to avoid any influences on the other components. As ACIS and SCOOT are the gateways to other systems and thereby to other network segments, they have to be deployed on separate servers for security reasons. In this scenario, there is only one possible deployment option, however, for capacity planning the utilisation of this central server as well as the maximal throughout needs to be analysed subject to the event rate. The maximal utilisation of the CPUs should not exceed 80% to guarantee a stable operation.

In this scenario, we have only one *System* and *Allocation Model*. To analyse and evaluate different load situations, we automatically reduced the timespan between two images emitted by the Cam component. The results (see Figure 6.7) show that the system can handle a traffic flow of up to 0.35 seconds between two cars and respectively a frequency of ≈2.86 cars per second until the limit of 80% resource utilisation is reached.

Scenario 2 - Growing Workload

In this scenario, we demonstrate the application of our performance evaluation to improve the system's deployment by analysing performance bottlenecks and analysing different deployment options. Compared to the previous scenario, the load on the system is increased as two additional streets are equipped with cameras to monitor the traffic resulting in a total of six Cam components sending images. Additionally, a second server is available. This server can be used to deploy some of the components on it in order to balance the load. In analogy to the previous scenario, we first analyse the deployment option with all processing components on a single machine, the *AllOnOne* deployment

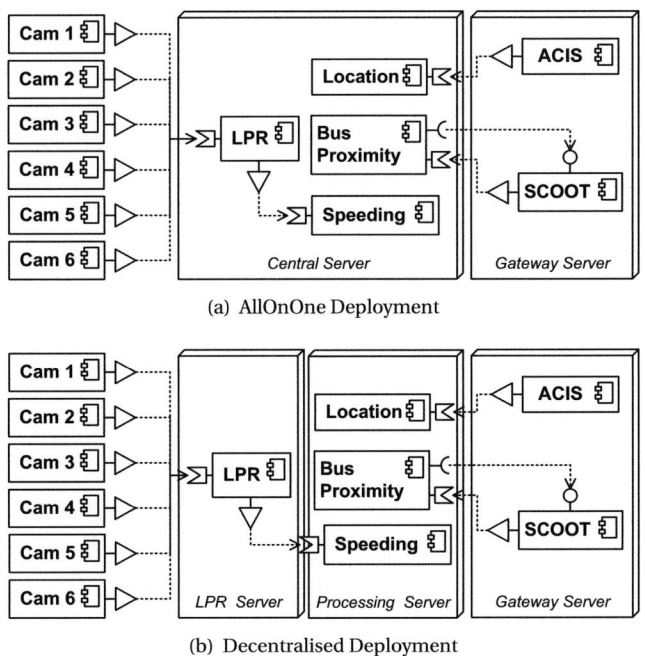

(a) AllOnOne Deployment

(b) Decentralised Deployment

Figure 6.8: Deployment Options of Scenario 2

233

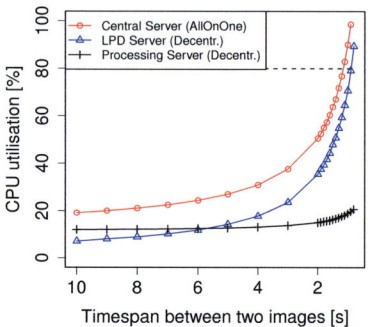

Figure 6.9: Predicted CPU Utilisation of Scenario 2

(see Figure 6.8(a)), to detect the component which induces most load. We add the new camera components to the System model and connect them with the LPR component. Again, we specify an automatic variation of the workload induced by the Cam components. The bottleneck analysis shows that the LPR component induces most load on the CPU, so this component is the best candidate to be deployed on the second server in which case we speak of a *Decentralised* deployment (see Figure 6.8(b)). We compare these two deployment options and deduce the maximum throughput of the two variants, namely all processing components on one system and LPR separated from the other processing components.

In Figure 6.9, the results of the prediction series are visualised. As the machine hosting the LPR component is still the bottleneck no further optimisation is possible in this scenario. Assuming an upper limit of 80% CPU utilisation for a stable state, the prediction results show that the *AllOnOne* deployment can handle up to 0.8 images per second and camera. The *Decentralised* deployment can handle up to 1 image per second. Thanks to the easy to use graphical editors, the required adaptations of the composition and allocation models could be done in less than 10 minutes.

Scenario 3 - New Components

The loose coupling of components in EBS improves the system extend-ability of the system by enabling the integration of new components with low effort. In this scenario, we demonstrate such an extension of the system involving the integration of new components analysing the performance influences caused by this extension. With the cameras added in the previous scenario, all arterial roads in and out of the city centre can be monitored for vehicles entering and leaving the inner city. This allows

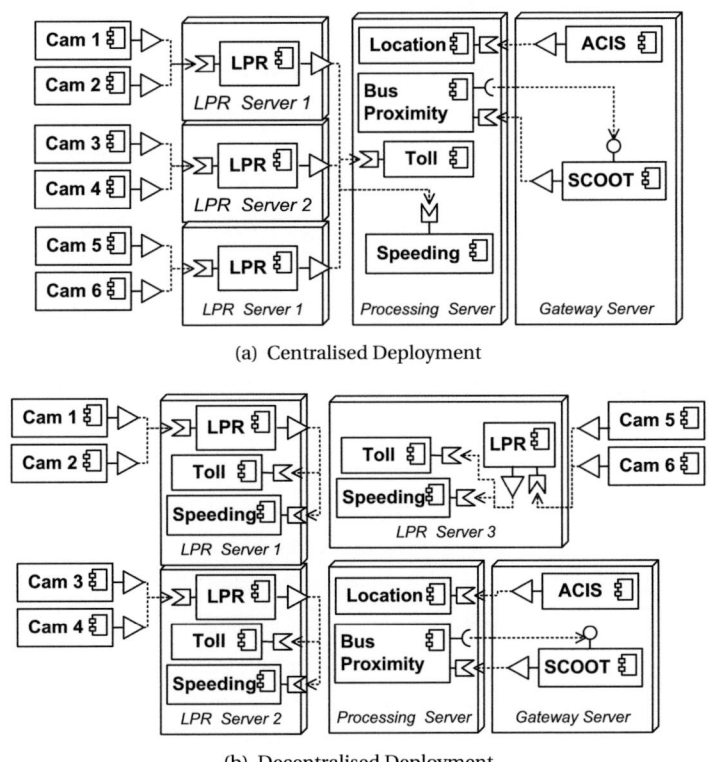

(a) Centralised Deployment

(b) Decentralised Deployment

Figure 6.10: Deployment Options in Scenario 3

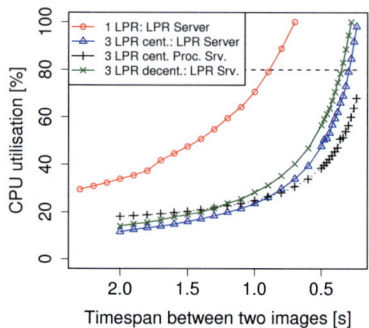

Figure 6.11: Predicted CPU Utilisation in Scenario 3

building up an automated toll collection system implemented using the Toll component. This component is the second component processing the events emitted by the LPR component. It induces additional load on the CPU of the Processing Server, which was not foreseen in the previous scenarios. To increase the system's throughput, an additional server is added allowing to run three independent instances of LPR on individual servers. In the first deployment option that we consider, the new hardware is not used and the LPR component is running isolated from all other components as in the previous scenario. Again, the LPR component is the bottleneck. Based on these results, we evaluated two further deployment options. In both options, three individual instances of LPR are running on different nodes each responsible for the events of two cameras. In the first option, all other components are running on the central Processing Server (*Centralised* deployment, see Figure 6.10(a)). In the second option, Speeding and Toll are deployed with three separate instances and co-located with the LPR instances on the three LPR Servers (*Decentralised* deployment, see Figure 6.10(b)).

The required adaptation effort of the model is slightly higher compared to the previous scenario. However, the adaptation can still be done in less than 20 minutes. The results of the prediction series are visualised in Figure 6.11. The *AllOnOne* deployment option with only one instance of the LPR has a maximum throughput of about 1 image per second and camera while the other two options (with three LPR instances) can handle up to 2.5 images per second and camera. Looking at the load balance between the machines hosting the LPR and the machine hosting the other components, the centralised deployment is preferable. The most efficient utilisation, i.e., equally balanced CPU utilisation, is at a load with an offset of roughly 0.9 seconds between two images.

Scenario 4 - Upgraded Sensors

In this last scenario, an additional street is equipped with two cameras. Furthermore, the existing cameras are replaced with a newer and improved model. The new cameras are able to take pictures with higher resolution and improved quality. With the improved quality, the detection error ratio can be reduced from 30% to 5%. It is known that the resource demand for processing images with undetectable license plates is significantly higher than for successfully recognised license plates. However, the resource demand D also depend on the image size p in pixels. In the following equation, the values of μ and σ are the same as the fitted values presented in Section 6.2.2, Δp is the difference of the image size, and ϕ a scaling factor with $\phi = 7.473 \cdot 10^{-4} \frac{ms}{px}$.

$$D = LogNorm(\mu, \sigma) + \phi \cdot \Delta p$$

The impacts on the system performance caused by the introduction of the new camera versions are the target of the evaluation in this scenario. The evaluation allows to decide if the investment into new cameras will improve the system performance. Similarly to the previous scenario, we evaluate a centralised and a decentralised deployment of the Toll and

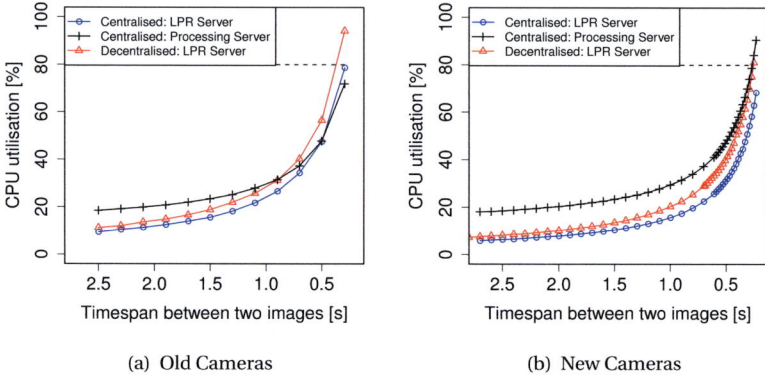

(a) Old Cameras (b) New Cameras

Figure 6.12: Predicted CPU Utilisation in Scenario 4

Speeding components. These two deployment options both have four instances of LPR as a new server node is available.

To represent the new cameras in the prediction model only two model parameters, the size of an image and the probability of an unsuccessful detection, must be changed. Furthermore, we need to adapt the *Stochastic Expression* (StoEx) representing the resource demand within the RD-SEFF of the LPR component to additionally consider the size of the images based on the equation shown above. Finally, the new Cam and LPR instances must be added to the System and Allocation models. Nevertheless, the required modelling time is less than 30 minutes. The results are visualised in Figure 6.12. In contrast to all other scenarios, the bottleneck in the *Centralised* deployment option with the new cameras is the machine hosting the event processing components and not the machines hosting the LPR components. This means that further replication of the LPR component has no influence on the maximum throughput. Comparing the new and old cameras, the maximum throughput can be slightly improved by introducing the new camera version.

6.2.4. Prediction Accuracy Evaluation

When applying the developed performance prediction techniques in the previous section, we assumed that the accuracy of the results is sufficient. In this section, we validate this assumption and compare measurements in our testbed with the predicted values. We set up all the previously presented scenarios in our experimental environment, which is depicted in Figure 6.4. We extended the implementations of the SCOOT, ACIS and Cam components with configurable and scalable event generators. The events emitted by SCOOT and ACIS are based on an event stream recorded in the city of Cambridge. The event generator added to the Cam component uses a set of real images of different vehicles including their license plates. All event generators have in common that the event rate can be specified using a configuration file.

A single run of the prediction series simulates about 100,000 images and its execution lasts about 3 minutes. On a real system, measuring such a set of data will last up to 5 hours or longer. For this reason, we had to limit the number of experiment runs and workload scenarios. For each scenario, we conducted up to seven experiments that cover the whole range from low to high system load. In the following, we present the results of these measurements compared to the predicted values.

Scenario 1: Throughput Analysis

In the base scenario, we used three machines of our experimental environment. On the first one, we deployed ACIS and SCOOT, on the second one the two Cam components, and on the last one the LPR component together with Speeding, Location, and Bus Proximity. In four experiments we ran the system with different event rates of the Cam components. Each experiment run lasts at least 20 minutes in which we measured the mean utilisation of the machine containing the event processing components. Table 6.3 lists the measured and predicted values combined with the calculated prediction error. Overall, the mean prediction error is less than 20% and the maximal error less than 25% and thus sufficient for capacity planning purposes and the evaluation of the maximal throughput.

(a) CPU Utilisation

Image rate per Cam [1/s]	0.67	1	1.43	2	3.33
Measurement [%]	24.78	33.9	54.64	68.63	92.5
Prediction [%]	21.8	30.7	42.4	56.9	92.8
Error	12%	9.4%	22.4%	17.1%	0.3%

(b) Processing Time

Image rate per Cam [1/s]	0.67	1	1.43	2	3.33
Measurement [s]	0.517	0.52	0.637	0.806	2.409
Prediction [s]	0.48	0.485	0.503	0.538	2.09
Error	7.3%	6.9%	21.1%	33.3%	13.2%

Table 6.3: Scenario 1: Model Predictions Compared to Measurements

Scenario 2: Growing Workload

We set up the *AllOnOne* as well as the *Decentralised* deployment option in our testbed. Figure 6.13 visualises the measured and predicted mean CPU utilisation of the LPR server hosting the LPR component as well as the Processing Server hosting the remaining components in the *Decentralised* deployment. Overall, the mean prediction error of the CPU utilisation in this scenario is less than 5%. In both deployment options, the prediction error increases with higher CPU load, which can be explained by caching effects since the algorithm used within the LPR component is very memory-intensive and the high CPU load leads to a higher number of context switches during execution. The measured utilisation under the highest load was lower than expected for both deployment options.

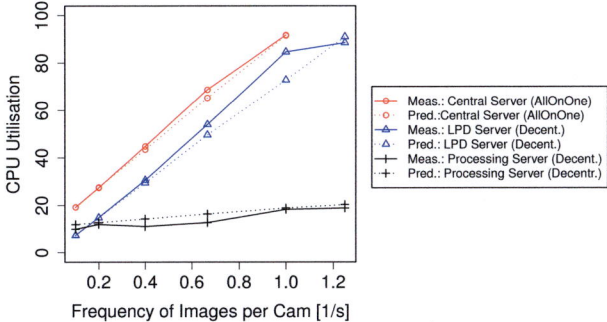

Figure 6.13: Scenario 2: Model Predictions Compared to Measurements

The analysis of the throughput measurements showed that some images were queued up and not processed by the LPR component in cases where the CPU utilisation was higher than 80%. This is an indicator for an overloaded and instable system state. We conducted some more experiments running the system continuously over several hours as well as with an increased event rate. In both cases, the system crashed, which confirms our assumption of an overloaded and instable system state.

Scenario 3: New Components

Again, we set up two deployment options in our testbed. In the centralised deployment, the event processing components with exception of the three instances of LPR are deployed on one machine. In the decentralised option, one instance of Toll and one instance of Speeding are deployed with one instance of LPR on the same machine. Figure 6.14(a) shows the measured and predicted mean utilisation of the machines hosting the LPR component for both deployment options. Additionally, it includes the utilisation of the machine hosting the processing components in the centralised deployment options. We leave out the values for the decentralised deployment options, as they are independent of the image frequency. Overall, the mean prediction error for the CPU utilisation of the machine hosting the LPR component is 11.52% and never exceeded 20%.

Additionally, we compared the measured and predicted processing time within the LPR component. The results are listed in Table 6.4 and vi-

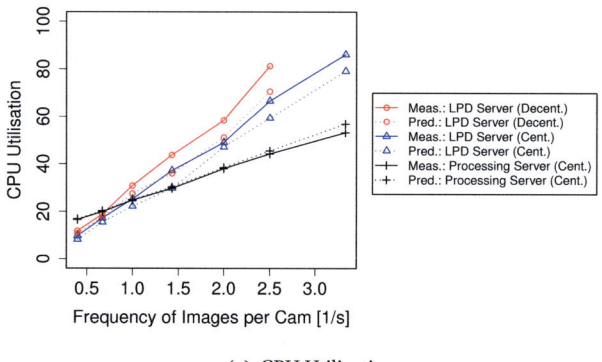

(a) CPU Utilisation

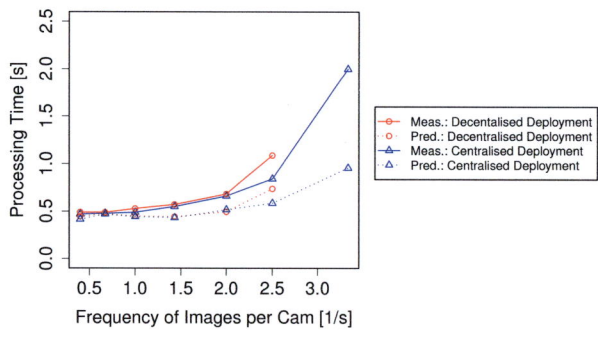

(b) Mean Processing Time of LPR

Figure 6.14: Scenario 3: Model Predictions Compared to Measurements

Image rate per Cam [1/s]		0.4	0.67	1	1.43	2	2.5	3.33
cent.	**Measurement [s]**	0.47	0.48	0.49	0.55	0.66	0.84	1.99
	Prediction [s]	0.41	0.47	0.44	0.43	0.52	0.59	0.96
	Error [%]	12.4	2.0	10.0	21.7	21.7	30.4	52.1
decent.	**Measurement [s]**	0.49	0.48	0.52	0.57	0.68	1.09	-
	Prediction [s]	0.44	0.47	0.44	0.44	0.49	0.73	-
	Error [%]	9.6	2.8	15.0	22.4	27.4	32.2	-

Table 6.4: Scenario 3: LPR Mean Processing Time

sualised in Figure 6.14(b). Under the highest workload, the decentralised deployment option was overloaded and thus these values are not present in the table and figure. Due to the caching effects, which cannot be predicted by the model, the prediction error increases with higher event rates and higher CPU utilisation respectively. However, the mean prediction error is still under 20%.

Scenario 4: Upgraded Hardware

In this scenario, we set up four different variants of the system, in which we varied between the new and the old version of the cameras by changing the images used as input and considering again a centralised and decentralised deployment. The results of the measurements and predictions of the mean CPU utilisation of the machines hosting an instance of the LPR component are shown in Figure 6.15(a). Again the prediction error increases with higher load due to the caching effects induced by the memory intensive algorithm of the LPR. However, the mean prediction error is only 5.56%.

We also analysed the measured and predicted mean processing time within the LPR component. In Figure 6.15(b), we present the processing times of LPR in the scenarios using the improved cameras. The mean prediction error was 5.36% and never exceeded 15%. Similarly to Sce-

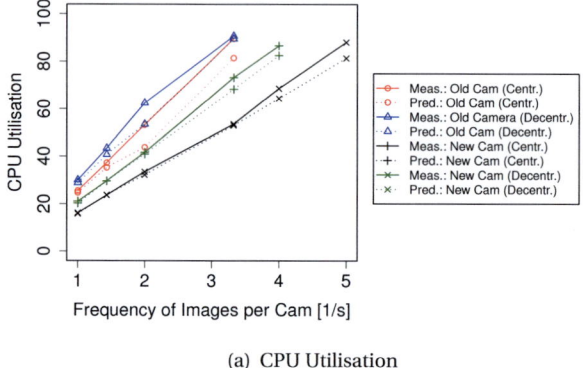

(a) CPU Utilisation

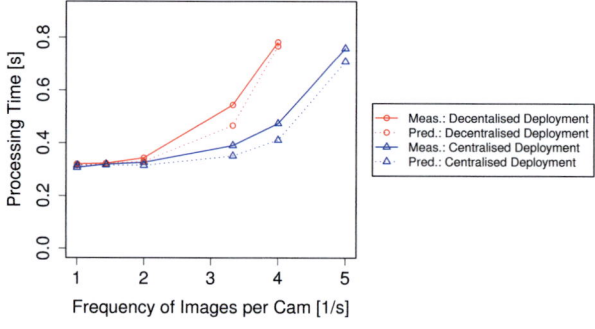

(b) Mean Processing Time of LPR with New Camera

Figure 6.15: Scenario 4: Model Predictions Compared to Measurements

nario 2, the measured CPU utilisation and processing time in the decentralised deployment option are lower than expected since again events were being queued up. The results for an even higher load that completely overloaded the system are not included. To further validate the prediction results, we analysed and compared the results in more detail. Beside the prediction of the aggregated mean processing times, the Pal-

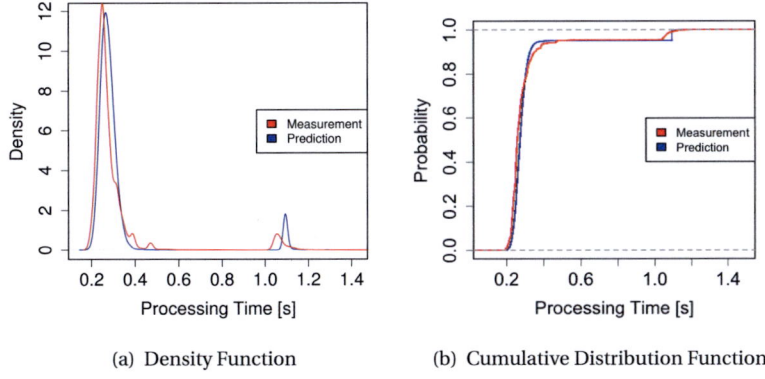

(a) Density Function   (b) Cumulative Distribution Function

Figure 6.16: Processing Time of LPR with 1 Image per Second

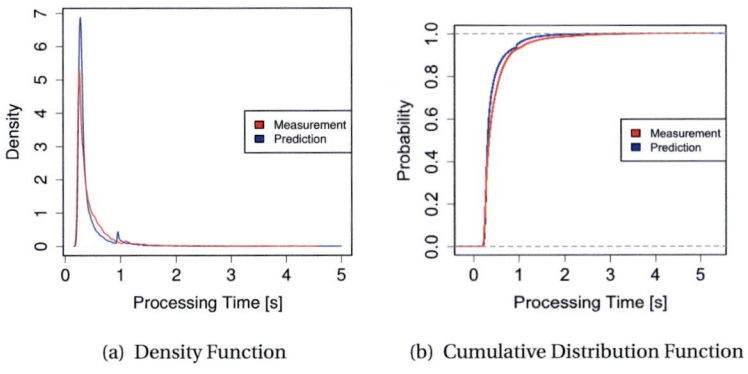

(a) Density Function   (b) Cumulative Distribution Function

Figure 6.17: Processing Time of LPR with 4 Images per Second

ladio approach additionally provides more detailed results in form of a set of individual response times, histograms, and distribution functions to support the analyse of varying response times. Since we measured the individual processing time in our experimental setup, we were able to compare the distributions of the predicted and measured response times. Figure 6.16(a) shows the density function and the *Cumulative Distribution Function* (CDF) of the LPR's processing time in the centralised deployment with new cameras with the load of one image per second for each camera while Figure 6.17(a) shows the same functions for a load of four images per second. The graphs highlight that in addition to the accurately predicted mean values the distributions of predicted and measured values fit quite well.

6.2.5. Evaluation of the Achieved Effort Reduction

To evaluate the improvement in terms of reduced modelling effort that can be achieved using our automated transformation-based modelling and prediction method, we compared the required modelling effort using the approach presented in this thesis with the modelling effort required in a previous manually conducted case study [Rathfelder 09c] based on a subset of the traffic monitoring system. As part of this previous case study, we demonstrated that it is possible to model event-based communication using the original PCM by utilising a set of manual modelling workarounds quite similar to the constructs automatically integrated by our transformations. These workarounds enable the architect to define performance equivalent structures emulating the behaviour of event-based communication. However, their modelling is very time consuming and at the architecture-level, they are semantically incorrect as they are based on synchronous interfaces combined with forks to emulate asynchronous behaviour. With the introduction of new modelling abstractions for an explicit modelling of events, source and sink ports, event channels as well as the respective connectors using our approach

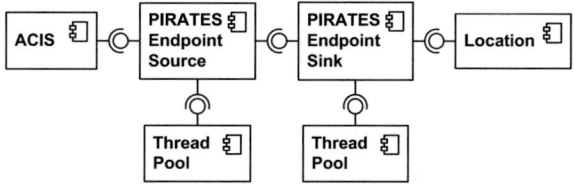

(a) Source to Sink Connection using the Workaround Approach

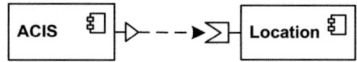

(b) Source to Sink Connection using the
Meta-Model Extension

Figure 6.18: Comparison of Source and Sink Modelling

it is now possible to model event-based interactions in a semantically correct fashion at the architecture-level. Figures 6.18(a) and 6.18(b) illustrate an event-based P2P connection using the workaround and using our modelling approach developed in this thesis. Using the workarounds based on synchronous interfaces combined with forks, event-based and RPC-style connections cannot be distinguished at the architecture-level. In contrast, the new elements make it possible for architects to explicitly differentiate between the two interaction styles.

In addition to enabling the semantically correct modelling of event-based interactions, the new elements significantly reduce the modelling effort. To evaluate this reduction, we tracked the effort in terms of number of elements that need to be created. We did not measure the time required for the creation of the individual elements in order to exclude any influence of the individual experience and training in the usage of Eclipse modelling tools in general and the PCM tool chain in particular. In the first scenario, we create a completely new direct P2P connection between two components. The second scenario adds a new sink to an existing connection and the third one adds a new source. This evaluation is a summary of the results presented in [Klatt 10].

Creation of a new connection We assume, that the source and sink components are already specified and the respective `Assembly-` and `AllocationContext` elements already exist. While the sink component is already equipped with the event handling behaviour and the respective `ProvidedRole`, the source component needs to be extended with the elements required for emitting an event.

Using the manual workarounds, modelling the PIRATES middleware requires three additional components between the sink and source components as depicted in Figure 6.18(a). Two of the components represent the PIRATES endpoints with the respective resource demands, while the third one, ThreadPool, is required to model the single threaded implementation of the PIRATES wrapper. The source and sink endpoint

Element	Manual Workarounds	Using the Model Extensions
Interface / EventGroup	2	1
Signature / EventType	3	1
BasicComponent	3	0
RequiredRole	5	1
ProvidedRole	3	0
RD-SEFF	3	0
ForkAction	1	0
ForkBehaviour	1	0
Call Action	5	1
VariableUsage	5	3
VariableCharacterisation	15	3
AssemblyContext	4	0
Connector	5	1
AllocationContext	4	0
Total	**59**	**11**

Table 6.5: Required Elements to Define a new P2P Connection

components contain the event-specific resource demands and thus are modelled individually for each event type. The ThreadPool component was modelled only once in the Repository and instantiated individually for each wrapper in the system. Thus, the effort tracking counted three new `BasicComponents` and four new `Assembly-` and `AllocationContext` elements. Assuming a new event type, new `OperationInterfaces` including an `OperationSignature` and `Parameter` need to be defined in the Repository model. The RD-SEFF of the source component is extended with an `ExternalCallAction` connected with the `OperationRequiredRole` representing the source port. Furthermore, the RD-SEFFs of the PIRATES endpoints need to be defined so that they forward the event content using multiple `VariableUsages` and `-Characterisations`. A list of all required elements is shown in Table 6.5.

Using our modelling extensions, specifying a new P2P connection requires the definition of an `EventGroup` with an `EventType`. Furthermore, a `SourceRole` that references this `EventGroup` is added to the component and the RD-SEFF is extended with an `EmitEventAction` that references this `SourceRole`. The `EmitEventActions` contain a `VariableUsage` with three `VariableCharacterisations` to instantiate the event. Finally, an `AssemblyEventConnector` links the new `SourceRole` with the `SinkRole` of the sink component.

In summary, the manual approach requires 59 new elements to model a source to sink connection, while using the introduced modelling constructs requires only 11 new elements.

Adding a new sink   In this scenario, we assume that there is already an existing event-based connection between two components and an additional sink component should be added to this interaction by connecting it with the source component.

Using the manual workarounds, adding a new sink requires the extension of the PIRATES EndpointSource component with an additional `OperationRequiredRole` as well as the integration of an additional `ForkedBehaviour` including an `ExternalCallAction` into the RD-SEFF of this component. The `ExternalCallAction` is connected with the new `OperationRequiredRole` and contains a `VariableUsage` and three `VariableCharacterisations` to forward the event content. The `OperationInterface` referenced by the `OperationRequiredRole` is already existing and thus can be reused. Furthermore, new `Assembly-` and `AllocationContexts` for the new components as well as `AssemblyConnectors` connecting them need to be created.

Using the proposed modelling extensions, only one new `AssemblyEventConnector` between the existing `SourceRole` and the `SinkRole` are necessary. As listed in Table 6.6, the workarounds re-

Element	Manual Workarounds	Using the Model Extensions
Interface / EventGroup	0	0
Signature / EventType	0	0
BasicComponent	0	0
RequiredRole	1	0
ProvidedRole	0	0
RD-SEFF	0	0
ForkAction	0	0
Fork Behaviour	1	0
CallAction	1	0
VariableUsage	1	0
VariableCharacterisation	3	0
AssemblyContext	2	0
Connector	3	1
AllocationContext	2	0
Total	**14**	**1**

Table 6.6: Required Elements to Add an Additional Sink

quire 14 new elements while using our extended meta-model requires only one new element.

Adding a new source In this last scenario, we assume an existing connection between a source and three sink components. This interaction should be extended by integrating a new source component and connecting it to the already existing sink.

In analogy to the first scenario, the manual approach requires a new `RequiredOperationRole` added to the source component referencing the `OperationInterface` already defined in the Repository model for the existing connection. Additionally, the RD-SEFF of the source needs to be extended with an `ExternalCallAction` and the required `VariableUsage` and `-Characterisation` elements. A new source component also implies a new EndpointSource component as each source component can be connected with a different num-

Element	Manual Workarounds	Using the Model Extensions
Interface / EventGroup	0	0
Signature / EventType	0	0
BasicComponent	1	0
RequiredRole	3	0
ProvidedRole	1	0
RD-SEFF	1	0
ForkAction	1	0
ForkBehaviour	1	0
Call Action	4	1
VariableUsage	4	1
VariableCharacterisation	12	3
AssemblyContext	2	0
Connector	3	1
AllocationContext	2	0
Total	**35**	**6**

Table 6.7: Required Elements for Adding a Source

ber of sinks. The new EndpointSource component contains two `Op-erationRequiredRoles`, one connected with the `OperationIn-terface` representing the event and one referencing the ThreadPool interface. The RD-SEFF includes a `ForkAction` with `ForkedBe-haviours` as well as three `ExternalCallActions`. One of these actions contains a `VariableUsage` and three `VariableCharacter-isations` to forward the event, while the remaining two actions call the require and release operations of the ThreadPool interface. Furthermore, the component contains an `OperationProvidedRole` to be connected with the source component. Several `Assembly-` and `Al-locationContexts` as well as `AssemblyConnectors` are required to describe the instantiation, composition and deployment of the components. All created elements are listed in Table 6.7.

Using the new modelling extensions, a new `SourceRole` is added to the source component and a new `EmitEventAction` with `Vari-ableUsage` and `-Characterisation` elements is integrated into the RD-SEFF. A new `AssemblyEventConnector` connecting the new `SourceRole` with the already existing `SinkRole` completes the model. Table 6.7 lists the created elements and shows that the modelling extensions reduce the modelling effort in term of required element creations from 35 down to only 6.

Summary of Modelling Effort Reduction   Table 6.8 summarises the effort reduction that can be achieved with our approach compared to using manual workarounds. The manual modelling approach reuses existing components as far as possible, but adding a new sink for example requires the extension of the component splitting the control-flow with an additional required interface and the respective specification of the component behaviour with an additional fork. For a completely new connection, the required effort was reduced from 59 to only 11 elements, which is an effort reduction of 81.3%. Adding an additional sink was re-

| Change Scenario | No. of Elements | | Effort Reduction |
	Manual	Extended	
New Connection	59	11	81,3%
Add Sink	14	1	92,8%
Add Source	35	6	82,8%

Table 6.8: Reduction of Modelling Effort

duced to create only one element instead of 14 with the old approach (effort reduction 92.8%). The effort for adding an additional source was reduced from 35 to 6 elements (effort reduction 82.8%). Although these numbers are only rough indicators of the overall effort in terms of time or money, they still demonstrate that the modelling effort is significantly reduced.

6.2.6. Summary of the Traffic Monitoring Case Study

As part of the presented traffic monitoring case study, all three evaluation goals established in Section 6.1 were considered. The evaluation of the prediction accuracy showed that the prediction error for CPU utilisation and response time is less than 20% in most cases and the maximum error of the always underestimated CPU utilisation never exceeded 25%. With this accuracy, the performance prediction can improve the system performance and efficiency significantly given that today's systems are normally over-provisioned by a factor of 2 or more [Kaplan 08].

The evaluation of multiple design alternatives in different system evolution stages, demonstrated the applicability of our approach to model and evaluate distributed EBS built on top of a decentralised peer-to-peer middleware. Thanks to the automated prediction process (Sec. 6.2.3), the only manual task that needs to be performed was the adaptation of the architecture-level model. As already mentioned in the different scenarios, the adaptation of the models could be done with a time effort of less than 30 minutes in all cases. The execution of the prediction process is then fully automated.

To evaluate the effort reduction achieved with our process automation in comparison to executing measurements on a test system, we compare the required time to execute the prediction with the time required to conduct equivalent measurements on our test system. One simulation run, which consists of 100000 simulated events, takes about 3 minutes on a MacBook Pro with Core i7 processor and 8 GB RAM. Assuming the highest event rate of five images per camera per second, this corresponds to a time span of 2.7 hours to collect the same amount of measurements in the testbed. For lower event rates the required time can be a whole day or more. Even neglecting the time required to setup the test system, the effort reduction using the proposed modelling and prediction approach compared to running experiments in the testbed was 98,7% or higher. Thanks to the automated parameter variation, different load situations can be evaluated automatically in less than one hour which might require several days of measurements on the test system to obtain the same results.

In [Rathfelder 10a], we presented a first proof-of-concept model demonstrating the use of manual modelling workarounds to realise a performance model of a simplified version of the traffic monitoring system. We compared the required modelling effort for typical modelling activities, like adding sinks or sources, using these manual workarounds as opposed to using the modelling extensions proposed in this thesis. The results indicate that the presented extensions combined with our automated model-to-model transformation reduce the modelling effort by up to 80% compared to using the original PCM.

6.3. SPECjms2007 Case Study

The application we consider in this case study is the SPECjms2007[1] standard benchmark [SPEC 07]. While the distributed traffic monitoring system used in the previous case study is based on a decentralised peer-to-peer based middleware, the SPECjms2007 benchmark is built on top of a centralised MOM server supporting the JMS standard. The two case studies are complementary and represent the two main classes of EBS and thus allow us to demonstrate the applicability of our modelling and prediction approach for a wide range of different EBS. The SPECjms2007 benchmark was developed by SPEC's Java Subcommittee with the participation of IBM, Sun, Oracle, BEA Systems, Sybase, Apache, JBoss, and TU Darmstadt. It is designed to be representative of real-world messaging applications based on a scenario in the supply chain management domain [Sachs 09]. The benchmark workload comprises a set of supply chain interactions between a supermarket company, its stores, its distribution centres, and its suppliers. The interactions represent a complex transaction mix exercising both P2P and Pub/Sub interactions including one-to-one, one-to-many and many-to-many communication [Sachs 09]. The benchmark covers the major message types used in practice including messages of different sizes and different delivery modes, i.e., persistent vs. non-persistent, transactional vs. non-transactional. Due to its high complexity, mix of different types of interactions, and workloads, and the involvement of different resources (e.g. CPU, network and hard disk), SPECjms2007 provides an ideal setting to further evaluate the applicability and expressiveness of our approach. Analysing the prediction accuracy, allows us to demonstrate that our prediction approach can handle very complex scenarios with differ-

---

[1]SPECjms2007 is a trademark of the *Standard Performance Evaluation Corporation* (SPEC). The results or findings in this thesis have not been reviewed or accepted by SPEC, therefore no comparison nor performance inference can be made against any published SPEC result. The official web site for SPECjms2007 is located at http://www.spec.org/osg/jms2007.

ent workload mixes and thus validate its applicability for realistic industrial systems. After introducing the general application scenario, we provide more details on the different interactions and the workload mixture within the benchmark.

6.3.1. Application and Scenario

The application scenario is the supply chain management of a supermarket company where *Radio-Frequency Identification* (RFID) technology is used to track the flow of goods. The participants involved are the supermarket company, its stores, its distribution centres and its suppliers. The scenario offers an excellent basis for defining interactions that stress different subsets of the functionality offered by MOM servers supporting event-based interactions, e.g., different message types as well as both P2P and Pub/Sub communication. Moreover, it offers a natural way to scale the workload, e.g., by scaling the number of supermarkets (horizontal) or by scaling the amount of products sold per supermarket (vertical). The participants involved can be grouped into the following four roles illustrated in Figure 6.19:

1. ***Company Headquarters* (HQ)** is responsible for managing the accounting of the company. The HQ monitors the flow of goods and money in the supply chain. It manages information about the goods and products offered in the supermarket stores and defines the selling prices of products.

2. ***Supermarket*s (SMs)** sell goods to end customers. In the SPECjms2007 scenario, the focus is set on the management of the inventory of supermarkets including their warehouses. Each SM is connected to at least one distribution centre responsible to supply the SM with products when they run out of stock.

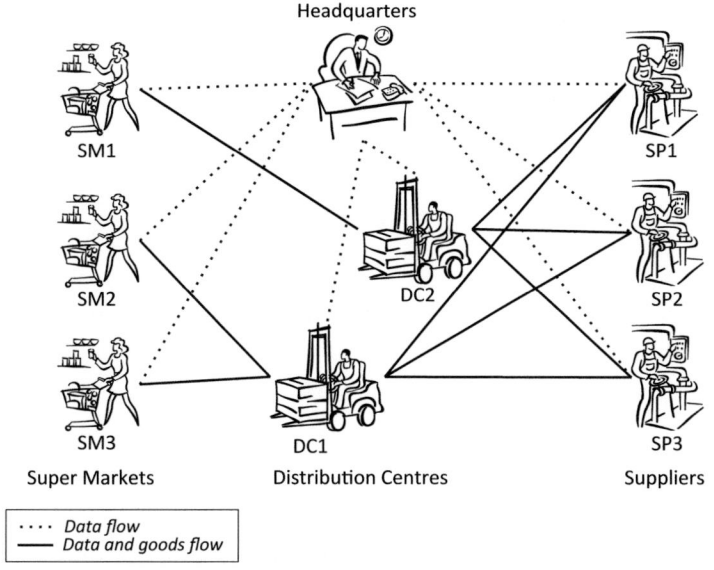

Figure 6.19: Overview of the SPECjms2007 Scenario

3. **Distribution Centres (DCs)** supply the supermarket stores. Each DC takes orders from SMs and if necessary orders products from suppliers and delivers them to the SM. Additionally, DCs are responsible to provide sale statistics to the HQ.

4. **Suppliers (SPs)** are specialised for different sets of products, which they supply to the DCs on demand. In contrast to SMs and DCs, SPs are independent companies and not part of the supermarket company. Their information systems are integrated into the supply chain management system of the supermarket company using standardised message formats.

SPECjms2007 is implemented as a Java application comprising multiple JVMs and threads distributed across a set of client nodes. For every destination, there is a separate Java class called *Event Handler* that encapsulates the application logic executed to process messages sent to that destination. In addition to the event handlers, for every physical location, a set of threads (referred to as *Driver Threads*) is launched to drive the benchmark interactions that are logically started at that location.

Interactions and Workload Characterisation

The SPECjms2007 benchmark defines several interactions that represent different types of messaging workloads stressing different aspects of the middleware including both workloads focused on P2P as well as workloads focused on Pub/Sub communication. The workflow of the seven interactions is shown in Figure 6.20-6.22. Interactions 1, 4 and 5 exercise P2P messaging whereas Interactions 3, 6 and 7 exercise Pub/Sub messaging. Interaction 2 contains both P2P and Pub/Sub communication. The interactions involve different components as described in the following based on the description given in [Sachs 07]:

- **Interaction 1: Order/Shipment Handling between SM and DC**
  This interaction exercises persistent P2P messaging between the SMs and DCs. The interaction is triggered when goods in the warehouse of a SM are depleted and the SM has to order from its DC to refill stock. The following steps are followed as illustrated in Figure 6.20:

  1. A SM sends an order to its DC.

  2. The DC sends a confirmation to the SM and ships the ordered goods.

  3. Goods are registered by RFID readers upon leaving the DC warehouse.

  4. The DC sends information about the transaction to the HQ (sales statistics).

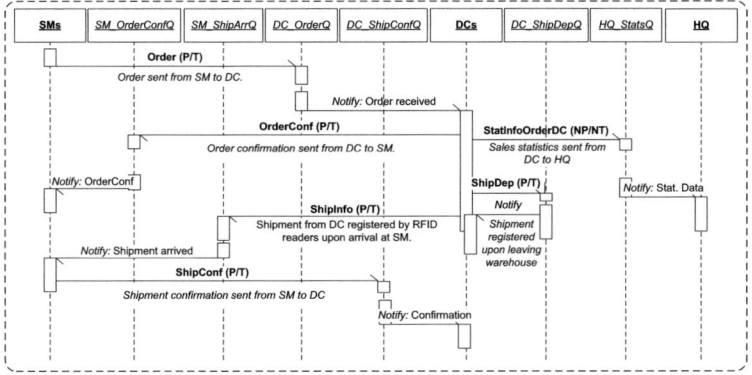

(N)P=(Non-)Persistent, (N)T=(Non-)Transactional

Figure 6.20: Workflow of the SPECjms2007 Interation 1 [Sachs 09]

5. The shipment arrives at the SM and is registered by RFID readers upon entering the SM warehouse.

6. A confirmation is sent to the DC.

- **Interaction 2: Order/Shipment Handling between DC and SP**

This interaction exercises persistent P2P and Pub/Sub (durable) messaging between the DCs and SPs. The interaction is triggered when goods in a DC are depleted and the DC has to order from a SP to refill stock. The following steps are followed as illustrated in Figure 6.21:

1. A DC sends a call for offers to all SPs that supply the types of goods that need to be ordered.

2. SPs that can deliver the goods send offers to the DC.

3. Based on the offers, the DC selects a SP and sends a purchase order to it.

4. The SP sends a confirmation to the DC and an invoice to the HQ. It then ships the ordered goods.

5. The shipment arrives at the DC and is registered by RFID readers upon entering the DC's warehouse.

6. The DC sends a delivery confirmation to the SP.

7. The DC sends transaction statistics to the HQ.

- **Interaction 3: Price Updates sent from HQ to SMs**
  This interaction exercises persistent, durable Pub/Sub messaging between the HQ and the SMs as illustrated in Figure 6.22. The interaction is triggered when selling prices are changed by the company administration. To communicate this, the company HQ sends messages with pricing information to the SMs.

- **Interaction 4: Inventory Management inside SMs**
  This interaction exercises persistent P2P messaging inside the SMs. The interaction is triggered when goods leave the warehouse of a SM (to refill a shelf). Goods are registered by RFID readers and the local warehouse application is notified so that inventory can be updated.

- **Interaction 5: Sales Statistics sent from SMs to HQ**
  This interaction, which is illustrated in Figure 6.22, exercises non-persistent P2P messaging between the SMs and the HQ. The interaction is triggered when a SM sends sales statistics to the HQ. HQ can use this data as a basis for data mining in order to study customer behaviour and provide useful information to marketing.

- **Interaction 6: New Product Announcements sent from HQ to SMs**
  This interaction exercises non-persistent, non-durable Pub/Sub

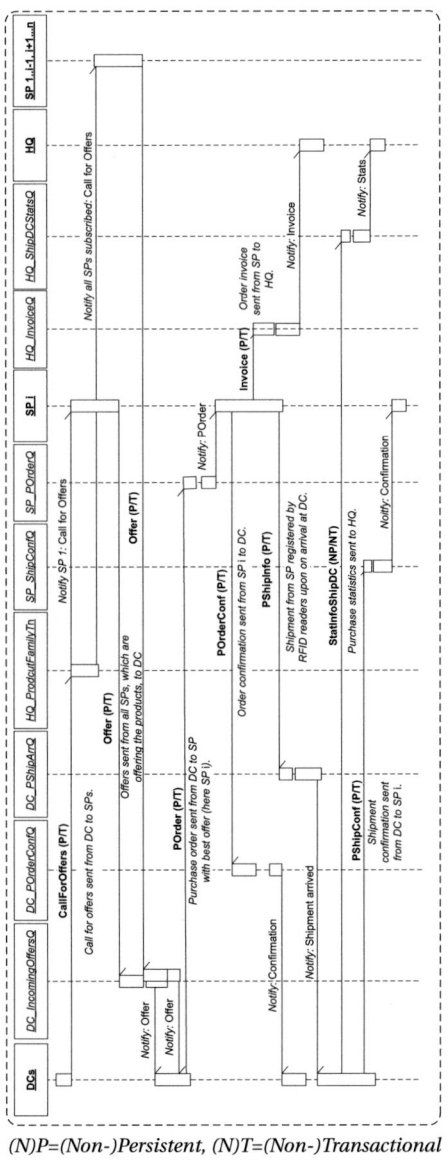

(N)P=(Non-)Persistent, (N)T=(Non-)Transactional

Figure 6.21: Workflow of the SPECjms2007 Interation 2 [Sachs 09]

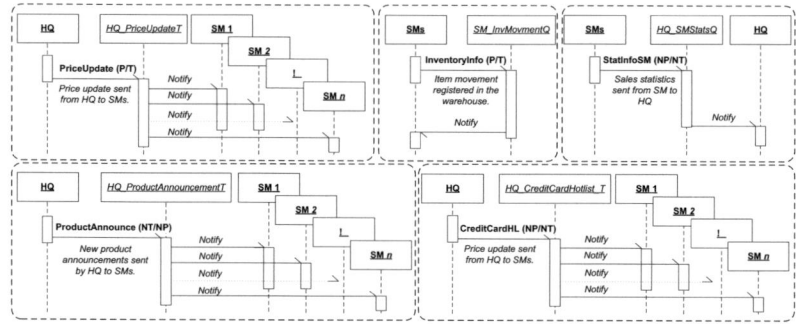

(N)P=(Non-)Persistent, (N)T=(Non-)Transactional

Figure 6.22: Workflow of the SPECjms2007 Interactions 3 to 7 [Sachs 09]

messaging between the HQ and the SMs. The interaction is triggered when new products are announced by the company administration. To communicate this, the HQ sends messages with product information to the SMs selling the respective product types.

- **Interaction 7: Credit Card Hot Lists sent from HQ to SMs**
  As illustrated in Figure 6.22, this interaction exercises non-
  persistent, non-durable Pub/Sub messaging between the HQ and
  the SMs. The interaction is triggered when the HQ sends credit
  card hot lists to the SMs (complete list once every hour and incre-
  mental updates as required).

As part of the interactions, a number of different event types with different characteristics (e.g., persistent vs. non-persistent, different message types) are used. Table 6.9 gives an overview on these events and
their individual characteristics. The size of messages depends on their
content structure (e.g., the number of order lines or the number of new
products that are announced). To reflect this variation of the message
size, the benchmark driver probabilistically varies the size of the generated messages between three values, namely size A with 95% probability,

Table 6.9: Message Types Overview [Sachs 11]

Intr.	Message	Type	Size (in KBytes)			Delivery	
			A (95%)	B (4%)	C (1%)	Destination	Prop.
1	order	Object	2.02	7.39	41.29	Queue (DC)	P, T
	orderConf	Object	0.22	1.67	10.83	Queue (SM)	P, T
	shipDep	Text	1.28	8.76	55.95	Queue (DC)	P, T
	statInfoOrder	Stream	1.12	8.59	55.79	Queue (HQ)	NP, NT
	shipInfo	Text	1.74	7.10	41.01	Queue (SM)	P, T
	shipConf	Object	0.81	2.73	14.83	Queue (DC)	P, T
2	callForOffer	Text	1.35	7.06	36.52	Topic (HQ)	P, T
	offer	Text	1.69	9.65	50.71	Queue (DC)	P, T
	pOrder	Text	1.86	9.85	51.07	Queue (SP)	P, T
	pOrderConf	Text	2.07	9.79	49.56	Queue (DC)	P, T
	invoice	Text	1.70	7.92	39.95	Queue (HQ)	P, T
	pShipInfo	Text	0.98	3.62	17.26	Queue (DC)	P, T
	pShipConf	Text	1.01	3.65	17.29	Queue (SP)	P, T
	statInfoShip	Stream	1.02	3.68	17.38	Queue (HQ)	NP, NT
3	priceUpdate	Map	0.24	0.24	0.24	Topic (HQ)	P, T
4	inventoryInfo	Text	1.48	10.22	49.03	Queue (SM)	P, T
5	statInfo	Object	Avg=5.27			Queue (HQ)	NP, NT
6	product-Announcement	Stream	1.21	2.80	10.51	Topic (HQ)	NP, NT
7	creditCardHL	Stream	1.01	8.49	50.00	Topic (HQ)	NP, NT

(N)P=(Non-)Persistent, (N)T=(Non-)Transactional

size B with 4% probability, and size C with 1% probability. A linear function is used to determine the size of a new message:

$$Size(m) = X_{m,T} \cdot a_m + b_m, \text{ with } T \in \{A, B, C\}$$

The coefficients a_m and b_m have fixed values defined as part of the benchmark specification, while the values of the matrix $X_{m,T}$ can be configured by the user running the benchmark. There are two exceptions of this variation mechanism. The priceUpdate messages of Interaction3 always have a constant size that cannot be changed and the statIn-foSM messages used in Interaction 5 are configured using two sizing parameters $X_{m,T}$ and $Y_{m,T}$. More details on the message size configuration and the values of the different coefficients can be found in [Sachs 11]. Table 6.9 lists the message sizes used in our benchmark configuration. The size of statInfoSM varies between 4.7 and 24.78 KBytes. As its size depends on two parameters, the table only lists the average values. The sizes of the messages used in the various interactions have been chosen to reflect typical message sizes in real-life applications.

SPECjms2007 was developed to support performance and scalability analysis of MOM systems. It allows to scale the system and its workload in two dimensions. In the *horizontal scaling*, the number of participating SMs, DCs and SPs and thus the number of destinations in the form of topics and queues is increased while the message rate per destination is kept constant. In the *vertical scaling*, the number of messages per destination is increased, while the number of queues and topics is kept constant. The SPECjms2007 benchmark provides two configurable topologies (*horizontal* and *vertical topology*) that support the analysis of the two scaling dimensions [Sachs 11]. In both topologies, a central parameter called *BASE* is used to specify and vary the load on the system. The rate (λ_i) at which each interaction is initiated is calculated using the following equation:

$$\lambda_i = BASE \cdot c_i$$

In this case study, we intentionally slightly deviate from the standard vertical topology to avoid presenting performance results that may be compared against standard SPECjms2007 results. The latter is prohibited by the SPECjms2007 run and reporting rules. Table 6.10 lists the factors that are required to calculate the individual interaction rates based on the value of the *BASE* parameter. The selected topology is based on the vertical topology with 10 SMs, 2 DCs, 1 HQ and 2 SPs.

Table 6.10: Interaction Scaling Factor

c_1	c_2	c_3	c_4	c_5	c_6	c_7
0.761905	0.213332	0.05	1.621622	5.77200	0.142315	0.102564

6.3.2. Architecture-level Model for Performance Evaluation

The architecture-level model of the SPECjms2007 benchmark consists of the following sub-models.

Component Repository

Figure 6.23 provides an overview on the *Component Repository* used the SPECjms2007 case study. For the sake of clarity, the illustration omits some elements, like component parameters, service effect specifications, or passive resources that are part of the graphical views provided by the PCM modelling tool. For each of the 19 messages used within the different interactions and listed in Table 6.9, we defined an individual event type. The different participants in the interactions, namely HQ, SM, DC, and SP are modelled as individual components. For each component, we specified the source and sink roles referring to the event type that can be emitted or received by the component. The focus of SPECjms2007 is on the evaluation of the underlying communication middleware. Therefore, in contrast to the traffic monitoring case study, the business logic of the different component implementations is simplified to reduce the influences of the component implementations on the overall system performance. For this reason, the RD-SEFF specifying the event handling do not include any resource demands. Nevertheless, they reflect the control flow of the interactions as described in the previous section and include one or more EventEmitActions to instantiate and emit events like the ShipConf event that is sent in response to a received ShipInfo event. In order to enable a centralised configuration of the events' characteristics, the components include individual Com-

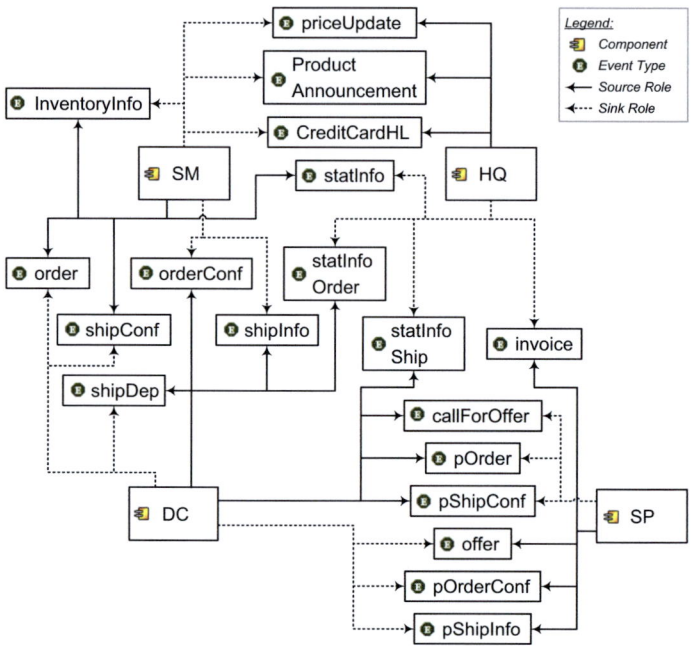

Figure 6.23: Component Repository of the SPECjms2007 Case Study

`ponentParameters` for each event they emit. Similarly to the traffic monitoring case study, we defined additional `OperationInterfaces` for each interaction that are later used to connect the components with the *Usage Model*.

Middleware Repository

The SPECjms2007 benchmark is focused on evaluating the performance and scalability of the MOM server implementations, thus the specification and calibration of the *Middleware Repository* is an important factor of the accuracy of our performance prediction models. For each event type, we measured the resource demands for CPU and HDD resources

Table 6.11: Event-specific Resource Demands on the Middleware Server [ms]

Intr.	Message	CPU			HDD		
		Size A	Size B	Size C	Size A	Size B	Size C
1	orderConf	0.973	0.987	1.846	0.081	0.067	0.146
	statInfoOrder	0.053	0.112	0.242	na		
	shipInfo	0.616	1.170	2.501	0.051	0.080	0.198
	shipDep	0.539	1.148	2.494	0.045	0.078	0.198
	order	0.838	0.948	1.833	0.065	0.069	0.145
	shipConf	0.390	0.365	0.663	0.032	0.025	0.053
2	callForOffers	0.343	0.403	0.946	0.045	0.077	0.117
	callForOffers Notification	0.130	0.153	0.359	0.017	0.029	0.044
	offer	0.452	0.831	1.945	0.033	0.056	0.176
	pOrder	0.921	1.097	2.580	0.121	0.209	0.318
	pShipConf	0.406	0.500	0.873	0.066	0.078	0.108
	statInfoShip	0.053	0.112	0.242	na		
	pOrderConf	1.025	1.090	2.504	0.134	0.208	0.309
	invoice	0.842	0.882	2.018	0.110	0.168	0.249
	pShipInfo	0.485	0.403	0.872	0.064	0.077	0.108
3	priceUpdate	0.501			0.118		
	priceUpdate Notification	0.458			0.027		
4	inventoryInfo	0.895	1.447	2.985	0.068	0.140	0.267
5	statInfo	0.444			na		
6	product-Announcement	0.164	0.177	0.168	na		
	product-Announcement Notification	0.034	0.024	0.177	na		
7	creditCardHL	0.096	0.364	0.430	na		
	creditCardHL Notification	0.039	0.144	0.841	na		

on the client and server side. In case of Pub/Sub communication, we differentiate between the resource demands caused by the event received from the source and the resource demands induced by the notifications sent to the subscribed sinks. We estimated the demands by running the interactions in isolation and measuring the utilisation of the respective resources using *Operating System* (OS) tools on the sender, middleware and sink sides. For interactions consisting of multiple messages, the demands of the individual messages were estimated by considering their relative fraction of the whole interaction. To derive the resource demands of notification messages, we repeated the experiments with different numbers of subscribers and used linear regression to estimate the resource demands. Table 6.11 lists the event-specific resource demands on CPU and HDD for the middleware server. Based on the utilisation measurements provided by OS tools and the data provided by the measurement framework of the benchmark, we could derive the resource demands on the network resource only at the granularity of complete interactions. Table 6.12 lists, the interaction-specific in- and outgoing network demands.

As illustrated in Figure 6.24, the *Middleware Repository* consists of three components providing the five middleware interfaces. The JMSSource components provides the interface handleSourcePort reflecting the event processing and resource consumption on the source side. The RD-SEFF implementing the interface contains a BranchAction with several GuardedBranchTransissions one for each event type. Within these branches the event-specific resource demands

Table 6.12: Interaction-specific Network Demands [ms]

Interaction		1	2	3	4	5	6	7
LAN	In	4.097	2.564	5.467	15.584	12.782	65.127	42.117
	Out	4.014	2.222	2.287	15.172	12.781	7.979	5.218

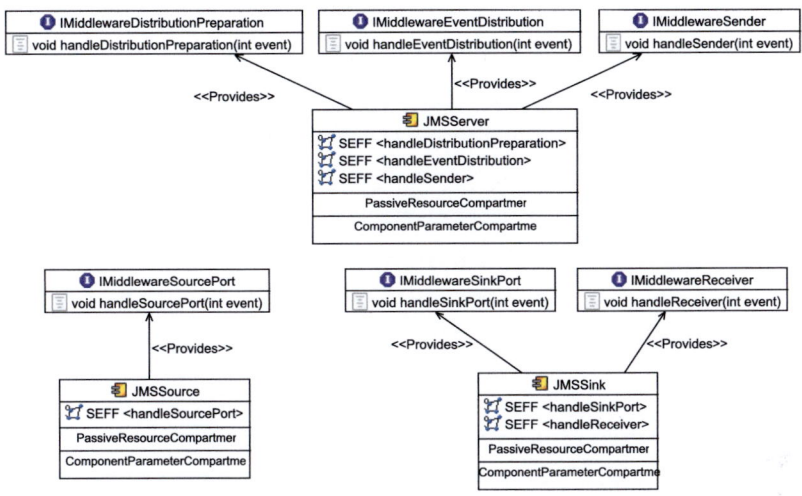

Figure 6.24: Middleware Repository of the SPECjms2007 Case Study

for CPU and HDD are specified. Similarly, the `JMSSink` component more precisely the RD-SEFF implementing the `handleSinkPort` operation includes the event-specific resource demands induced on the sink side. The `JMSServer` component, which represents the event processing within the JMS server, needs to distinguish between the resource demands induced by a message received from sources and the messages sent to the subscribed sinks. Especially in the case of Pub/Sub communication, this separation is essential, as the resource demands for forwarding messages to the subscribed sinks depend on the number of connected sinks. The RD-SEFF implementing the `handleSource-Communication` interface includes event type and size dependent resource demands for CPU and HDD required for processing the message received from the respective source. Furthermore, it includes the demands on the LAN resource representing the inbound network traffic. The RD-SEFF implementing the `handleSinkCommunication` interface contains the resource demands required for delivering the message to one of the subscribed sinks. In analogy to the other RD-SEFFs, we use a combination of `BranchAction` with `GuardedBranchTransissions` to model the event-specific resource demands. We use an exponential distribution function $Exp(\lambda)$ with $1/\lambda = D$ to specify the resource demand D. The expressiveness of the StoEx language allows us to specify messagesize-dependent resource demands within an `InternalAction` using the ?-operator. As an example, the following expression shows the specification of the CPU demands induced for processing the `inventoryInfo` message:

```
(event.TYPE=="A" ?  Exp(1.11732844):0) +
(event.TYPE=="B" ?  Exp(0.691085):0) +
(event.TYPE=="C" ?  Exp(0.33500838):0)
```

System Model

Corresponding to the SPECjms2007 system topology, we instantiated the components SM, DC, HQ, and SP within the *System Model*. For each Pub-/Sub communication, we defined a dedicated `EventChannel`. For the sake of clarity, Figure 6.25 only shows an excerpt from the *System Model* covering Interactions 1 and 3. In case of P2P communication, the event connector directly connects sinks and sources, while in case of Pub/Sub communication, we first defined a `EventChannel` and then connected the respective sources and sinks with this channel.

Resource Environment and Allocation Model

The *Resource Environment* consists of several `ResourceContainers`. We defined the available resources according to the hardware available in our experimental environment, depicted in Figure 6.26. For example, the `ResourceContainer` hosting the middleware server contains a `ProcessingResource` representing the CPU with processor sharing on 8

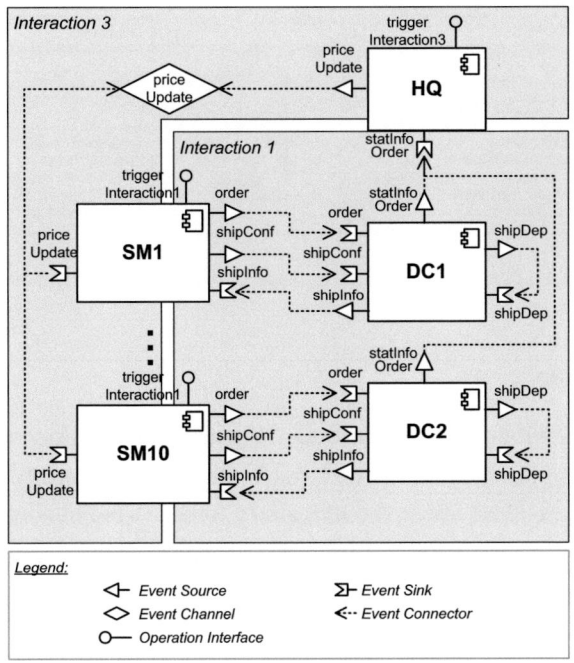

Figure 6.25: System Model Covering Interaction 1 and 3

cores as scheduling strategy. The LAN and HDD resources are modelled as `ProcessingResources` with *first-come-first-serve* (FCFS) scheduling. As all resource demands are specified in milliseconds, we set the processing rate of all resources to 1000 working units per second. In the allocation model, we deployed the different component instances of the system (HQ, SMs, DCs, and SPs) on `ResourceContainers` matching the deployment of the benchmark in our experimental environment. All `EventChannels` are allocated on the central middleware server. The deployment of the middleware specific-components is automatically generated by the transformation described in Chapter 5.

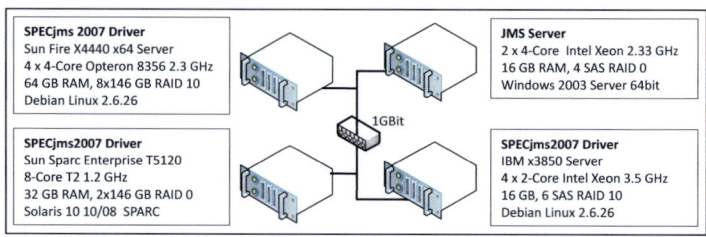

Figure 6.26: Experimental Environment of the SPECjms2007 Benchmark

Usage Model

The *Usage Model* contains a dedicated `UsageProfile` for each interaction. Each of these `UsageProfiles` includes a call of one of the trigger interfaces specified within the *Repository Model*. Using separate `Usage-Profiles` enables us to specify individual rates for each interaction or completely deactivate them if necessary.

6.3.3. Prediction Accuracy Evaluation

As already mentioned, we use a slightly adapted system topology to avoid presenting performance results that may be compared against standard SPECjms2007 results, which is prohibited by the SPECjms2007 run and reporting rules. We use a topology based on the benchmark's vertical topology with the number of DC and HQ instances each set to 10. With the aim to evaluate the accuracy of the model predictions individually for P2P and Pub/Sub communication but also for mixed workloads, we defined the following scenarios as combinations of the different benchmark interactions:

- *Scenario 1:* A mix of all seven interactions exercising both P2P and Pub/Sub messaging.

Table 6.13: Scenario Transaction Mix

			Sc. 1			Sc. 2	Sc. 3
			In	Out	Overall		
No. of Msg.	P2P	P/T	49.2%	40.7%	44.6%	21.0%	-
		NP/NT	47.2%	39.0%	42.8%	79.0%	-
	Pub/Sub	P/T	1.8%	6.0%	4.1%	-	17.0%
		NP/NT	1.7%	14.2%	8.5%	-	83.0%
	Overall	P/T	51.1%	46.7%	48.7%	21.0%	17.0%
		NT/NP	48.9%	53.3%	51.3%	79.0%	83.0%
Traffic	P2P	P/T	32.2%	29.5%	30.8%	11.0%	-
		NP/NT	66.6%	61.0%	63.5%	89.0%	-
	Pub/Sub	P/T	0.5%	2.3%	1.6%	-	3.0%
		NP/NT	0.8%	7.2%	4.1%	-	97.0%
	Overall	P/T	32.7%	31.8%	32.4%	11.0%	3.0%
		NT/NP	67.3%	68.2%	67.6%	89.0%	97.0%
Avg. Size (in KBytes)	P2P	P/T	2.13			2.31	-
		NP/NT	4.59			5.27	-
	Pub/Sub	P/T	1.11			-	0.24
		NP/NT	1.49			-	1.49
	Overall	P/T	2.00			2.31	0.24
		NT/NP	3.76			5.27	1.49

For Scenario 2 & 3: In = Out

- *Scenario 2:* A mix of Interactions 4 and 5 focused on P2P messaging.

- *Scenario 3:* A mix of Interactions 3, 6 and 7 focused on Pub/Sub messaging.

Table 6.13 and Figure 6.27 provide a detailed workload characterisation of the three scenarios to illustrate the differences in terms of transaction mix and message size distribution.

Experimental Environment

To evaluate the accuracy of our modelling and prediction approach, we conducted an experimental analysis of the modelled application in the

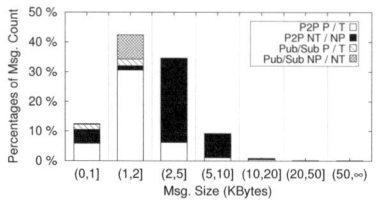
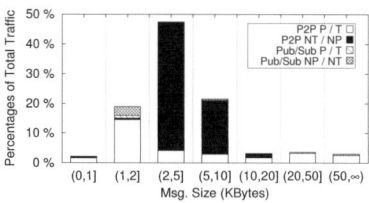

(a) Scenario 1

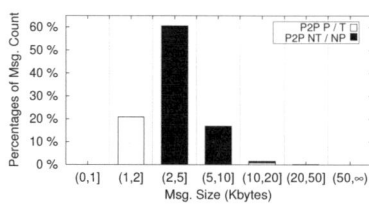
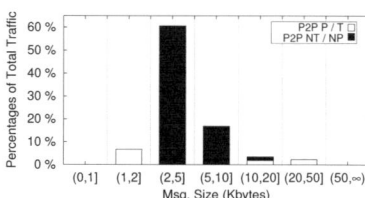

(b) Scenario 2

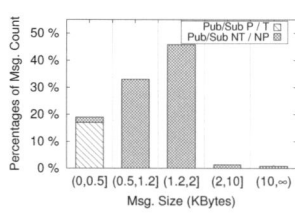
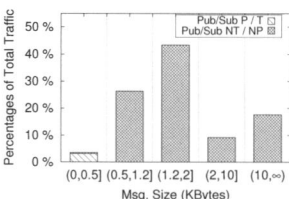

(c) Scenario 3

Figure 6.27: Message Size Distribution

environment depicted in Figure 6.26. A leading commercial message-oriented middleware platform was used as a centralised JMS server installed on a machine with two quad-core Intel Xeon 2.33 GHz CPUs and 16 GB of main memory. The server ran in a 64-bit 1.5 JVM with 8 GB of heap space. A RAID 0 disk array comprised of four disk drives was used for maximum performance. The JMS Server was configured to use a file-based store for persistent messages with a 3.8 GB message buffer. The SPECjms2007 drivers were distributed across three machines: i) one Sun Fire X4440 x64 server with four quad-core Opteron 2.3 GHz CPUs and 64 GB of main memory, ii) one Sun Sparc Enterprise T5120 server with one 8-core T2 1.2 GHz CPU and 32 GB of main memory and iii) one IBM x3850 server with four dual-core Intel Xeon 3.5 GHz CPUs and 16 GB of main memory. All machines were connected to a 1 GBit network.

Experimental Results

In each case, the model was analysed using simulations with at least 100000 simulated transactions in each simulation run. The SPECjms2007 benchmark provides a central parameter named $BASE$ to configure the workload intensity. Figure 6.28 shows the predicted and measured CPU utilisation of the MOM server for the considered cus-

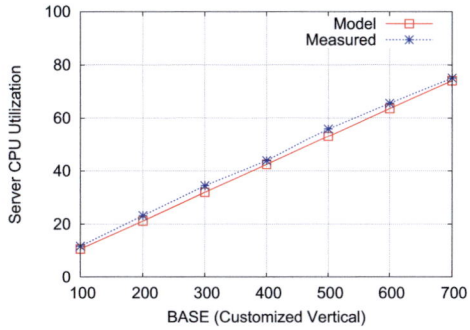

Figure 6.28: Server CPU Utilisation for Customised Vertical Topology

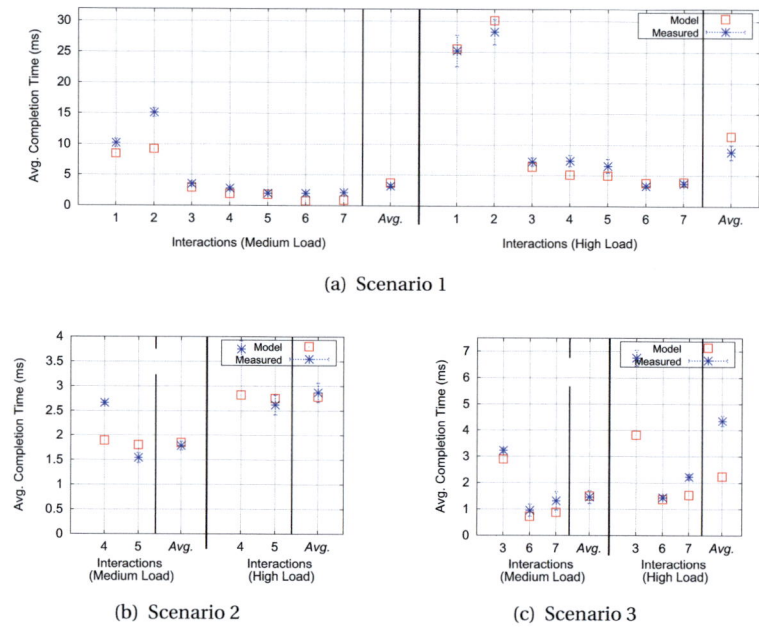

(a) Scenario 1

(b) Scenario 2   (c) Scenario 3

Figure 6.29: Predicted and Measured Completion Time

tomised vertical topology when varying the $BASE$ between 100 and 700. As we can see, the model predicts the server CPU utilisation very accurately as the workload is scaled. In the following, we present a more detailed evaluation of the three scenarios under different load intensities considering further performance metrics such as interaction throughput and completion time.

The detailed results for the scenarios are presented in Table 6.14 and illustrated in Figure 6.29. For each scenario, we consider two workload intensities corresponding to medium and high load conditions configured using the $BASE$ parameter. The first scenario represents the vertical interaction mix for $BASE$ 300 and 550, respectively. The second scenario is a mix of Interactions 4 and 5 focused on P2P communication, while

Table 6.14: Detailed Results for Scenario 1, 2 and 3

(a) Scenario 1

Input BASE	Inter-action	Rate p. sec	Avg. Completion T (ms)	
			Model	Meas. (95% c.i.)
	1	226.36	8.41	10.17 +/- 0.68
	2	66.9	9.18	15.10 +/- 0.71
	3	14.92	2.9	3.49 +/- 0.41
300	4	483.4	1.89	2.76 +/- 0.31
med. load	5	1734.7	1.79	1.97 +/- 0.27
	6	43.45	0.72	1.96 +/- 0.29
	7	30.65	0.87	2.10 +/- 0.24
	1	418.1	25.51	25.19 +/- 2.56
	2	120.15	30.12	28.27 +/- 2.05
	3	26.0	6.36	7.20 +/- 0.67
550	4	887.5	5.09	7.35 +/- 0.89
high load	5	3189.4	4.94	6.52 +/- 1.13
	6	81.73	3.77	3.26 +/- 0.26
	7	56.9	3.89	3.67 +/- 0.34

(b) Scenario 2

Input BASE	Inter-action	Rate p. sec	Avg. Completion T (ms)	
			Model	Meas. (95% c.i.)
600	4	977.8	1.89	2.66 +/- 0.04
med. load	5	3474.8	1.80	1.54 +/- 0.10
800	4	1289.1	2.82	3.75 +/- 0.17
high load	5	4637.62	2.75	2.62 +/- 0.20

(c) Scenario 3

Input BASE	Inter-action	Rate p. sec	Avg. Completion T (ms)	
			Model	Meas. (95% c.i.)
6000	3	304.1	2.89	3.22 +/- 0.09
med. load	6	852.2	0.72	0.95 +/- 0.23
	7	617.9	0.87	1.31 +/- 0.35
10000	3	498.3	3.81	6.75 +/- 0.30
high load	6	1418.2	1.37	1.44 +/- 0.07
	7	1025.53	1.53	2.22 +/- 0.10

the third scenario is a mix of Interactions 3, 6 and 7 focused on Pub/Sub communication. For each scenario, the interaction rates and the average interaction completion times are shown. The *interaction completion time* is defined as the time between the beginning of the interaction and the time when the last message has been processed. The difference between the predicted and measured interaction rates was negligible (with an error below 1%) and therefore we only show the predicted interaction rates. For completion times, we show both, the predicted and measured mean values, where for the latter we provide a 95% confidence interval from 5 repetitions of each experiment. Given that the measured mean values were computed from a large number of observations, their respective confidence intervals were quite narrow. The prediction error was less than 25% in most cases. In the cases where the interaction completion times were below 3 ms, e.g., for Interactions 6 and 7 in the first scenario, the prediction error was higher. In such cases, a small absolute difference of say 1 ms between the measured and predicted values (e.g., due to some synchronisation aspects not captured by the model) appears high when considered as a percentage of the respective mean value given that the latter is very low. However, when considered as an absolute value, the error is still quite small.

Figure 6.29 depicts the predicted and measured interaction completion times for the three scenarios. The results reveal the accuracy of the model when considering different types of messaging. For P2P messaging, the modelling error is independent of whether persistent or non-persistent messages are sent. However, for the Pub/Sub case under high load (Scenario 3), the prediction error is much higher for the case of persistent messages than for the case of non-persistent messages. In Scenario 1 where all interactions are running at the same time, Interactions 1 and 2 exhibited the highest modelling error (with exception of the interactions with very low completion times). This is due to the fact that each of these interactions comprise a complex chain of multiple messages of different types and sizes. Finally, looking at the mean completion time over all interactions, we see that the prediction is optimistic as the predicted completion times are lower than the measured ones. This behaviour is typical for performance models in general since no matter how representative they are, they normally cannot capture all factors causing delays in the system.

6.3.4. Summary of the SPECjms2007 Case Study

The SPECjms2007 case study demonstrates the applicability of our approach to a representative industrial supply-chain management system. In contrast to the distributed traffic monitoring case study, the SPECjms2007 scenario is built on top of a centralised JMS server executing a complex mix of P2P and Pub/Sub interactions with different event types and sizes. The prediction results proved to be very accurate in predicting the system performance, especially considering the size and complexity of the system that was modelled. The prediction error does not exceed 25% in most cases. As discussed above, in cases where interaction completion times were below 3 ms, the relative prediction error was higher. Nevertheless, the absolute prediction error was less than 2 ms.

6.4. Further External Case Studies

Beside the two case studies presented in the previous sections, the modelling abstractions and prediction techniques developed in this thesis are currently applied in two external projects. In these projects, software engineers, which have not directly been involved in the development of the presented approach, apply the modelling and prediction techniques to evaluate two different systems. This application by external users, demonstrates the intuitive applicability of our approach and highlights the need for performance predictions for EBS using architecture-level models by research and industry. In the following, we provide a short overview of the two projects.

The first project was recently started as a cooperation between the *Forschungszentrum Informatik* (FZI) and a large manufacturer for industrial control systems for power plants. The goal of this project is the application of model-based predictions based on the Palladio approach to their large and distributed control system for power plants. The control system has a tree-based structure. A central root server is connected to multiple data collection and aggregation servers, which again are connected to plenty of different field devices. While the central server is responsible for visualising the collected data and providing a configuration interface for the different field devices, the data collection and aggregation servers are responsible to encapsulate the communication with the field devices and aggregate the provided data. Each field device is equipped with sensors specialised for a certain measuring domain. These domains range from the flow and fill level of liquids over temperature and pressure up to electrical voltage and current to mention only some of them. Within the control system multiple different messages are exchanged that are for example used to configure sensors, transfer measured and aggregated data but also to raise alarms if a sensor detects the excess of a configured threshold. Such messages are exchanged between the collection and aggregation servers and the central server but also between data collection and aggregation servers and the individual field devices. The availability and responsiveness of the whole control system is mission-critical as failures of the power plant can result in monetary and physical damage, which is the reason why the manufacturer evaluates model-based prediction approaches.

With support of the FZI, the manufacturer currently evaluates the applicability of the Palladio approach to model and analyse the control system. As part of an initial modelling workshop, the modelling abstractions developed in this thesis, which have been part of the official PCM release since version 3.3, were successfully used by a performance modelling expert only familiar with the original PCM. The results of the workshop highlighted the importance of modelling capabilities for event-based interactions and the necessity of supporting the modelling of Pub/Sub communication using one or multiple event channels. The manufacturer emphasised its interest in our modelling extensions and the developed prediction techniques. Unfortunately, due to confidentiality constraints, we cannot provide further details on this running project.

The second project, the contributions presented in this thesis are applied in, is the development of a solar orbiter more specific the *Instrument Control System* (ICU) for the *Energetic Particle Detector* (EPD) onboard of this orbiter [Prieto 12]. The ICU controls the EPD and communicates with the spacecraft to receive new tele-commands and to transfer data collected by the EPD back to earth. Additionally, it is connected to multiple sensors providing telemetry data and information about the system state. The ICU is implemented on top of a real-time operating system and the communication between components is realised by means of clocked messages. Depending on their importance, different priorities are assigned to the messages to ensure that system critical messages like failure detections or control commands are always transferred in time. The *Space Research Group at the University of Alcalá* (SRG) in Spain extended the simulation-based prediction of Palladio with a new priority based real-time scheduler with the aim to evaluate the software design and the impact of different scheduling algorithms on the system behaviour.

SRG's first approach to model the ICU was based on the original version of PCM. The communication channel was modelled as a central component all components are connected to. This approach resulted in a very complex component and the connections between individual components were hidden in this central component and spread over multiple RD-SEFFs. Although the performance prediction were accurate enough to evaluate the system design, the complexity of the model and the effort for adapting the model to different design alternatives was very high as this central component has to be manually adapted each time. In a second iteration, the SRG has used the modelling extensions developed in this thesis. The different components of the ICU and the sensors were directly connected using event-based interactions without explicitly modelling the communication component in the system model. The behaviour of the communication layer in terms of different delivery delays for messages was specified as separate middleware components. Applying the two-step refinement transformation presented in this thesis automatically integrates these middleware components. Using the developed extensions for EBS, the modelling effort could significantly reduced. Since the two-step transformation was designed to be compatible with existing prediction techniques, the SRG's extended simulation could directly be used without any adaptations. SRG plans to submit and publish a report describing the case study and the application of PCM in the next months.

6.5. Evaluation Summary

In Section 1.3, we identified the five characteristics expressiveness, accuracy, efficiency, scalability, and automation as essential success criteria for any model-based prediction approach. To evaluate our approach with respect to these characteristics, we defined three evaluation goals, which focus on the prediction capabilities and their accuracy, the applicability of the introduced modelling elements, and finally the integration and automation of the modelling and prediction techniques.

We selected two complementary real-world case studies that represent the two major classes of EBS. The traffic monitoring case study is a resource intensive distributed system built on top of a decentralised peer-to-peer middleware, while the SPECjms2007 benchmark is designed as a representative supply-chain scenario with a complex mix of P2P and Pub/Sub interactions typically implemented using a centralised MOM. In combination, the case studies cover most characteristics of EBS, which have been introduced in Section 2.1.1, and thus can be considered as representative for a large set of existing EBS. Applying our modelling approach to these systems demonstrates the *expressiveness* of the proposed modelling abstractions for event-based interactions. Using two existing real-world case studies with realistic workloads allows us to demonstrate the *scalability* of our approach and its ability to handle systems of realistic size and complexity.

To evaluate the *accuracy* of the prediction results, we deployed both systems in realistic test environments. Using configureable load-drivers that emit real-world data collected at the running system with a predefined event rate, we measured resource utilisations as well as processing times for different workloads. In the case of the traffic monitoring system, we deployed and measured the system in a number of different settings corresponding to different design alternatives. The comparison of predicted and measured performance metrics exhibited a prediction error of mostly less than 20% respectively 25% for the two case studies. According to [Menascé 04], prediction errors of up to 35% are considered acceptable for capacity planning, which confirms the accuracy of our prediction approach.

The applicability of performance modelling and evaluation based on the original PCM, has already been shown in an empirical study [Martens 08a, Martens 08b]. Evaluating different evolution stages of the traffic monitoring system allows us to demonstrate the *efficiency* of our modelling approach. All required modelling adaptations with exception of the initial component definition could be performed in less than 30 minutes. The use of the proposed modelling extensions in combination with the *automation* of the developed refinement transformations reduced the modelling effort by up to 80%.

The two external case studies, which have already started before finishing this thesis, highlight the high demand for architecture-level quality evaluation approaches for EBS both in industry and research. The
application by users not involved in the development of our approach
demonstrates the intuitive applicability of the developed methodology
and techniques for standard software engineers. Furthermore, these case
studies show the significant improvement in terms of effort reductions
compared to existing approaches and thus are an additional indicator
for the Type III validity of the results presented in this thesis.

7. Conclusions

This chapter concludes with a summary of the contributions presented in this thesis. Afterwards, we discuss ongoing and future research topics in the area of architecture-level modelling and performance prediction techniques for *Event-based Systems* (EBS).

7.1. Summary

With the growing proliferation of event-based interactions in business- and mission-critical systems, the assurance of certain *Quality-of-Service* (QoS) levels with regard to availability, performance, or scalability play an important role. System architects require tools and methodologies supporting them in evaluating and predicting the system behaviour and its QoS attributes for certain situations, i.e., different design alternatives, varying workloads as well as variable deployments and resource environments.

In this thesis, we proposed a novel modelling and prediction approach combining architecture-level modelling of event-based interactions with detailed and platform-aware QoS prediction techniques. The developed **modelling abstractions for event-based interactions** allow architects to describe EBS at the architecture-level abstracting platform- and implementation-specific details. While being platform-independent and hiding as much details related to the underlying communication middleware as possible, the developed modelling abstractions still contain sufficient information to enable an in-depth analysis of the system behaviour and QoS. We developed the abstractions with the goal to be independent of a certain *Architecture Description Language* (ADL) and thus being applicable to extend different existing ADLs for component-based systems with support for modelling event-based interactions. Introducing events as first class entities enables architects to explicitly specify events and individual source and sink ports of components. The presented modelling approach enables to differentiate between direct *Point-to-Point* (P2P) and decoupled *Publish/Subscribe* (Pub/Sub) communication using intermediate event channels. Supporting P2P delivery as well as different subscription models (i.e., channel-based, content-based, and type-based), our approach allows modelling most existing EBS and covers the major classes of EBS. Besides proposing generic modelling abstractions, we applied them to the *Palladio Component Model* (PCM), a mature and representative ADL for component-based systems accompanied by multiple different QoS evaluation and prediction techniques.

To enable a **detailed and platform-aware QoS prediction** based on architecture-level models, we developed a **two-step refinement transformation** method. The transformation is partitioned into a platform-independent and a platform-specific part. In the first step, event-based interactions are refined by integrating several components representing different event processing stages. Using the resulting refined model as a basis, the second transformation step integrates platform-specific components specified in a separate middleware model. These components encapsulate the performance relevant influence factors of the employed transmission system. The strict separation of platform-independent and platform-specific aspects, which is a novel aspect compared to existing refinement approaches, simplifies the evaluation of different transmission systems in terms of their influence on the system performance, and vice versa, it eases the evaluation of different design and deployment options as platform-specific details are abstracted at the architecture-level and later integrated automatically. Since the refinement substitutes all event related elements, the resulting model is compatible to the original ADL and can thus serve as input for all existing prediction techniques defined for the base ADL. As part of this thesis, we implemented the two-step refinement in the context of PCM as a model-to-model transformation. We integrated the transformation into PCM's modelling and prediction tool making it being automatically executed before running the respective prediction technique.

We evaluated our approach in the context of **two representative real-world case studies**: A distributed traffic monitoring system built on top of a peer-to-peer middleware developed for the city of Cambridge and the official SPECjms2007 benchmark, a representative supply chain management system using a centralised *Message-Oriented Middleware* (MOM) server. We selected the case studies to be complementary and to represent different types of EBS, i.e., distributed peer-to-peer systems and centralised systems executing a mixture of P2P and Pub/Sub interactions. Since the two case-studies represent the major classes of EBS, they can be considered as representative for a large set of existing EBS. Following the developed evaluation plan, we conduct several experiments and applied the developed methodology and framework in multiple architecture evaluation scenarios.

The results of the evaluation showed that system variations and evolutions typical for loosely coupled EBS can be reflected in architecture-level models in less than 30 minutes. Compared to the use of manual modelling workarounds as demonstrated in [Rathfelder 10a], the modelling effort could be reduced by more than 80%. The application in different scenarios demonstrated that the presented modelling and prediction approach can be applied at design time to evaluate and compare different design alternatives, as well as at deployment time to analyse different deployment options and to determine the required hardware resources. The evaluation of the prediction accuracy highlighted that the prediction error was less than 20% and 25% in most cases of the two case studies and thereby significantly better than 35%-40%, which is the value generally considered as acceptable for model-based performance prediction techniques [Menascé 04]. Furthermore, the application of our approach in several external projects demonstrates the applicability and highlights the need for architecture-level modelling and prediction techniques supporting the evaluation of EBS.

7.2. Ongoing and Future Work

The results presented in this thesis form the basis for several areas of future work. In the following overview, we summarise ongoing research and present opportunities for future work.

Reliability and Tradeoff Analysis   The presented validation of our approach focuses on the accuracy of performance predictions, however, the general approach is not limited to performance. Recently, a new prediction technique for PCM enabling reliability analysis for component-based systems has been developed [Brosch 12]. Combining our approach with this prediction technique is a logical next step. Several transmission systems support the configuration of a reliable event delivery, however, mostly at the cost of higher resource demands and transmission overheads. Supporting a combined analysis and prediction of performance and reliability aspects will allow further analysis of the tradeoffs between these properties.

Support for Embedded Systems   In embedded systems, components often interact in an asynchronous manner using event-based interactions ranging from triggers and interrupts over simple sensor data values up to complex data sets. With the traffic-monitoring case study and the application of the developed modelling and prediction techniques in the context of a satellite control system as described in Section 6.4, we demonstrated the applicability of our approach in the context of embedded systems. However, especially applying PCM to the satellite control system identified several limitations of PCM in terms of its support for embedded systems, e.g., the lack of real-time schedulers or the missing support of additional quality attributes of particular importance in the area of embedded system such as energy consumption. However, with the support for modelling and evaluating event-based interactions, the extensions presented in this thesis eliminates one of PCM's most crucial limitations related to the support of embedded systems, which was a prerequisite for starting research on topics that specifically address the area of embedded systems.

Automated Model Extractions The presented prediction technique requires the existence of a middleware model describing the platform-specific components. These components have to be specified manually by a middleware expert based on benchmark results or measurements conducted on test systems. Especially, the identification and specification of parameterised resource demands is a complex task and requires structured measurements. The Performance Cockpit approach [Westermann 11] developed by Westermann et al. supports the identification of parameterised resource demands based on a set of automatically executed experiments. Extending the Performance Cockpit with a standardised set of experiments combined with generic workload drivers for event-based interactions, will enable the automated generation of platform-specific components based on reproducible experiments that can be applied to different middleware implementations to automatically derive the platform-specific middleware model.

Dynamic and Mobile Ad-hoc Systems Because of its loose coupling between components, event-based interactions are a promising technique to implement dynamic and mobile adhoc systems. Such systems are used in different domains, e.g., sensor networks, car-to-car communication, or ubiquitous computing, in which interacting components dynamically appear and disappear. Supporting the modelling and prediction of dynamic adhoc systems requires an additional modelling view to describe the dynamics and variability of these systems. With regard to event-based interactions, this support includes the specification of dynamic subscriptions that can be created and removed at run-time as well as supporting the dynamic appearance or disappearance of event sources and sinks. Although our approach assumes a static architecture, it provides a basis to be extended with additional elements supporting the modelling of dynamic architectures.

Self-aware Run-time Systems Management The Descartes Research Group[1] is working on enhancing design-time models to specify dynamic aspects of the environment and making them an integral part of the system [Kounev 10a]. Beside the support for modelling component-based architectures, the *Descartes Meta-Model* (DMM) [Brosig 12a] provides additional views to capture run-time aspects like the integration of online monitoring data [Brosig 12b], modelling dynamic resource landscapes [Huber 12a], or specifying run-time adaptations [Huber 12b]. The loose coupling between components in EBS, simplifies the dynamic relocation of components on different servers to handle peak loads or to improve the system's efficiency. For this reason, large and distributed systems with event-based interactions provide an ideal basis for applying self-aware system management techniques in general and the Descartes approach in particular. Based on the modelling abstractions presented in this thesis, we are currently extending DMM with native support for specifying event-based interactions. Beside enabling the application of the Descartes approach to the domain of EBS, these extensions additionally open new opportunities and research topics like for example the

---

[1]http://www.descartes-research.net

dynamic adaptation of subscriptions to reflect component relocations or the instantiation of event-channels and replication of components at run-time for load balancing purposes.

A. Remaining MOLA Transformation Procedures

A.1. Sub-Procedure `createSinkPortContexts`

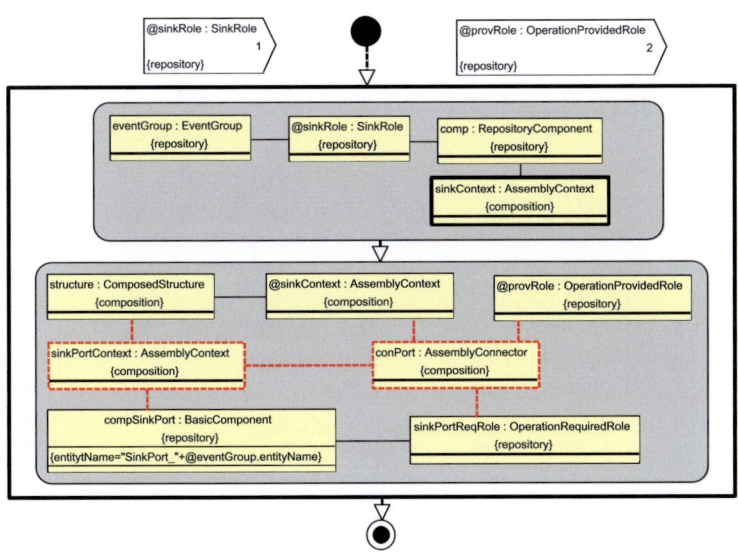

Figure A.1: Sub Procedure `createSinkPortContexts`

A.2. Middleware Integration Procedures

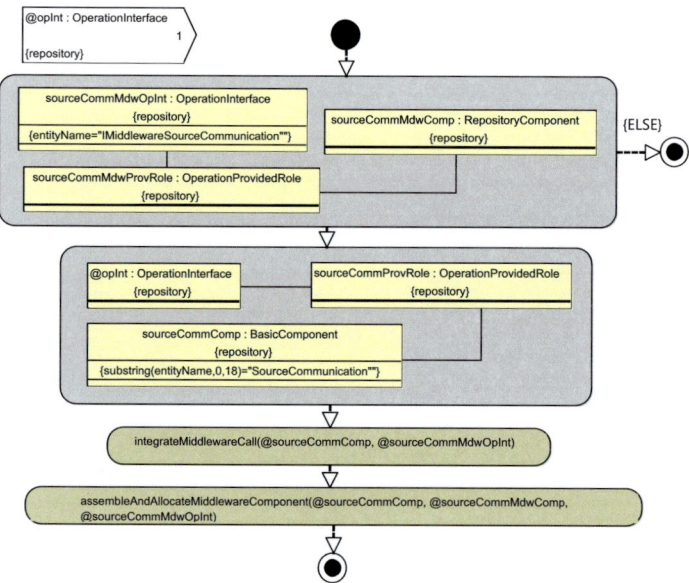

Figure A.2: Sub Procedure integrateSourceCommMiddleware

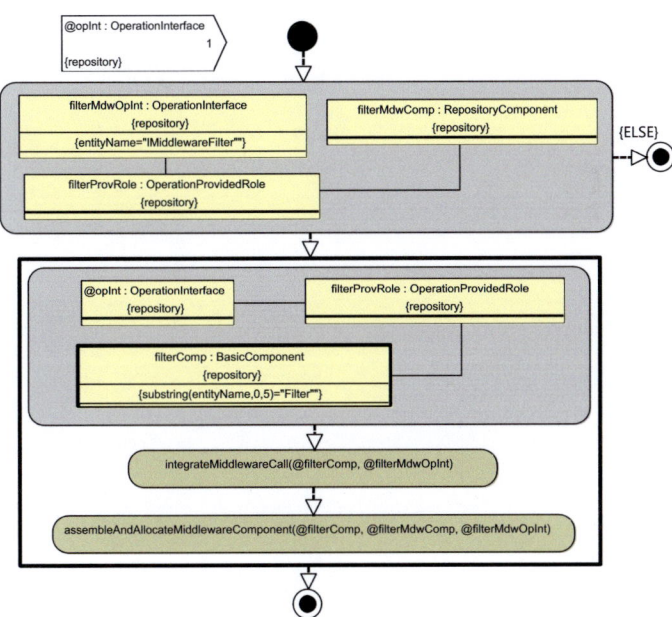

Figure A.3: Sub Procedure `integrateFilterMiddleware`

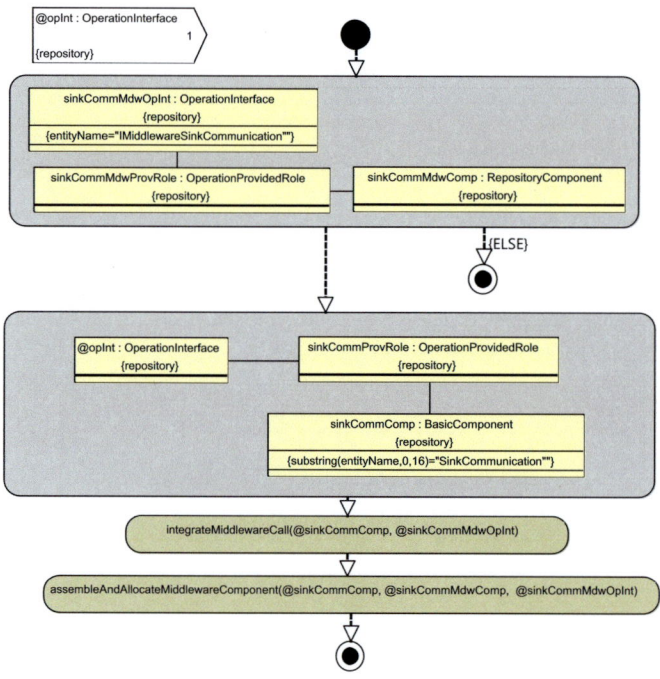

Figure A.4: Sub Procedure `integrateSinkCommMiddleware`

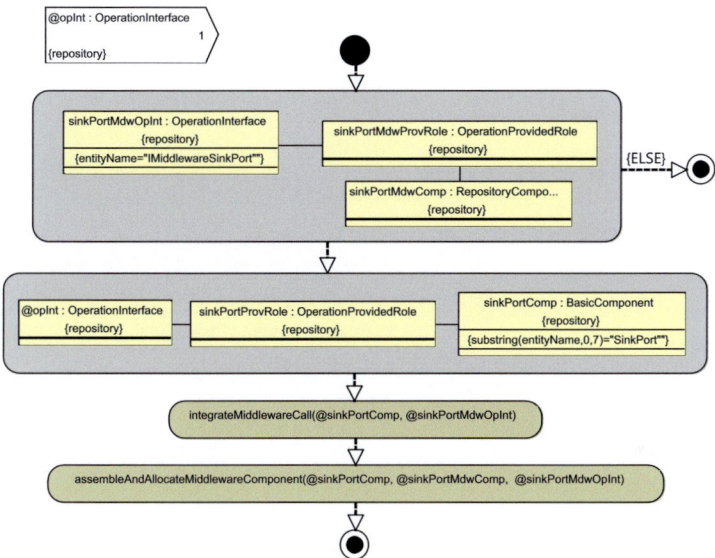

Figure A.5: Sub Procedure `integrateSInkPortMiddleware`

Acronyms

Java EE	*Java Platform, Enterprise Edition*
QVT-O	*QVT Operational Mapping Language*
QVT-R	*QVT Relations Language*
RD-SEFF	*Resource Demanding Service Effect Specification*
ADL	*Architecture Description Language*
ADM2	*Architecture Documentation Maturity Model*
API	*Application Programming Interface*
ATL	*Atlas Transformation Language*
AUTOSAR	*Automotive Open System Architecture*
CBSE	*Component-based Software Engineering*
CCM	*CORBA Component Model*
CDF	*Cumulative Distribution Function*
CEA	*Cambridge Event Architecture*
CEP	*Complex Event Processing*
COM	*Component Object Model*
CORBA	*Common Object Request Broker Architecture*
CoSMIC	*Component Synthesis with Model Integrated Computing*

DC	*Distribution Centre*
DMM	*Descartes Meta-Model*
EBS	*Event-based Systems*
EDA	*Event-Driven Architecture*
EJB	*Enterprise JavaBeans*
EMF	*Eclipse Modeling Framework Project*
EPD	*Energetic Particle Detector*
ER	*Entity Relationship*
FCFS	*first-come-first-serve*
FZI	*Forschungszentrum Informatik*
GMF	*Graphical Modeling Framework*
HOT	*Higher Order Transformation*
HQ	*Company Headquarters*
ICU	*Instrument Control System*
IDL	*Interface Definition Language*
iSOAMM	*independent SOA Maturity Model*
JEDI	*Java Event-based Distributed Infrastructure*
JMS	*Java Message Service*
KIT	*Karlsruhe Institute of Technology*
KLAPER	*Kernel LAnguage for PErformance and Reliability analysis*

LHS	*left-hand-side*
LITMUS	*Language of Interface Types for Messages in Underlying Streams*
LQN	*Layered Queueing Network*
M2M	*Model-2-Model*
M2T	*Model-2-Text*
MDA	*Model-Driven Architecture*
MDE	*Model-driven Engineering*
MDSD	*Model-driven Software Development*
MOF	*Meta Object Facility*
MOLA	*MOdel transformation LAnguage*
MOM	*Message-Oriented Middleware*
OASIS	*Organisation for the Advancement of Structured Information Standards*
OCL	*Object Constraint Language*
OMG	*Object Management Group*
OO	*object-oriented*
OS	*Operating System*
P2P	*Point-to-Point*
PCM	*Palladio Component Model*
PICML	*Platform-independent Component Modeling Language*
PIM	*platform-independent model*
PIRATES	*Peer-to-peer Implementation of Reconfigurable Architecture for Typed Event Streams*
PSM	*platform-specific model*
Pub/Sub	*Publish/Subscribe*

QImPrESS	*Quality Impact Prediction for Evolving Service-oriented Software*
QoS	*Quality-of-Service*
QPN	*Queueing Petri Net*
QVT	*Query/View/Transformation*
RFID	*Radio-Frequency Identification*
RHS	*right-hand-side*
RMI	*Remote Method Invocation*
RPC	*Remote Procedure Call*
SAMM	*Service Architecture Meta-Model*
SCA	*Service Component Architecture*
SIENA	Scalable Internet Event Notification Architecture
SLA	*Service Level Agreement*
SM	*Supermarket*
SOA	*Service-Oriented Architecture*
SOAP	*Simple Object Access Protocol*
SP	*Supplier*
SPE	*Software Performance Engineering*
SPEC	*Standard Performance Evaluation Corporation*
SRG	*Space Research Group at the University of Alcalá*
StoEx	*Stochastic Expression*
TDE	*Transformation Definition Environment*

TEE	*Transformation Execution Environment*
TIME	*Transport Information Monitoring Environment*
UML	*Unified Modeling Language*
URL	*Uniform Resource Locator*
VIATRA2	*VIsual Automated model TRAnsformations framework*
W3C	*World Wide Web Consortium*
WS-Addressing	*Web Service Addressing*
WS-BaseNotification	*Web Service Base Notification*
WS-BrokeredNotification	*Web Service Brokered Notification*
WS-Eventing	*Web Service Eventing*
WS-Topics	*Web Service Topics*
WSN	*Web Service Notification*
XMI	*XML Metadata Interchange*
XML	*Extensible Markup Language*

List of Figures

List of Tables

List of Listings

Bibliography

[Andries 96] Marc Andries, Gregor Engels, Annegret Habel, Berthold Hoffmann, Hans-Jörg Kreowski, Sabine Kuske, Detlef Plump, Andy Schürr & Gabriele Taentzer. *Graph Transformation for Specification and Programming.* Science of Computer Programming, vol. 34, pages 1–54, 1996.

[Appel 10] Stefan Appel, Kai Sachs & Alejandro Buchmann. *Quality of Service in Event-based Systems.* In 22nd GI-Workshop on Foundations of Databases (GvD), May 2010.

[Arendt 10] Thorsten Arendt, Enrico Biermann, Stefan Jurack, Christian Krause & Gabriele Taentzer. *Henshin: Advanced Concepts and Tools for In-Place EMF Model Transformations.* In Dorina Petriu, Nicolas Rouquette & Øystein Haugen, editors, Model Driven Engineering Languages and Systems, volume 6394 of *Lecture Notes in Computer Science*, pages 121–135. Springer Berlin / Heidelberg, 2010.

[ASFINAG 11] ASFINAG. *Videomaut - ASFINAG.* http://www.videomaut.at, 2011.

[ATLAS Group 07]   ATLAS Group. *Atlas Transformation Language (ATL) Homepage.* http://www.eclipse.org/m2m/atl/, 2007.

[aut 07]   *AUTOSAR Specification Release 3.1*, 2007.

[Bacon 00]   Jean Bacon, Ken Moody, John Bates, Richard Hayton, Chaoying Ma, Andrew McNeil, Oliver Seidel & Mark Spiteri. *Generic Support for Distributed Applications.* Computer, vol. 33, no. 3, pages 68–76, 2000.

[Bacon 08]   Jean Bacon, Alastair R. Beresford, David Evans, David Ingram, Niki Trigoni, Alexandre Guitton & Antonios Skordylis. *TIME: An open platform for capturing, processing and delivering transport-related data.* In Proceedings of the IEEE consumer communications and networking conference, pages 687–691, 2008.

[Balasubramanian 07]   Krishnakumar Balasubramanian, Jaiganesh Balasubramanian, Jeff Parsons, Aniruddha Gokhale & Douglas C. Schmidt. *A Platform-Independent Component Modeling Language for Distributed Real-time and Embedded Systems.* J. Comput. Syst. Sci., vol. 73, no. 2, pages 171–185, March 2007.

[Baldoni 05]   R. Baldoni, R. Beraldi, S. Tucci Piergiovanni & A. Virgillito. *On the modelling of publish/subscribe communication systems.* Concurrency and Computation: Practice and Experience, vol. 17, no. 12, pages 1471–1495, 2005.

[Baldoni 06] R. Baldoni & A. Virgillito. *Distributed Event Routing in Publish/Subscribe Communication Systems: a Survey (revised version)*. technical report, MIDLAB 1/2006 - Dipartimento di Informatica e Sistemistica A.Ruberti, Università di Roma la Sapienza, 2006.

[Balsamo 03] Simonetta Balsamo & Moreno Marzolla. *A Simulation-Based Approach to Software Performance Modeling*. In Proceedings of the 9th European Software Engineering Conference held jointly with 11th ACM SIGSOFT international symposium on Foundations of Software Engineering, pages 363–366. ACM Press, 2003.

[Banks 04] Jerry Banks, John Carson, Barry L. Nelson & David Nicol. *Discrete-Event System Simulation (4th Edition)*. Prentice Hall, 4 edition, 2004.

[Barzdins 06] J. Barzdins, G. Barzdins, R. Balodis, K. Cerans, A. Kalnins, M. Opmanis & K. Podnieks. *Towards Semantic Latvia*. In O.Vasileckas, J.Eder & A.Caplinskas, editors, Baltic DB&IS 2006, Communications, pages 203–218, 2006.

[Bause 93] Falko Bause. *Queueing Petri Nets-A formalism for the combined qualitative and quantitative analysis of systems*. In Petri Nets and Performance Models, 1993. Proceedings., 5th International Workshop on, pages 14 –23, oct 1993.

[Becker 06a] Steffen Becker, Lars Grunske, Raffaela Mirandola & Sven Overhage. *Performance Prediction of Component-Based Systems: A Survey from an*

Engineering Perspective. In Ralf Reussner, Judith Stafford & Clemens Szyperski, editors, Architecting Systems with Trustworthy Components, volume 3938 of *Lecture Notes in Computer Science*, pages 169–192. Springer-Verlag Berlin Heidelberg, 2006.

[Becker 06b] Steffen Becker, Jens Happe & Heiko Koziolek. *Putting Components into Context: Supporting QoS-Predictions with an explicit Context Model.* In Ralf Reussner, Clemens Szyperski & Wolfgang Weck, editors, Proc. 11th International Workshop on Component Oriented Programming (WCOP'06), pages 1–6, July 2006.

[Becker 08a] Steffen Becker. *Coupled Model Transformations for QoS Enabled Component-Based Software Design*, volume 1 of *Karlsruhe Series on Software Design and Quality*. Universitätsverlag Karlsruhe, 2008.

[Becker 08b] Steffen Becker, Lubomìr Bulej, Tomas Bures, Petr Hneetynka, Lucia Kapova, Jan Kofron, Heiko Koziolek, Johan Kraft, Raffaella Mirandola, Johannes Stammel, Giordano Tamburrelli & Mircea Trifu. *Q-ImPrESS Project Deliverable D2.1 - Service Architecture Meta-Model (SAMM).* Project Deliverable, 2008.

[Becker 09] Steffen Becker, Heiko Koziolek & Ralf Reussner. *The Palladio component model for model-driven performance prediction.* Journal of Systems and Software, vol. 82, pages 3–22, 2009.

[Behnel 06] Stefan Behnel, Ludger Fiege & Gero Mühl. *On Quality-of-Service and Publish/Subscribe.* In Fifth International Workshop on Distributed Event-based Systems (DEBS06), July 2006.

[Bertolino 04] Antonia Bertolino & Raffaela Mirandola. *CB-SPE Tool: Putting Component-Based Performance Engineering into Practice.* In Ivica Crnkovic, Judith A. Stafford, Heinz W. Schmidt & Kurt C. Wallnau, editors, Proc. 7th International Symposium on Component-Based Software Engineering (CBSE 2004), Edinburgh, UK, volume 3054 of *Lecture Notes in Computer Science*, pages 233–248. Springer-Verlag, Berlin, Germany, 2004.

[Bloomberg 12] Bloomberg. *Nasdaq Chief Blames Software for Delayed Facebook Debut.* http://bloom.bg/ L9wCwW, May 2012.

[Böhme 08] Rainer Böhme & Ralf Reussner. *Validation of Predictions with Measurements.* In Dependability Metrics, volume 4909 of *Lecture Notes in Computer Science*, 3, pages 14–18. Springer-Verlag Berlin Heidelberg, 2008.

[Bondarev 04] Egor Bondarev, Johan Muskens, Peter de With, Michel Chaudron & Johan Lukkien. *Predicting Real-Time Properties of Component Assemblies: A Scenario-Simulation Approach.* In Proceedings of the 30th EUROMICRO Conference (EUROMICRO'04), pages 40–47, Washington, DC, USA, 2004. IEEE Computer Society.

[Briegleb 07]   Volker Briegleb. *Bericht: Probleme bei SAPs neuer Mittelstandssoftware.* Heise online news, http://www.heise.de/newsticker/meldung/ 88300/, 2007.

[Brosch 12]   Franz Brosch. *Integrated Software Architecture-Based Reliability Prediction for IT Systems : Characterization and applications.* PhD thesis, Karlsruhe Institute of Technology (KIT), Karlsruhe, 2012.

[Brosig 12a]   Fabian Brosig, Nikolaus Huber & Samuel Kounev. *Descartes Meta-Model (DMM).* technical report, Karlsruhe Institute of Technology (KIT), 2012. To be published (http://descartes.ipd.kit.edu/research_and_ profile/descartes_meta_model).

[Brosig 12b]   Fabian Brosig, Nikolaus Huber & Samuel Kounev. *Modeling Parameter and Context Dependencies in Online Architecture-Level Performance Models.* In Proceedings of the 15th ACM SIGSOFT International Symposium on Component Based Software Engineering (CBSE 2012), June 26–28, 2012, Bertinoro, Italy, June 2012.

[Carzaniga 98a]   Antonio Carzaniga. *Architectures for an Event Notification Service Scalable to Wide-area Networks.* PhD thesis, Politecnico di Milano, Milano, Italy, December 1998.

[Carzaniga 98b]   Antonio Carzaniga, Elisabetta Di Nitto, David S. Rosenblum & Alexander L. Wolf. *Issues in supporting event-based architectural styles.* In Proceedings of the third international workshop on Software architecture, ISAW '98, pages 17–20, New York, NY, USA, 1998. ACM.

[Carzaniga 01] Antonio Carzaniga, David S. Rosenblum & Alexander L. Wolf. *Design and evaluation of a wide-area event notification service.* ACM Transactions on Computer Systems, vol. 19, pages 332–383, August 2001.

[Castro 02] M. Castro, P. Druschel, A.-M. Kermarrec & A.I.T. Rowstron. *Scribe: a large-scale and decentralized application-level multicast infrastructure.* Selected Areas in Communications, IEEE Journal on, vol. 20, no. 8, pages 1489 – 1499, oct 2002.

[Chandy 06] Mani K. Chandy. *Event-Driven Applications: Costs, Benefits and Design Approaches.* Gartner Application Integration and Web Services Summit 2006, 2006.

[Chandy 10] W. Roy Chandy Kanianthra Mani ; Schulte. *Event processing : designing IT systems for agile companies.* McGraw-Hill, 2010.

[Cheesman 00] John Cheesman & John Daniels. *UML Components: A Simple Process for Specifying Component-based Software.* Addison-Wesley, Reading, MA, USA, 2000.

[Cherkasova 09] Ludmila Cherkasova, Kivanc Ozonat, Ningfang Mi, Julie Symons & Evgenia Smirni. *Automated anomaly detection and performance modeling of enterprise applications.* ACM Trans. Comput. Syst., vol. 27, pages 6:1–6:32, Nov 2009.

[Ciancone 10] Andrea Ciancone. *Mapping the Service Architecture Meta-Model to the Palladio Component Model.* Master's thesis, Politecnico di Milano and Universität Karlsruhe (TH), 2010.

[Clements 96] P.C. Clements & L.M. Northrop. *Software Architecture: An Executive Overview.* technical report CMU/SEI-96-TR-003, Software Engineering Institute, Carnegie Mellon University, 1996.

[Corsaro 06] Angelo Corsaro, Leonardo Querzoni, Sirio Scipioni, Sara Tucci Piergiovanni & Antonino Virgillito. volume 8, *Quality of Service in Publish/Subscribe Middleware,* page 0. Emerging communication: Studies in new technologies and practices in communication, Roberto Baldoni, Giovanni Cortese, Fabrizio Davide & Angelo Melpignano, editors. IOS Press, Amsterdam, Netherlands, 1 edition, 2006.

[Cortellessa 05] Vittorio Cortellessa. *How far are we from the definition of a common software performance ontology?* In WOSP '05: Proceedings of the 5th International Workshop on Software and Performance, pages 195–204, New York, NY, USA, 2005. ACM Press.

[Cortellessa 07a] Vittorio Cortellessa, Antinisca Di Marco & Paola Inverardi. *Integrating Performance and Reliability Analysis in a Non-Functional MDA*

Framework. In Matthew B. Dwyer & Antónia Lopes, editors, Fundamental Approaches to Software Engineering, 10th International Conference, FASE 2007, Held as Part of the Joint European Conferences, on Theory and Practice of Software, ETAPS 2007, Braga, Portugal, March 24 - April 1, 2007, Proceedings, volume 4422 of *Lecture Notes in Computer Science*, pages 57–71. Springer, 2007.

[Cortellessa 07b] Vittorio Cortellessa, Pierluigi Pierini & Daniele Rossi. *Integrating Software Models and Platform Models for Performance Analysis.* IEEE Transactions on Software Engineering, vol. 33, no. 6, pages 385–401, June 2007.

[Crnkovic 11] I. Crnkovic, S. Sentilles, A. Vulgarakis & M.R.V. Chaudron. *A Classification Framework for Software Component Models.* IEEE Transactions on Software Engineering, vol. 37, no. 5, pages 593–615, sept.-oct. 2011.

[Cugola 01] Gianpaolo Cugola, Elisabetta Di Nitto & Alfonso Fuggetta. *The JEDI event-based infrastructure and its application to the development of the OPSS WFMS.* IEEE Transaction on Software Engineering, vol. 27, no. 9, pages 827–850, 2001.

[Czarnecki 00] Krysztof Czarnecki & Ulrich W. Eisenecker. *Generative Programming.* Addison-Wesley, Reading, MA, USA, 2000.

[Czarnecki 03] Krzysztof Czarnecki & Simon Helsen. *Classification of Model Transformation Approaches.* In

OOPSLA 2003 Workshop on Generative Techniques in the context of Model Driven Architecture, oct 2003.

[Czarnecki 06]   K. Czarnecki & S. Helsen. *Feature-based survey of model transformation approaches.* IBM Systems Journal, vol. 45, no. 3, pages 621–645, July 2006.

[DeMichiel 06]   Linda DeMichiel & Michael Keith. *Enterprise JavaBeans,Version 3.0.* Standard JSR 220, May 2006.

[DESMO-J 12]   DESMO-J. *DESMO-J project.* website: http://desmoj.sourceforge.net/home.html, 2012.

[Di Marco 04]   Antinisca Di Marco & Paola Inveradi. *Compositional Generation of Software Architecture Performance QN Models.* In Proceedings of WICSA 2004, pages 37–46, 2004.

[Eclipse Foundation 12]   Eclipse Foundation. *Eclipse Modeling Project.* http://wiki.eclipse.org/Modeling, 2012.

[Eisenhauer 06]   G. Eisenhauer, K. Schwan & F.E. Bustamante. *Publish-subscribe for high-performance computing.* Internet Computing, IEEE, vol. 10, no. 1, pages 40 – 47, jan.-feb. 2006.

[Ernst 99]   Johannes Ernst. *What is metamodeling, and what is it good for?* http://infogrid.org/trac/wiki/Reference/WhatIsMetaModeling, 1999.

[etr 10]   *407 ETR - Express Toll Route.* http://www.407etr.com, 2010. last checked March 2012.

[Etzion 11] Opher Etzion & Peter Niblett. *Event processing in action.* Manning, Stamford, 2011.

[Eugster 01] Patrick Eugster. *Type-based Publish/Subscribe.* PhD thesis, Ecole Polytechnique Federale de Lausanne (EPFL), 2001.

[Eugster 03] Patrick Th. Eugster, Pascal A. Felber, Rachid Guerraoui & Anne-Marie Kermarrec. *The many faces of publish/subscribe.* ACM Computing Surveys, vol. 35, pages 114–131, June 2003.

[Evans 10] David Evans, Jean Bacon, Alastair R. Beresford, Richard Gibbens & David Ingram. *Time for change.* In Intertraffic World, Annual Showcase, pages 52–56, 2010.

[extendsim 12] extendsim. *ExtendSim tool website.* http://www.extendsim.com, 2012.

[Feljan 09] Juraj Feljan, Luka Lednicki, Josip Maras, Ana Petričić & Ivica Crnkovic. *Classification and survey of component models.* technical report No. 03/07, Dices Technical Report, 2009.

[Fiege 04] L. Fiege, A. Zeidler, A. Buchmann, R. Kilian-Kehr & G. Mühl. *Security Aspects in Publish/-Subscribe Systems.* In Third Intl. Workshop on Distributed Event-based Systems (DEBS'04). IEEE, 2004.

[Fromm 09] Thilo Fromm. *Ahkera.* Project website: http://t-lo.github.com/ahkera/, 2009.

[Gal 10]   Avigdor Gal & Ethan Hadar. *Generic Architecture of Complex Event Processing Systems*, pages 1–18. Principles and applications of distributed event-based systems, Annika Hinze & Alejandro Buchmann, editors. IGI Global, 2010.

[Gamma 95]   Erich Gamma, Richard Helm, Ralph Johnson & John Vlissides. *Design Patterns: Elements of Reusable Object-Oriented Software*. Addison-Wesley, Reading, MA, USA, 1995.

[Gelissen 03]   Jean Gelissen & Ronan Mac Laverty. *ROBOCOP: Revised specification of framework and models (Deliverable 1.5)*. technical report, Information Technology for European Advancement, 2003.

[Glass 98]   Robert L. Glass. *Software Runaways: Monumental Software Disasters*. Prentice Hall, Englewood Cliffs, NJ, USA, 1998.

[Goble 97]   John Goble. *Modsim III- A Tutorial*. In Simulation Conference, 1997., Proceedings of the 1997 Winter, pages 601 –605, dec 1997.

[Gokhale 02]   Anirudda Gokhale, Balachandran Natarjan, Douglas C. Schmidt, Andrey Nechypurenko, Nanbor Wang, Jeff Gray, Sandeep Neema, Ted Bapty & Jeff Parsons. *CoSMIC: An MDA Generative Tool for Distributed Real-time and Embdedded Component Middleware and Applications*. In Proceedings of the OOPSLA 2002 Workshop on Generative Techniques in the Context of Model Driven Architecture, Seattle, WA, 2002.

[Goldschmidt 08] Thomas Goldschmidt & Guido Wachsmuth. *Refinement transformation support for QVT Relational transformations.* In Proceedings of the 3rd Workshop on Model Driven Software Engineering (MDSE 2008), 2008.

[Gordon 78] Geoffrey Gordon. *The development of the General Purpose Simulation System (GPSS).* SIGPLAN Not., vol. 13, no. 8, pages 183–198, August 1978.

[Gouvêa 12] Daniel Dominguez Gouvêa, Cyro Muniz, Gilson Pinto, Alberto Avritzer, Rosa Maria Meri Leão, Edmundo de Souza e Silva, Morganna Carmem Diniz, Luca Berardinelli, Julius C. B. Leite, Daniel Mossé, Yuanfang Cai, Mike Dalton, Lucia Happe & Anne Koziolek. *Experience with Model-based Performance, Reliability and Adaptability Assessment of a Complex Industrial Architecture.* Journal of Software and Systems Modeling, 2012. accepted for the special issue on Performance Modeling, to appear.

[Grassi 05] Vincenzo Grassi, Raffaela Mirandola & Antonino Sabetta. *From Design to Analysis Models: a Kernel Language for Performance and Reliability Analysis of Component-based Systems.* In WOSP '05: Proceedings of the 5th international workshop on Software and performance, pages 25–36, New York, NY, USA, 2005. ACM Press.

[Grassi 06] Vincenzo Grassi, Raffaela Mirandola & Antonino Sabetta. *A Model Transformation Ap-*

proach for the Early Performance and Reliability Analysis of Component-Based Systems. In Ian Gorton, George T. Heineman, Ivica Crnkovic, Heinz W. Schmidt, Judith A. Stafford, Clemens A. Szyperski & Kurt C. Wallnau, editors, Component-Based Software Engineering, 9th International Symposium, CBSE 2006, Västerås, Sweden, June 29 - July 1, 2006, Proceedings, volume 4063 of *Lecture Notes in Computer Science*, pages 270–284. Springer, 2006.

[Grassi 08] Vincenzo Grassi, Raffaela Mirandola, Enrico Randazzo & Antonino Sabetta. *The Common Component Modeling Example. KLAPER: An Intermediate Language for Model-Driven Predictive Analysis of Performance and Reliability*, pages 327–356. Springer-Verlag, Berlin, Heidelberg, 2008.

[Gruber 00] R.E. Gruber, B. Krishnamurthy & E. Panagos. *READY: a high performance event notification service.* In Proceedings of 16th International Conference on Data Engineering, 2000., pages 668 –669, 2000.

[Guduric 09] P. Guduric, A. Puder & R. Todtenhofer. *A Comparison between Relational and Operational QVT Mappings.* In Information Technology: New Generations, 2009. ITNG '09. Sixth International Conference on, pages 266 –271, april 2009.

[Haber 12] Arne Haber, Jan Oliver Ringert & Bernhard Rumpe. *MontiArc – Architectural Modeling of Interactive Distributed and Cyber-Physical Systems*. Aachener Informatik-Berichte AIB-2012-03, RWTH Aachen - Department of Computer Science, February 2012.

[Hapner 02] Mark Hapner, Rich Burridge, Rahul Sharma, Joseph Fialli & Kate Stout. *Java Message Service Specification Final Release 1.1*. JSR-000914, 2002.

[Happe 08] Jens Happe, Holger Friedrich, Steffen Becker & Ralf H. Reussner. *A Pattern-Based Performance Completion for Message-Oriented Middleware*. In Proceedings of the 7th International Workshop on Software and Performance (WOSP '08), pages 165–176, New York, NY, USA, 2008. ACM.

[Happe 09] Jens Happe. *Predicting software performance in symmetric multi-core and multiprocessor environments*, volume 3 of *The Karlsruhe Series on Software Design and Quality*. Universitätsverlag Karlsruhe, 2009.

[Happe 10] Jens Happe, Steffen Becker, Christoph Rathfelder, Holger Friedrich & Ralf H. Reussner. *Parametric Performance Completions for Model-Driven Performance Prediction*. Performance Evaluation, vol. 67, no. 8, pages 694–716, 2010.

[Happe 11] Jens Happe, Heiko Koziolek & Ralf Reussner. *Facilitating Performance Predictions Using Soft-*

ware Components. IEEE Software, vol. 28, no. 3, pages 27 –33, may-june 2011.

[He 07] Fei He, Luciano Baresi, Carlo Ghezzi & Paola Spoletini. *Formal Analysis of Publish-Subscribe Systems by Probabilistic Timed Automata.* In 27th IFIP WG 6.1 Intl. Conf. on Formal Techniques for Networked and Distributed Systems, volume 4574 of *LNCS*, pages 247–262, 2007.

[Henjes 06a] Robert Henjes, Michael Menth & Sebastian Gehrsitz. *Throughput Performance of Java Messaging Services Using FioranoMQ.* In 13th GI/ITG Conference on Measuring, Modelling and Evaluation of Computer and Communication Systems (MMB), Nürnberg, Germany, March 2006.

[Henjes 06b] Robert Henjes, Michael Menth & Christian Zepfel. *Throughput Performance of Java Messaging Services Using WebsphereMQ.* In Distributed Computing Systems Workshops, 2006. ICDCS Workshops 2006. 26th IEEE International Conference on, 2006.

[Henjes 07a] Robert Henjes, Michael Menth & Valentin Himmler. *Impact of Complex Filters on the Message Throughput of the ActiveMQ JMS Server.* Managing Traffic Performance in Converged Networks, pages 192–203, 2007.

[Henjes 07b] Robert Henjes, Michael Menth & Valentin Himmler. *Throughput Performance of the BEA*

WebLogic JMS Server. International Transactions on Systems Science and Applications, vol. Volume 3, Number 3, October 2007.

[Hinze 09] Annika Hinze, Kai Sachs & Alejandro Buchmann. *Event-based applications and enabling technologies.* In Proceedings of the Third ACM International Conference on Distributed Event-Based Systems, DEBS '09, pages 1:1–1:15, New York, NY, USA, 2009. ACM.

[Hinze 10a] Annika Hinze, Jean Bacon, Alejandro Buchmann, Sharam Chakravarthy, Mani Chandi, Avigdor Gal, Dieter Gawlick & Richard Tibbetts. *Panel: Current State and Future of Event-Based Systems,* pages 432–454. Principles and applications of distributed event-based systems, Annika Hinze & Alejandro Buchmann, editors. IGI Global, 2010.

[Hinze 10b] Annika Hinze & Alejandro P. Buchmann, editors. *Principles and Applications of Distributed Event-Based Systems.* IGI Global, 2010.

[Hohpe 08] Gregor Hohpe & Bobby Woolf. *Enterprise integration patterns.* Addison-Wesley, 2008.

[Huber 10] Nikolaus Huber, Steffen Becker, Christof Rathfelder, Jochen Schweflinghaus & Ralf Reussner. *Performance Modeling in Industry: A Case Study on Storage Virtualization.* In ACM/IEEE 32nd International Conference on Software Engineering, Software Engineering in Practice Track, Capetown, South Africa, pages 1–10, New

York, NY, USA, 2010. ACM. Acceptance Rate: 23% (16/71).

[Huber 12a] Nikolaus Huber, Fabian Brosig & Samuel Kounev. *Modeling Dynamic Virtualized Resource Landscapes*. In Proceedings of the 8th ACM SIGSOFT International Conference on the Quality of Software Architectures (QoSA 2012), Bertinoro, Italy, June 25-28 2012.

[Huber 12b] Nikolaus Huber, André van Hoorn, Anne Koziolek, Fabian Brosig & Samuel Kounev. *S/T/A: Meta-Modeling Run-Time Adaptation in Component-Based System Architectures*. In 9th IEEE International Conference on e-Business Engineering (ICEBE 2012), Hangzhou, China, September 9-11 2012.

[Hunt 81] P. B. Hunt, D. I. Robertson, R. D. Bretherton & R. I. Winton. *SCOOT—a traffic responsive method of coordinating signals*. technical report LR1014, Transport and Road Research Laboratory, 1981.

[IBM 01] TJ Watson Reasearch Center IBM. *The Gryphon Project*. website: http://www.research.ibm.com/distributedmessaging/gryphon.html, 2001.

[ikv++ 12] ikv++. *mediniQVT project website*. http://projects.ikv.de/qvt/, 2012.

[Ingram 09a] David Ingram. *PIRATES Data Representation*. http://www.cl.cam.ac.uk/research/time/pirates/docs/datarepr.pdf, August 2009.

[Ingram 09b] David Ingram. *Reconfigurable middleware for high availability sensor systems.* In Proceedings of the Third ACM International Conference on Distributed Event-Based Systems, DEBS '09, pages 20:1–20:11, New York, NY, USA, 2009. ACM.

[ISO/IEC 03] ISO/IEC. *Software Engineering – Product Quality – Part 1: Quality Model.* ISO Standard 9126-1, ISO/IEC, 2003.

[Iwai 00] M. Iwai, J. Nakazawa & H. Tokuda. *Dragon: soft real-time event delivering architecture for networked sensors and appliances.* In Proceedings of the Seventh International Conference on Real-Time Systems and Applications (RTCSA'00). IEEE, 2000.

[JGraLab 12] Project JGraLab. *JGraLab Project Homepage.* https://github.com/jgralab, 2012.

[Kaiser 05] Jörg Kaiser, Cristiano Brudna & Carlos Mitidieri. *COSMIC: A real-time event-based middleware for the CAN-bus.* J. Syst. Softw., vol. 77, pages 27–36, July 2005.

[Kalnins 04] Audris Kalnins, Janis Barzdins & Edgars Celms. *Model transformation language MOLA.* In in: Proceedings of MDAFA 2004 (Model-Driven Architecture: Foundations and Applications 2004, pages 14–28, 2004.

[Kalnins 06] Audris Kalnins, Edgars Celms & Agris Sostaks. *Tool support for MOLA.* Electron. Notes Theor. Comput. Sci., vol. 152, pages 83–96, 2006.

[Kaplan 08] James M. Kaplan, William Forrest & Noah Kindler. *Revolutionizing Data Center Energy Efficiency.* technical report, McKinsey&Company, 2008.

[Kapova 09] Lucia Kapova & Thomas Goldschmidt. *Automated Feature Model-based Generation of Refinement Transformations.* In Proceedings of the 35th EUROMICRO Conference on Software Engineering and Advanced Applications (SEAA). IEEE, 2009.

[Kapova 10a] Lucia Kapova & Steffen Becker. *Systematic Refinement of Performance Models for Concurrent Component-based Systems.* In 7th International Workshop on Formal Engineering approaches to Software Components and Architectures (FESCA), Electronic Notes in Theoretical Computer Science. Elsevier, 2010.

[Kapova 10b] Lucia Kapova, Thomas Goldschmidt, Steffen Becker & Joerg Henss. *Evaluating Maintainability with Code Metrics for Model-to-Model Transformations.* In George Heineman, Jan Kofron & Frantisek Plasil, editors, Research into Practice - Reality and Gaps (Proceeding of QoSA 2010), volume 6093 of *LNCS*, pages 151–166. Springer-Verlag Berlin Heidelberg, 2010.

[Kapova 11] Lucia Kapova. *Configurable Software Per-formance Completions through Higher-Order Model Transformations.* PhD thesis, Karlsruher Instituts für Technologie (KIT), 2011.

[Kelton 10] W. David Kelton, Randall P. Sadowski & Nancy B. Swets. *Simulation with Arena.* McGraw-Hill, 5th edition edition, 2010.

[Klatt 10] Benjamin Klatt. *Modelling and Prediction of Event-Based Communication in Component-Based Architectures.* Master's thesis, Karlsruhe Institute of Technology, Germany, 2010.

[Klatt 11a] Benjamin Klatt, Franz Brosch, Zoya Durdik & Christoph Rathfelder. *Quality Prediction in Ser-vice Composition Frameworks.* In 5th Work-shop on Non-Functional Properties and SLA Management in Service-Oriented Computing (NFPSLAM-SOC'11), December 5–8, 2011, Pa-phos, Cyprus, December 2011.

[Klatt 11b] Benjamin Klatt, Christoph Rathfelder & Samuel Kounev. *Integration of Event-Based Communi-cation in the Palladio Software Quality Predic-tion Framework.* In 7th ACM SIGSOFT Inter-national Conference on the Quality of Software Architectures (QoSA 2011), Boulder, Colorado, USA, June 20-24 2011.

[Kleppe 07] Anneke G. Kleppe, Jos B. Warmer & Wim Bast. *MDA explained : the model driven architecture; practice and promise.* Addison-Wesley object technology series. Addison-Wesley, Boston, 5. print. edition, 2007.

[Kounev 06] Samuel Kounev & Alejandro Buchmann. *SimQPN - a tool and methodology for analyzing queueing Petri net models by means of simulation*. Performance Evaluation, vol. 63, no. 4-5, pages 364–394, May 2006.

[Kounev 08] Samuel Kounev, Kai Sachs, Jean Bacon & Alejandro Buchmann. *A Methodology for Performance Modeling of Distributed Event-Based Systems*. In Proc. of the 11th IEEE Intl. Symposium on Object/Component/Service-oriented Real-time Distributed Computing, May 2008.

[Kounev 09a] Samuel Kounev. *Software Performance Evaluation*. Wiley Encyclopedia of Computer Science and Engineering, edited by Benjamin W. Wah. Wiley-Interscience, John Wiley & Sons Inc., January 2009.

[Kounev 09b] Samuel Kounev & Kai Sachs. *Benchmarking and Performance Modeling of Event-Based Systems*. it - Information Technology, vol. 5, September 2009.

[Kounev 10a] Samuel Kounev. *Engineering of Next Generation Self-Aware Software Systems: A Research Roadmap*. In Emerging Research Directions in Computer Science. Contributions from the Young Informatics Faculty in Karlsruhe. KIT Scientific Publishing, July 2010. ISBN: 978-3-86644-508-6.

[Kounev 10b] Samuel Kounev, Simon Spinner & Philipp Meier. *QPME 2.0 - A Tool for Stochastic Modeling and Analysis using Queueing Petri Nets.* In Pablo Guerrero, Ilia Petrov & Kai Sachs, editors, Active Data Management: From active databases to event-based systems and more. Springer, 2010.

[Kounev 12a] Samuel Kounev, Nikolaus Huber, Simon Spinner & Fabian Brosig. *Model-based Techniques for Performance Engineering of Business Information Systems.* In Boris Shishkov, editor, Business Modeling and Software Design, volume 0109 of *Lecture Notes in Business Information Processing (LNBIP)*, pages 19–37. Springer-Verlag, 2012.

[Kounev 12b] Samuel Kounev, Christoph Rathfelder & Benjamin Klatt. *Modeling of Event-based Communication in Component-based Architectures.* In 9th International Workshop on Formal Engineering Approaches to Software Components and Architectures (FESCA @ ETAPS 2012), Electronic Notes in Theorethical Computer Science (ENTCS), Satellite event of ETAPS, Tallinn, Estonia, March 31, 2012.

[Koziolek 06] Heiko Koziolek & Jens Happe. *A QoS Driven Development Process Model for Component-Based Software Systems.* In Ian Gorton, George T. Heineman, Ivica Crnkovic, Heinz W. Schmidt, Judith A. Stafford, Clemens A. Szyperski &

Kurt C. Wallnau, editors, Proc. 9th Int. Symposium on Component-Based Software Engineering (CBSE'06), volume 4063 of *Lecture Notes in Computer Science*, pages 336–343. Springer-Verlag Berlin Heidelberg, 2006.

[Koziolek 08a] Heiko Koziolek. *Parameter Dependencies for Reusable Performance Specifications of Software Components*, volume 2 of *The Karlsruhe Series on Software Design and Quality*. Universitätsverlag Karlsruhe, 2008.

[Koziolek 08b] Heiko Koziolek & Ralf Reussner. *A Model Transformation from the Palladio Component Model to Layered Queueing Networks*. In Performance Evaluation: Metrics, Models and Benchmarks, SIPEW 2008, volume 5119 of *Lecture Notes in Computer Science*, pages 58–78. Springer-Verlag Berlin Heidelberg, 2008.

[Koziolek 10] Heiko Koziolek. *Performance evaluation of component-based software systems: A survey*. Elsevier Performance Evaluation, vol. 67, no. 8, pages 634–658, August 2010.

[Koziolek 11a] Anne Koziolek. *Automated Improvement of Software Architecture Models for Performance and Other Quality Attributes*. PhD thesis, Karlsruhe Institute of Technology (KIT), 2011.

[Koziolek 11b] Anne Koziolek & Ralf Reussner. *Towards a generic quality optimisation framework for component-based system models*. In Proceedings of the 14th international ACM Sigsoft symposium on Component based software engineering, CBSE '11, pages 103–108, New York, NY, USA, June 2011. ACM, New York, NY, USA.

[Koziolek 11c] Heiko Koziolek, Bastian Schlich, Carlos Bilich, Roland Weiss, Steffen Becker, Klaus Krogmann, Mircea Trifu, Raffaela Mirandola & Anne Koziolek. *An Industrial Case Study on Quality Impact Prediction for Evolving Service-Oriented Software*. In Proceeding of the 33rd international conference on Software engineering, Software Engineering in Practice Track, ICSE '11, pages 776–785, New York, NY, USA, 2011. ACM, New York, NY, USA. Acceptance Rate: 18% (18/100).

[Krafzig 06] Dirk Krafzig, Karl Banke & Dirk Slama. *Enterprise SOA*. Prentice Hall PTR, reprint. edition, 2006.

[Landau 09] E. Landau. *Handbuch der Lehre von der Verteilung der Primzahlen*. B. G. Teubner, Leipzig, 1909. 2 volumes. Reprinted by Chelsea, New York, 1953.

[Latvia 12] University of Latvia. *Mola Project*. http://mola.mii.lu.lv/, 2012.

[Lau 06] K.-K. Lau & Z. Wang. *A Survey of Software Component Models*. technical report, School of Computer Science, The University of Manchester, May 2006.

[Lau 07]   Kung-Kiu Lau & Zheng Wang. *Software Component Models*. IEEE Transactions on Software Engineering, vol. 33, no. 10, pages 709–724, October 2007.

[Law 99]   Averill Law & W. David Kelton. *Simulation Modeling and Analysis (Industrial Engineering and Management Science Series)*. McGraw-Hill Science/Engineering/Math, 3 edition, December 1999.

[Liu 03]   Ying Liu & Beth Plale. *Survey of publish subscribe event systems*. Technical Report TR574, Indiana University, 2003.

[Liu 05a]   Yan Liu, Alan Fekete & Ian Gorton. *Design-Level Performance Prediction of Component-Based Applications*. IEEE Transactions on Software Engineering, vol. 31, no. 11, pages 928–941, 2005.

[Liu 05b]   Yan Liu & Ian Gorton. *Performance Prediction of J2EE Applications Using Messaging Protocols*. Component-Based Software Engineering, pages 1–16, 2005.

[MacNair 94]   E. A. MacNair & R. F. Gordon. *An introduction to the RESearch Queueing Package for modeling contention systems*. SIGSIM Simul. Dig., vol. 24, no. 2, pages 40–70, December 1994.

[Mahambre 08]   Shruti P. Mahambre, Madhu Kumar S. D & Umesh Bellur. *A Taxonomy and Classification of Adaptive Event Based Middleware with Support for Service Guarantees*. technical report, KRe-SIT, IIT Bombay, 2008.

[Martens 08a] Anne Martens, Steffen Becker, Heiko Koziolek & Ralf Reussner. *An Empirical Investigation of the Applicability of a Component-Based Performance Prediction Method.* In Proceedings of the 5th European Performance Engineering Workshop (EPEW'08), Palma de Mallorca, Spain, volume 5261 of *Lecture Notes in Computer Science*, pages 17–31. Springer-Verlag Berlin Heidelberg, 2008.

[Martens 08b] Anne Martens, Steffen Becker, Heiko Koziolek & Ralf Reussner. *An Empirical Investigation of the Effort of Creating Reusable Models for Performance Prediction.* In Proceedings of the 11th International Symposium on Component-Based Software Engineering (CBSE'08), Karlsruhe, Germany, volume 5282 of *Lecture Notes in Computer Science*, pages 16–31. Springer-Verlag Berlin Heidelberg, 2008.

[Martens 09] Anne Martens, Franz Brosch & Ralf Reussner. *Optimising multiple quality criteria of service-oriented software architectures.* In Proceedings of the 1st international workshop on Quality of service-oriented software systems (QUASOSS), pages 25–32. ACM, New York, NY, USA, 2009.

[Martens 11] Anne Martens, Heiko Koziolek, Lutz Prechelt & Ralf Reussner. *From monolithic to component-based performance evaluation of software ar-*

chitectures. Empirical Software Engineering, vol. 16, no. 5, pages 587–622, 2011.

[Martinsky 06] Ondrej Martinsky. *JavaANPR - automatic number plate recognition system.* http://javaanpr.sourceforge.net/, 2006.

[Marzolla 04] Moreno Marzolla. *Simulation-Based Performance Modeling of UML Software Architectures.* PhD Thesis TD-2004-1, Dipartimento di Informatica, Università Ca' Foscari di Venezia, Mestre, Italy, February 2004.

[Meier 10] Philipp Meier. *Automated Transformation of Palladio Component Models to Queueing Petri Nets.* Master's thesis, Karlsruhe Institute of Technology (KIT), 2010.

[Meier 11] Philipp Meier, Samuel Kounev & Heiko Koziolek. *Automated Transformation of Palladio Component Models to Queueing Petri Nets.* In In 19th IEEE/ACM International Symposium on Modeling, Analysis and Simulation of Computer and Telecommunication Systems (MASCOTS 2011), Singapore, July 25-27 2011.

[Menascé 04] D. A. Menascé, V. A. F. Almeida & L. W. Dowdy. *Performance by Design.* Prentice Hall, 2004.

[Mens 06] Tom Mens & Pieter Van Gorp. *A Taxonomy of Model Transformation.* Electronic Notes in Theoretical Computer Science, vol. 152, no. 0, pages 125 – 142, 2006.

[Menth 06]   Michael Menth & Robert Henjes. *Analysis of the Message Waiting Time for the FioranoMQ JMS Server*. In Proc. of ICDCS '06, Washington, DC, USA, 2006.

[Microsoft 07]   Microsoft. *COM Website*. http://www.microsoft.com/com/default.mspx, 2007.

[Mühl 02]   Gero Mühl. *Large-Scale Content-Based Publish/Subscribe Systems*. PhD thesis, Technische Universität Darmstadt, 2002.

[Mühl 06]   Gero Mühl, Ludger Fiege & Peter R. Pietzuch. *Distributed Event-Based Systems*. Springer, 2006.

[Mühl 09]   Gero Mühl, Arnd Schröter, Helge Parzyjegla, Samuel Kounev & Jan Richling. *Stochastic Analysis of Hierarchical Publish/Subscribe Systems*. In Proceedings of the 15th International European Conference on Parallel and Distributed Computing (Euro-Par 2009), Delft, The Netherlands, August 25-28, 2009. Springer Verlag, 2009.

[Nolte 10]   Siegfried Nolte. *QVT - Operational Mappings: Modellierung mit der Query Views Transformation*. Xpert.pressSpringerLink : Bücher. Springer-Verlag Berlin Heidelberg, Berlin, Heidelberg, 2010.

[OASIS 04]   OASIS. *OASIS Web Services Notification (WSN) TC*. https://www.oasis-open.org/committees/tc_home.php?wg_abbrev=wsn, 2004.

[OASIS 06a] OASIS. *Web Services Base Notification 1.3 (WS-BaseNotification)*. OSASIS standard: wsn-ws_-base_notification-1.3-spec-os, 2006.

[OASIS 06b] OASIS. *Web Services Brokered Notification 1.3 (WS-BrokeredNotification)*. OASIS standard: wsn-ws_brokered_notification-1.3-spec-os, 2006.

[OASIS 06c] OASIS. *Web Services Topics 1.3 (WS-Topics)*. OASIS standard: wsn-ws_topics-1.3-spec-os, 2006.

[OASIS 07a] OASIS. *JMS Binding Specification, SCA Version 1.00*, 2007.

[OASIS 07b] OASIS. *The Service Component Architecture homepage*. http://www.oasis-opencsa.org/sca, 2007.

[Oki 93] Brian Oki, Manfred Pfluegl, Alex Siegel & Dale Skeen. *The Information Bus: an architecture for extensible distributed systems*. SIGOPS Oper. Syst. Rev., vol. 27, pages 58–68, December 1993.

[OMG 94] Object Management Group OMG. *Common Object Services Specification Volume I*. OMG document 1994/94-01-01, 1994.

[OMG 03] Object Management Group OMG. *MDA Guide V1.0.1*. http://www.omg.org/cgi-bin/doc?omg/03-06-01, 2003.

[OMG 04a] Object Management Group OMG. *Event Service Specification v1.2*. OMG document formal/2004-10-02, 2004.

[OMG 04b] Object Management Group OMG. *Notification Service Specification, Version 1.1.* OMG document formal/2004-10-11, 2004.

[OMG 05] Object Management Group OMG. *UML Profile for Schedulability, Performance, and Time (SPT), v1.1,* January 2005.

[OMG 06a] Object Management Group OMG. *CORBA Component Model, v4.0 (formal/2006-04-01),* 2006.

[OMG 06b] Object Management Group OMG. *Model Driven Architecture - Specifications,* 2006.

[OMG 06c] Object Management Group OMG. *MOF 2.0 Core Specification (formal/2006-01-01),* 2006.

[OMG 06d] Object Management Group OMG. *Object Constraint Language, v2.0 (formal/06-05-01),* 2006.

[OMG 06e] Object Management Group OMG. *UML Profile for Modeling and Analysis of Real-Time and Embedded systems (MARTE),* May 2006.

[OMG 07] Object Management Group OMG. *Meta Object Facility (MOF) 2.0 Query/View/Transformation Specification (formal/2011-01-01),* 2007.

[OMG 10] Object Management Group OMG. *OMG Unified Modeling Language TM (OMG UML), Superstructure Specification: Version 2.3 (formal/2010-05-05),* 2010.

[OMG 11] Object Management Group OMG. *The Common Object Request Broker: Architecture and*

Specification: Version 3.2. http://www.omg.org/ spec/CORBA/, 2011.

[OMNeT 12] OMNeT. *OMNeT++ Network Simulation Framework.* http://www.omnetpp.org/, 2012.

[Palladio 12] Palladio. *Palladio Release 3.3.* http://www. palladio-simulator.com/tools/download/, 2012.

[Pallickara 03] Shrideep Pallickara & Geoffrey Fox. *NaradaBrokering: a distributed middleware framework and architecture for enabling durable peer-to-peer grids.* In Proceedings of the ACM/IFIP/USENIX 2003 International Conference on Middleware, Middleware '03, pages 41–61, New York, NY, USA, 2003. Springer-Verlag New York, Inc.

[Parzyjegla 10] Helge Parzyjegla, Daniel Graff, Arnd Schröter, Jan Richling & Gero Mühl. *Design and Implementation of the Rebeca Publish/Subscribe Middleware.* In Kai Sachs, Ilia Petrov & Pablo Guerrero, editors, From Active Data Management to Event-Based Systems and More, volume 6462 of *Lecture Notes in Computer Science,* pages 124–140. Springer Berlin / Heidelberg, 2010.

[PCM 12] PCM. *Palladio Simulator.* project website http://www.palladio-simulator.com/, 2012.

[Petriu 00] D. C. Petriu & X. Wang. *From UML Description of High-level Software Architecture to LQN Performance Models.* In M. Nagl, A. Schürr

& M. Münch, editors, Proc. of AGTIVE'99 Kerkrade, volume 1779. Springer, 2000.

[Petriu 07] Dorin B. Petriu & Murray Woodside. *An intermediate metamodel with scenarios and resources for generating performance models from UML designs.* Software and Systems Modeling, vol. 6, no. 2, pages 163–184, 2007.

[Pietzuch 04] Peter Robert Pietzuch. *Hermes: A Scalable Event-Based Middleware.* PhD thesis, University of Cambridge, 2004.

[Pietzuch 07] Peter Pietzuch, David Eyers, Samuel Kounev & Brian Shand. *Towards a Common API for Publish/Subscribe.* In Hans-Arno Jacobsen, Gero Mühl & Michael A. Jaeger, editors, Proceedings of the 2007 Inaugural International Conference on Distributed Event-Based Systems (DEBS 2007), Toronto, Canada, June 20-22, 2007, volume 233 of *ACM International Conference Proceeding Series,* pages 152–157. ACM, New York, NY, USA, June 2007.

[Prieto 12] Sebastián Sánchez Prieto, Manuel Prieto Mateo, Oscar Rodríguez Polo, Pablo Parra Espada, Óscar Gutiérrez Molina, Ronald Castillo Rivas & Javier Fernández Salgado. *Instrument Control Unit for the Energetic Particle Detector onboard Solar Orbiter.* Advances in Space Research (ASR), 2012. Planned to be submitted.

[Ramasubramanian 06] Venugopalan Ramasubramanian, Ryan Peterson & Emin Gün Sirer. *Corona: a high perfor-*

mance publish-subscribe system for the world wide web. In Proceedings of the 3rd conference on Networked Systems Design & Implementation - Volume 3, NSDI'06, pages 2–2, Berkeley, CA, USA, 2006. USENIX Association.

[Rathfelder 07] Christoph Rathfelder & Henning Groenda. *Geschäftsprozessorientierte Kategorisierung von SOA.* In 2. Workshop Bewertungsaspekte serviceorientierter Architekturen, pages 11–22. SHAKER Verlag, November 2007.

[Rathfelder 08a] Christoph Rathfelder & Henning Groenda. *iSOAMM: An independent SOA Maturity Model.* In Proc. of 8th IFIP International Conference on Distributed Applications and Interoperable Systems (DAIS'08), volume 5053/2008 of *Lecture Notes in Computer Science*, pages 1–15. Springer-Verlag Berlin Heidelberg, 2008.

[Rathfelder 08b] Christoph Rathfelder & Henning Groenda. *Towards an Architecture Maintainability Maturity Model (AM3).* Softwaretechnik-Trends, vol. 28, no. 4, pages 3–7, November 2008.

[Rathfelder 08c] Christoph Rathfelder, Henning Groenda & Ralf Reussner. *Software Industrialization and Architecture Certification.* In Georg Herzwurm & Martin Mikusz, editors, Industrialisierung des Software-Managements, volume P-139 of *Lecture Notes in Informatics*, pages 169–180, 2008.

[Rathfelder 09a] Christoph Rathfelder & Henning Groenda. *The Architecture Documentation Maturity Model*

ADM2. In Proc. 3rd Workshop MDD, SOA und IT-Management (MSI'09), pages 65–80. GiTO-Verlag, 2009.

[Rathfelder 09b] Christoph Rathfelder & Samuel Kounev. *Model-based Performance Prediction for Event-driven Systems (Fast Abstract)*. In 3rd ACM International Conference on Distributed Event-Based Systems (DEBS2009), Nashville, TN, USA, July 2009.

[Rathfelder 09c] Christoph Rathfelder & Samuel Kounev. *Modeling Event-Driven Service-Oriented Systems using the Palladio Component Model*. In Proceedings of the 1st International Workshop on the Quality of Service-Oriented Software Systems (QUASOSS), pages 33–38. ACM, New York, NY, USA, 2009.

[Rathfelder 10a] Christoph Rathfelder, David Evans & Samuel Kounev. *Predictive Modelling of Peer-to-Peer Event-driven Communication in Component-based Systems*. In Alessandro Aldini, Marco Bernardo, Luciano Bononi & Vittorio Cortellessa, editors, Proceedings of the 7th European Performance Engineering Workshop (EPEW'10), University Residential Center of Bertinoro, Italy, volume 6342 of *Lecture Notes in Computer Science*, pages 219–235. Springer-Verlag Berlin Heidelberg, 2010.

[Rathfelder 10b] Christoph Rathfelder, Benjamin Klatt, Samuel Kounev & David Evans. *Towards Middleware-*

aware Integration of Event-based Communication into the Palladio Component Model (Poster Paper). In Proceedings of the 4th ACM International Conference on Distributed Event-Based Systems (DEBS-2010), Cambridge, United Kingdom, July 2010. ACM, New York, USA.

[Rathfelder 11a] Christoph Rathfelder & Benjamin Klatt. *Palladio Workbench: A Quality-Prediction Tool for Component-Based Architectures*. In Proceedings of the 9th Working IEEE/IFIP Conference on Software Architecture (WICSA), 2011.

[Rathfelder 11b] Christoph Rathfelder, Benjamin Klatt, Franz Brosch & Samuel Kounev. *Performance Modeling for Quality of Service Prediction in Service-Oriented Systems*. Handbook of Research on Service-Oriented Systems and Non-Functional Properties: Future Directions, Stephan Reiff-Marganiec & Marcel Tilly, editors. IGI Global, 2011.

[Rathfelder 11c] Christoph Rathfelder, Samuel Kounev & David Evans. *Capacity Planning for Event-based Systems using Automated Performance Predictions*. In 26th IEEE/ACM International Conference On Automated Software Engineering (ASE 2011), Oread, Lawrence, Kansas, November 2011. Acceptance Rate (Full Paper): 14.7% (37/252).

[Rathfelder 12] Christoph Rathfelder, Stefan Becker, Klaus Krogmann & Ralf Reussner. *Workload-aware System Monitoring Using Performance Predictions Applied to a Large-scale E-Mail System.* In Proceedings of the Joint 10th Working IEEE/IFIP Conference on Software Architecture (WICSA) & 6th European Conference on Software Architecture (ECSA), Helsinki, Finland, 2012. Acceptance Rate (Full Paper): 19.8%.

[Rathfelder 13] Christoph Rathfelder, Benjamin Klatt, Kai Sachs & Samuel Kounev. *Modeling Event-based Communication in Component-based Software Architectures for Performance Predictions.* Journal on Software and Systems Modeling (SoSyM) – Theme Issue on Models for Quality of Software Architecture, 2013. under publication.

[Rentschler 06] Andreas Rentschler. *Model-To-Text Transformation Languages.* In Seminar: Modellgetriebene Software-Entwicklung Architekturen, Muster und Eclipse-basierte MDA. Fakultät für Informatik, Universität Karlsruhe (TH), Germany, 2006.

[Reussner 11] Ralf Reussner, Steffen Becker, Erik Burger, Jens Happe, Michael Hauck, Anne Koziolek, Heiko Koziolek, Klaus Krogmann & Michael Kuperberg. *The Palladio Component Model.* technical report, Karlsruhe, 2011.

[Rose 12] Louis Rose, Markus Herrmannsdoerfer, Steffen Mazanek, Pieter Van Gorp, Sebastian Buchwald, Tassilo Horn, Elina Kalnina, Andreas Koch, Kevin Lano, Bernhard Schätz & Manuel Wimmer. *Graph and model transformation tools for model migration.* Software and Systems Modeling, pages 1–37, 2012.

[Rowstron 01] Antony I. T. Rowstron & Peter Druschel. *Pastry: Scalable, Decentralized Object Location, and Routing for Large-Scale Peer-to-Peer Systems.* In Proceedings of the IFIP/ACM International Conference on Distributed Systems Platforms Heidelberg, Middleware '01, pages 329–350, London, UK, UK, 2001. Springer-Verlag.

[Sachs 07] Kai Sachs, Samuel Kounev, Jean Bacon & Alejandro Buchmann. *Workload Characterization of the SPECjms2007 Benchmark.* In Katinka Wolter, editor, Formal Methods and Stochastic Models for Performance Evaluation, Proceedings of the 4th European Performance Engineering Workshop (EPEW 2007), Berlin, Germany, September 27-28, 2007, number 4748 in Lecture Notes in Computer Science (LNCS), pages 228–244, Heidelberg, Germany, September 2007. Springer Verlag.

[Sachs 09] Kai Sachs, Samuel Kounev, Jean Bacon & Alejandro Buchmann. *Performance evaluation of message-oriented middleware using the SPECjms2007 benchmark.* Performance Evaluation, vol. 66, no. 8, pages 410–434, Aug 2009.

[Sachs 11] Kai Sachs. *Performance Modeling and Benchmarking of Event-Based Systems.* PhD thesis, TU Darmstadt, 2011.

[Sachs 12] Kai Sachs, Samuel Kounev & Alejandro Buchmann. *Performance modeling and analysis of message-oriented event-driven systems.* Software and Systems Modeling, pages 1–25, February 2012.

[Schmidt 06] Douglas C. Schmidt. *Guest Editor's Introduction: Model-Driven Engineering.* Computer, vol. 39, no. 2, pages 25–31, 2006.

[Schmidt 08] Kay-Uwe Schmidt, Darko Anicic & Roland Stühmer. *Event-driven Reactivity: A Survey and Requirements Analysis.* In SBPM2008: 3rd international Workshop on Semantic Business Process Management in conjunction with the 5th European Semantic Web Conference (ESWC'08). CEUR Workshop Proceedings (CEUR-WS.org, ISSN 1613-0073), June 2008.

[Schröter 10] Arnd Schröter, Gero Mühl, Samuel Kounev, Helge Parzyjegla & Jan Richling. *Stochastic performance analysis and capacity planning of publish/subscribe systems.* In Proceedings of the Fourth ACM International Conference on Distributed Event-Based Systems, DEBS '10, pages 258–269, New York, NY, USA, 2010. ACM.

[Schuster 10] Thomas Schuster, Christoph Rathfelder, Nelly Schuster & Jens Nimis. *Comprehensive tool support for iterative SOA evolution.* In International Workshop on SOA Migration and Evolution 2010 (SOAME 2010) as part of the 14th European Conference on Software Maintenance and Reengineering (CSMR), 2010, 2010.

[Sheldon 02] Frederick T. Sheldon, Kshamta Jerath & Hong Chung. *Metrics for maintainability of class inheritance hierarchies*. Journal of Software Maintenance, vol. 14, pages 147–160, May 2002.

[Simard 11] Richard Simard. *SSJ: Stochastic Simulation in Java*. http://www.iro.umontreal.ca/~simardr/ssj/indexe.html, 2011.

[Skjeksvik 10] Katrine Stemland Skjeksvik, Vera Goebel & Thomas Plagemann. *Event-Based Interaction for Rescue and Emergency Applications in Mobile and Disruptive Environments*, pages 411–431. Principles and applications of distributed event-based systems, Annika Hinze & Alejandro Buchmann, editors. IGI Global, 2010.

[Slominski 02] Aleksander Slominski, Yogesh Simmhan, Albert Louis Rossi, Matthew Farrellee & Dennis Gannon. *XEVENTS/XMESSAGES: Application Events and Messaging Framework for Grid*. technical report, Indiana University Computer Science Department, 2002.

[Smith 90] Connie U. Smith. *Performance Engineering of Software Systems*. Addison-Wesley Longman Publishing Co., Inc., Boston, MA, USA, 1990.

[Smith 02] Connie U. Smith & Lloyd G. Williams. *Performance Solutions: A Practical Guide to Creating Responsive, Scalable Software.* Addison-Wesley, 2002.

[Sostaks 10] Agris Sostaks. *Implementation of model transformation languages.* PhD thesis, University of Latvia, 2010.

[SPEC 07] Standard Performance Evaluation Corporation SPEC. *SPECjms2007 benchmark.* http://www.spec.org/jms2007/, 2007.

[Stachowiak 73] Herbert Stachowiak. *Allgemeine Modelltheorie.* Springer Verlag, Wien, 1973.

[(Sun) 09] Sun Microsystems Corp. (Sun). *JavaTM Platform, Enterprise Edition (Java EE) Specification, v6.* JSR-000316, 2009.

[Szyperski 02] Clemens Szyperski, Dominik Gruntz & Stephan Murer. *Component Software: Beyond Object-Oriented Programming.* ACM Press and Addison-Wesley, New York, NY, 2 edition, 2002.

[Uhl 07] Axel Uhl. *Model-Driven Architecture, MDA.* In Handbuch der Software-Architektur, 6, pages 106–123. dPunkt.verlag, Heidelberg, 2007.

[Varro 07] Daniel Varro & Andras Balogh. *The model transformation language of the VIATRA2 framework.* Science of Computer Programming, Special Issue on Model Transformation, vol. 68, no. 3, pages 214 – 234, 2007.

[Verdickt 05] Tom Verdickt, Bart Dhoedt, Frank Gielen & Piet Demeester. *Automatic Inclusion of Middleware Performance Attributes into Architectural UML Software Models.* IEEE Transactions on Software Engineering, vol. 31, no. 8, pages 695–711, 2005.

[Virgillito 03] Antonino Virgillito. *Publish/Subscribe Communication Systems: From Models to Applications.* PhD thesis, Universita La Sapienza, 2003.

[Vogel 12] Christian Vogel. *Rapid Performance Modeling by Transforming Use Case Maps to Palladio Component Models.* Master's thesis, Karlsruhe Institute of Technology (KIT), 2012.

[Völter 06] Markus Völter & Thomas Stahl. *Model-Driven Software Development.* Wiley & Sons, New York, NY, USA, 2006.

[von Detten 12] M. von Detten, C. Heinzemann, M. Platenius, J. Rieke, J. Suck, D. Travkin & S. Hildebrandt. *Story Diagrams - Syntax and Semantics.* technical report tr-ri-12-320, Software Engineering Group, Heinz Nixdorf Institute, 2012.

[W3C 04] W3C. *Web Services Addressing (WS-Addressing).* W3C standard: http://www.w3.org/Submission/ws-addressing/, 2004.

[W3C 06] W3C. *Web Services Eventing (WS-Eventing).* W3C standard: http://www.w3.org/Submission/WS-Eventing/, 2006.

[Wang 02]   C. Wang, A. Carzaniga, D. Evans & A. Wolf. *Security Issues and Requirements for Internet-Scale Publish-Subscribe Systems*. In Proceedings of the 35th Annual Hawaii International Conference on System Sciences (HICSS'02)-Volume 9 - Volume 9, HICSS '02, pages 303–, Washington, DC, USA, 2002. IEEE Computer Society.

[Webster 09]   Ben Webster. *Average speed cameras mean no escape for drivers*. The Times online, 2009.

[Weikum 02]   Gerhard Weikum, Axel Moenkeberg, Christof Hasse & Peter Zabback. *Self-tuning Database Technology and Information Services: from Wishful Thinking to Viable Engineering*. In In VLDB Conference, pages 20–31, 2002.

[Westermann 11]   Dennis Westermann & Jens Happe. *Performance Cockpit: Systematic Measurements and Analyses*. In ICPE'11: Proceedings of the 2nd ACM/SPEC International Conference on Performance Engineering, New York, NY, USA, 2011. ACM.

[Williams 03]   Lloyd G. Williams & Connie U. Smith. *Making the Business Case for Software Performance Engineering*. In Proceedings of the 29th International Computer Measurement Group Conference, December 7-12, 2003, Dallas, Texas, USA, pages 349–358. Computer Measurement Group, 2003.

[Woodside 95]   C. Murray Woodside, John E. Neilson, Dorina C. Petriu & Shikharesh Majumdar. *The Stochas-*

tic Rendezvous Network Model for Performance of Synchronous Client-Server-like Distributed Software. IEEE Trans. Comput., vol. 44, no. 1, pages 20–34, January 1995.

[Woodside 02] Murray Woodside, Dorina C. Petriu & Khalid H. Siddiqui. *Performance-related Completions for Software Specifications.* In Proceedings of the 22rd International Conference on Software Engineering, ICSE 2002, 19-25 May 2002, Orlando, Florida, USA, pages 22–32. ACM, 2002.

[Wu 04] Xiuping Wu & C. Murray Woodside. *Performance modeling from software components.* In Jozo J. Dujmovic, Virgílio A. F. Almeida & Doug Lea, editors, Proceedings of the Fourth International Workshop on Software and Performance, WOSP 2004, Redwood Shores, California, USA, January 14-16, 2004, pages 290–301. ACM, 2004.

All websites were last retrieved on 2013-01-18

The Karlsruhe Series on Software Design and Quality

Edited by Prof. Dr. Ralf Reussner // ISSN 1867-0067

Die Bände sind unter www.ksp.kit.edu als PDF frei verfügbar oder als Druckausgabe bestellbar.

The Karlsruhe Series on Software Design and Quality

Edited by Prof. Dr. Ralf Reussner // ISSN 1867-0067

Die Bände sind unter www.ksp.kit.edu als PDF frei verfügbar oder als Druckausgabe bestellbar.